BUILDING BETTER BOARDS

A Handbook for Board Members in Catholic Education

Lourdes Sheehan, RSM, Ed.D.

Copyright 1990 by the National Catholic Educational Association, Washington, DC. All rights reserved. Published in the United States of America by the National Catholic Educational Association.
ISBN #1-55833-042-9

TABLE OF CONTENTS

	page
Preface	vi
Introduction	viii

Chapter 1: What is a Catholic School Board?	1
Types of Catholic Schools	1
Types of Boards	2
Areas of Board Responsibility	5
Catholic School Boards Differ from Public School Boards	6

Chapter 2: Planning	7
One Practical Planning Approach	8
Roles and Responsibilities in Planning	9
Plan Format	10
Developing the Long-Range Plan	10
Using the Long-Range Plan	14
Annual Update of Long-Range Plan	14

Chapter 3: Policy Formulation and Enactment	15
Relationship: Law/Policy/Regulation	15
Significance of Policies	17
The Board and Policy	17
Areas Which Need Policies	23
Diocesan Policies	24

Chapter 4: The Role of the Board in Finances	25
How Schools Are Funded	25
Budget	26
Tuition	29
Daily Financial Management	31

Chapter 5: Appointment/Selection of the Principal	33
Clarifying the Charge	33
Laying the Foundation for the Search	34
Searching	34
Arriving at Decisions	36

Chapter 6: Development/Public Relations/Marketing	37
What Is Development?	37
Public Relations	40
Marketing	41

Chapter 7: Evaluation	**45**
The Role of the Board in the Evaluation of the Administrator	45
The Board and Its Own Evaluation	49
Evaluating the Instructional Program	49
Chapter 8: Roles and Relationships	**51**
Roles	51
Relationships	52
Boards for Interparish/Regional Schools	54
Boards for Diocesan Schools	55
Boards for Private Schools	56
Diocesan Boards	57
Chapter 9: Membership	**61**
Eligibility Requirements	61
Membership Qualifications	62
Orientation of New Members	64
Specific Issues Regarding Membership	64
Most Difficult Things for Board Members to Learn	66
Chapter 10: Board Meetings	**67**
Responsibility of Members	67
Committees	68
Preparation for Board Meetings	68
Steps to More Successful Meetings	69
Decision-Making	70

APPENDICES

A.	**Consultative Boards**—sample constitutions/bylaws	
	A1 - Parish School Board	75
	A2 - Parish Board of Education	79
	A3 - Regional/Interparish School Board	83
	A4 - Diocesan Secondary School	89
	A5 - Diocesan School Board	93
	A6 - Archdiocesan Board of Education	98
B.	**Boards with Limited Jurisdiction**—sample constitutions/bylaws	
	B1 - Catholic Central School Board	102
	B2 - Interparish School Boards	107
	B3 - Private Secondary School (sponsored by religious congregation)	112
	B4 - Private Secondary School (owned by parents)	119
	B5 - Diocesan Secondary School	125

C.	**Schools Constituted as Separate Juridic Persons**	
	C1 - Interparish Schools	128
	C2 - A Letter Concerning the Catholic School System (including statutes for diocesan high schools)	132
D.	**The Catholic School Principal**	
	D1 - Principal's Job Description	139
	D2 - Outline of a Portrait of the Catholic School Principal	141
	D3 - The Principal's Leadership of and Service to the Board	143
	D4 - Guidelines for Principal Evaluation	144
	D5 - Principal Contract	152
	D6 - Sample Interview Questions	154
E.	**The Board and Evaluation**	
	E1 - Principal's Evaluation	155
	E2 - The Internal Functions of the Board	157
	E3 - The External Functions of the Board	158
F.	**Board Membership**	
	F1 - Board Members Profile Grid	160
	F2 - Code of Ethics for Catholic School Board Members	161
	F3 - A Board Member's Prayer	162
G.	**Meetings**	
	G1 - Checklist for Planning a Meeting	163
	G2 - Meeting Evaluation Form	164
	G3 - Minute Taking Reminders	166
H.	Alternative Tuition Plans	167
I.	Five-Year Development Plan	168
J.	Church Documents on Catholic Education	169
K.	Catholic Regional School Systems: Pros, Cons and Alternatives	172
L.	Sample Diocesan Policies	178

Bibliography and Resources	182
About the Author	186

PREFACE

A survey of members of the NCEA Department of Chief Administrators indicated a need for a handbook which would consolidate information in one publication for school board members. Although the primary focus of this handbook is Catholic school boards and boards of trustees, the principles and much of the materials are easily adaptable to councils, commissions, and committees for other diocesan, parish and religious education programs. Sample constitutions for a variety of educational governance structures are in the appendices.

The basic question about various types of governance structures is: Why does the structure exist? For example, the focus of this handbook communicates that the author, while supporting the church's one educational mission, believes that each Catholic school needs a governance group specifically charged with shared responsibility for the present and future life of that institution.

Practicing subsidiarity and collaboration, school boards and other diocesan, parish and educational councils and commissions can effectively and efficaciously serve the church's educational mission.

Policies regarding diocesan and local governance are promulgated by each diocesan bishop through the (arch)diocesan education offices. Given the needs and preferences of the local church, educational governance groups are known by a variety of names and function under differing models. However, experiences and the 1983 Code of Canon Law have contributed to the recognition that boards in Catholic education may be constituted as either consultative or with limited jurisdiction. Therefore, the materials, suggestions, and types and models of boards offered in this handbook should be adapted to meet (arch)diocesan and religious congregation policies and regulations.

Some of the material in this handbook was published previously in issues of *PolicyMaker,* in other articles and talks by the author, in the workshop series "14 x 7—Building Better Boards," and in other publications of the National Catholic Educational Association.

Special acknowledgement and gratitude are due to those Catholic educators who with the author developed the board workshop series "14 x 7—Building Better Boards": Dr. Lois K. Draina, Director of

Graduate Education, Marywood College; Bro. Adrian Gaudin, SC, Educational Consultant, Brothers of the Sacred Heart; Dr. Carolyn M. Jurkowitz, Associate Director, Department on Education, Catholic Conference of Ohio; Rev. J. Stephen O'Brien, Executive Director, CACE/NCEA; Bro. Michael O'Hern, FSC, President and CEO, Christian Brothers Investment Services; Sr. JoCeal Young, SM, Associate Superintendent, Diocese of San Jose. The author is also grateful to Lorie Catsos, administrative assistant at NCEA/NABE, for typing the manuscript.

Lourdes Sheehan, RSM
February, 1990

INTRODUCTION

Boards and commissions have been an important part of Catholic education for a long time. They were called for by the Councils of Baltimore in the late 1800's and experienced a significant revival in the decades following Vatican Council II. Approximately 68 percent of the Catholic schools in the United States have some form of educational governance structure. (Ganley, 1988)

Boards Prior to Vatican Council II

The early Councils of Baltimore called for education boards and commissions primarily to assist the bishop in the administration of the schools in the diocese. Diocesan priests were members of these first education boards. The position of superintendent of schools did not develop until the first decades of this century.

Vatican Council II and the Renewal of Boards

Following Vatican Council II, the proponents of a renewed Catholic board movement, convinced that support for Catholic schools needed to be broadened beyond bishops, clergy, and professionals, offered the following three arguments for involving the laity more directly in decision-making boards:

1. **The Role of the Laity and the Future of Catholic Schools**
The proponents of the board movement were primarily Catholic school superintendents who believed that the spirit and documents of Vatican Council II called for the church to put into practice its statements regarding parents as the first and foremost educators of their children. They argued that parents should have a voice in the formal education of their children in Catholic schools by participating in school boards similar to public school boards.

2. **Financial Support from Government and Community**
Addressing the financial needs of the schools, the superintendents suggested that increased involvement by the laity (some even argued for full legal autonomy and jurisdiction for boards) would increase the financial base of support for schools from both the Catholic community and from federal and state governments.

3. **Response to Vatican Council II and a New Image for Catholic Schools**
Vatican Council II called for more involvement by the laity

in the life of the church; therefore, many board proponents commented that Catholic schools had the opportunity to project a post-Vatican II image by representation in policy-making. Shared responsibility and participatory decision-making were seen as directions in church government and were used to support the board of education movement.

One major obstacle to the boards' successful flourishing immediately following the Council was the absence of tested and appropriate models. Neither the clerical model of the pre-Vatican II church nor the public school board model was suited for post-conciliar Catholic education.

Current Status of School Boards

While there is much validity in the initial reasons for promoting Catholic education boards, subsequent events and insights have raised new issues, clarified some issues, and offered reasons why the church needs Catholic education boards today. Some of the reasons which motivate establishing and fostering of boards are:

1. **To promote the concept of lay ministry**

    The church is indeed the People of God. Each baptized person has a responsibility to use talents and gifts for the building of community. Participation in the ministry of Catholic education is one of the ways individuals can participate in the life of the church in a significant way. This realization is the first and primary reason for having Catholic education boards which provide concrete means for people to contribute to Catholic education and thereby build the kingdom of God.

2. **To develop ownership and stability for the future**

    Participation in the life of any organization is bound to bring with it an increase of pride and ownership. Many adult Catholics enjoy the benefits of a Catholic school education and welcome the chance to provide the same opportunities for this generation of children and youth. People appreciate recognition of their expertise and are eager to offer their services as board members. Boards with well-developed plans and policies provide stability when parish and school administrators are changed.

3. **To offer financial advice**

    Given the complexities which currently face educational institutions, schools need the talents and interests of many people. It is no longer possible nor desirable for the principal to feel the total responsibility for the life of the school. Neither is it a good thing when the pastor thinks that the financial challenges of the parish are his alone. Educational administrators need assistance and boards can be a positive force for dealing with the financial needs of today and planning for the future.

4. **To develop and defend policy**

    Policies give general direction to administrators. They communicate what should be done, not how it should be done.

Board members have the responsibility to develop and defend local policies, as well as to insure that diocesan educational policies are implemented at the local level.

5. **To serve as a good public relations source**

    Involvement, information, and commitment will provide board members with the opportunity to be positive voices on behalf of the Catholic school they represent.

6. **To enable the principal to spend adequate time as an educational leader**

    Many demands are placed on Catholic school principals today. To the extent that an active, involved board participates appropriately in the life of the school, the principal is freer to spend more time as the educational leader of the institution.

7. **To provide parents/guardians with a voice in their children's education**

    Parents, as the first and foremost educators of their children, need a formal systematic forum to participate in decisions affecting them.

8. **To encourage strategic planning**

    Every institution needs a group charged with planning responsibilities. The diocesan or local board is a logical body to assume this charge.

Chapter 1
WHAT IS A CATHOLIC SCHOOL BOARD?

A Catholic school board is a body whose members are selected and/or elected to participate in decision-making in designated areas of responsibility. Usually these areas include planning, policy formulation/enactment, finances, the selection or appointment of the principal, development including public relations and marketing, and evaluation. Board members also include the administrator (principal/superintendent) and canonical administrator (pastor/bishop).

Types of Catholic Schools

The organizational structure of the school will almost always dictate how the school board is constituted. For example, models which are appropriate for the parish elementary school may not be appropriate for the diocesan secondary school or regional school, and are usually not appropriate for most private schools.

Most Catholic schools function within the traditional organization of parish, diocese or religious congregation.

A parish school is part of the educational mission of the parish for which the pastor is the canonical administrator. He delegates, according to diocesan policy, administrative responsibilities to the school principal, who is accountable to him.

Diocesan schools function as part of the diocese and the principal is usually accountable to the bishop through the superintendent of schools.

Private Catholic schools are part of the mission of the religious congregation and the principal is responsible to the elected/appointed community administrators. Some private Catholic schools are owned and operated by lay boards of trustees. In order to call themselves Catholic, these institutions receive formal approval from the diocesan bishop and commit themselves to follow diocesan norms regarding religious education programs and the Catholicity of the school.

An exception to this traditional organizational pattern is the **regional or interparish** school, that is, a school supported by more than one parish. Some dioceses appoint one of the pastors of a contributing parish as the school's canonical administrator. This person, representing the other pastors, is the one to whom the principal is accountable. Some dioceses constitute boards of regional schools with limited jurisdiction. Board constitutions clearly state the canonical relationship between these schools and the parishes and/or dioceses. Other dioceses formally erect this type of school as a separate juridic person and appoint the principal as the canonical administrator.

Types of Boards

Four types of school boards are often referred to in governance literature. They are jurisdictional boards, boards with limited jurisdiction, consultative boards, and regulatory boards. In *A Primer on Educational Governance in the Catholic Church,* these types are defined as follows:

Jurisdictional—a board which not only legislates but also controls. It has final authority and total jurisdiction for all areas of educational policy and administration, as well as the legislative power to enact policy. There are no jurisdictional boards in the Catholic Church.

Board with Limited Jurisdiction—a board which has power limited to certain areas of educational concern. It has final, but not total jurisdiction, since the diocesan bishop has jurisdiction over the religious education and Catholicity of all schools including private schools, and most religious congregations have canonically reserved powers.

Consultative—a board which operates in the policy-making process by formulating and adapting, but never enacting policy. This type of board is more in keeping with shared decision-making in the Catholic church because of the consultative status of the diocesan presbyteral council and the diocesan finance council. The constituting authority establishes those areas where the board is to be consulted. Such action is usually made effective by the board's constitution.

Regulatory—a board which enacts or uses existing rules and regulations to govern the operation of its institutions. This type of board is considered administrative rather than policy-making or consultative. Public school boards are usually designated as regulatory.

Only consultative boards and boards with limited jurisdiction are appropriate models for Catholic school boards.

In order to appreciate the role of these boards, it is necessary to understand the nature of consultation within the church.

Consultative Bodies in the Church

The 1983 Code of Canon Law requires several consultative bodies in each diocese and parish. Each diocese has a presbyteral council and college of consultors (cc. 495, 502), and a finance council (c. 492), and every parish has a finance council (c. 537). Other consultative bodies, such as a diocesan pastoral council and parish pastoral councils, are recommended by the Code. Although not specifically mentioned, education boards, councils, and commissions are certainly within the spirit of the Code and should be constituted within the norms given for the mandated consultative bodies.

Consultation implies that the administrator(s) will listen to the advice of the properly convened body in certain designated matters prior to a decision being made. The operating principle is that the administrator(s) will not act contrary to the advice which has been given, especially when there is a consensus, unless the administrator(s) has an overriding reason. It is customary for the administrator(s) to communicate this reason to the consultative body.

Civil Incorporation

Catholic school boards may or may not be incorporated according to the civil laws of the state and the policies of the diocese or religious congregation. Board members should know and understand the status of the civil corporation with which the board is affiliated.

A diocesan bishop exercises his authority in accord with Canon Law and in accord with all applicable civil law, federal, state, and local. In regard to church property, there are three major systems which states use to legislate ownership: They are: the bishop-as-trustee, the bishop-as-corporation-sole, and the corporation aggregate. In the bishop-as-trustee method, the title to the property is vested in the bishop as trustee and the equitable title is vested in the members of the parish. (The state statutes that apply in this case are the ones that govern nonprofit or religious corporations.) The bishop-as-trustee holds the title for the benefit of the parish. Although he retains the right of supervision and the right to govern in accord with church law, the trustee can delegate the control of the property to the administrator of the parish.

In the bishop-as-corporation-sole method, the bishop holds absolute title to the church's property until he is transferred, retires, or dies. In civil law, the bishop can do anything he wishes with the property as long as it is in compliance with church law. The person who is appointed the new bishop becomes the corporation sole.

In the corporation aggregate method, there are two different ways the property may be owned. In the first, legal title is vested in incorporated trustees with equitable title vested in the non-incorporated parish. In the second, legal title is vested directly in the corporate officers of the parish who are elected and act as a board of directors or trustees. In this case, they are the agents of the corporation. The state statutes that apply here are the ones which govern a charitable trust or an aggregation of charitable trusts.

Religious congregations hold property in their own right according to the laws of the state. The articles of incorporation define the role and authority of the agents of the corporation. According to church law (Canon 1290), all administrators are bound to observe the civil laws of any given territory "with the same effects in a matter which is subject to the governing power of the Church, unless the civil regulations are contrary to divine law or canon law makes some other provision..." (*A Primer on Educational Governance in the Catholic Church*, NCEA, 1987.)

Most diocesan and parish school boards are not separately incorporated while many boards of private and diocesan/regional schools are. The preferred model for private schools of religious congregations and those of diocesan schools is the two-tiered board composed of both corporate members and boards of directors (cf. Appendix for model).

Consultative Boards

A consultative board is one which cooperates in the policy-making process by formulating and adapting, but never enacting policy. To call a group "consultative" does not diminish its importance; rather, it indicates that the body is inserted into the governance structure of the organization in a significant way.

The pastor or canonical administrator related to the school enacts policy developed by a consultative board before it can be promulgated and implemented.

Boards with Limited Jurisdiction

A board with limited jurisdiction has authority limited to certain areas of educational concern. It has final, but not total jurisdiction. The constitutions of boards with limited jurisdiction should clearly state the areas in which the board has authority and those which are reserved to the bishop and/or to the religious congregation. For example, these boards have no authority to change the diocesan philosophy of education or to formulate local policies which are not in concert with diocesan policies in religious education. Most religious congregations reserve such powers as approval to change the philosophy and mission of the school, approval of debts over a certain amount, ownership of property, and others (cf. Appendix for sample constitutions).

Diocesan Boards

Diocesan school boards are usually constituted as consultative to the diocesan bishop. The policies which they develop are enacted/approved by the bishop and promulgated by him for implementation in the diocese.

Areas of Board Responsibility

Those areas in which all Catholic school boards should be involved are:

Planning — establishing a mission statement and a strategic plan.

Policy Formulation/Enactment — to give general direction for administrative action.

Finances — developing plans and means to finance ongoing educational programs including setting tuition, negotiating subsidy, and developing the annual budget.

Selection/appointment of the principal — participating according to its constitution and the policies of the diocese and/or religious congregation in determining the principal.

Development, including public relations and marketing — includes understanding the school's mission, a commitment to that vision, the involvement of people, the formulation of a plan, the development and presentation of a case statement to the public, and finally the acquisition of funds to bring the plan to fruition.

Evaluation — determining whether goals and plans are being met, not evaluating individual staff members, administrators or students, except the principal's relationship with the board, and determining the board's own effectiveness.

Chapters two through seven detail these responsibilities.

Decision-Making

Consensus-building is the appropriate mode of decision-making for a Catholic school board. Consensus means that all board members agree to support the decision which appears to be the best, under the present circumstances, for the greatest number of people. In those cases where a vote needs to be recorded for legal purposes, *Roberts Rules of Order Revised* should be followed.

Catholic School Boards Differ from Public School Boards

A public school board is constituted as regulatory, one which enacts or uses existing rules and regulations to govern the operation of its institution. This type of board is considered administrative and differs significantly from the consultative or limited-jurisdiction board appropriate for Catholic schools.

PUBLIC SCHOOL BOARDS	CATHOLIC SCHOOL BOARDS
End: provide free education to all	End: provide Catholic education to those who choose it
Responsibility: for school system's general operation	Responsibility: specific operation and religious dimension of one particular school or diocese
Orientation: civic, societal	Orientation: Catholic Church
Type: Regulatory	Type: Consultative or With Limited Jurisdiction
Entity: Legal	Entity: Legal entity only if separately incorporated
Establishment: by law	Establishment: by episcopal mandate or by religious congregation
Membership: elected or appointed to represent constituencies	Membership: elected or appointed to serve educational mission of church
Impact: own locality	Impact: the entire Church

Chapter 2
PLANNING

Catholic schools are involved in planning activities in a variety of ways. For example, each year the faculty plans inservice opportunities and curriculum development. The school itself usually participates in a type of planning in conjunction with its regular evaluation and accreditation process. The board, usually through its long-range planning committee, assesses where the school is currently and where it hopes to be in the next three to five years. The rationale for board planning is best expressed in the adage, "If you don't know where you're going, any plan will do" (Drucker). Long-range or strategic planning is an absolute necessity for Catholic schools, especially in terms of development and effective budgeting. The chair of the long-range planning committee is a member of the board, but committee members need not be.

Some Pitfalls of Planning

- If preparations are not made carefully, planning can cause groups to focus on problems without ever coming up with solutions. Some problems seem so insurmountable that people give up. Planning has to be done in such a way that the group has small successes along the way.
- Planning may heighten interpersonal tensions within a group or organization. When these tensions surface, they may obstruct the planning process. Some means has to be built in that will diffuse interpersonal problems.
- Planning can allow people to concentrate on paper solutions or on ideas instead of action. Sometimes organizations get so caught up in the planning process that they never get to the implementation stage. It is very easy to push paper around; it is not as easy to motivate and lead people.
- Planning that involves goal setting and the writing of objectives (for example, management by objective) can tend to lower standards after it has been used more than one year. People recognize very quickly that they will be judged only on the objectives they write. Therefore, they tend to write objectives that will not make as many demands on them as the ones they wrote

in the previous year. Management by objectives usually works very well the first year, but tends to help people slide into mediocrity thereafter.
- Planning can lead to inflated budgets. People tend to budget according to all the contingencies they thought of during the planning process, which in turn tends to raise they amount of money they request for any given project. Group planning includes good budgeting which will help keep the budget realistic.

One Practical Planning Approach

Successful planning includes the steps listed below in the order they are given. The amount of time that any group spends on each of the steps is a part of the planning process. The board is responsible for its own planning and should work closely with the principal in planning for the school.

A. Develop ideal goals

The best way to start out any planning process is to develop the ideal picture of what things should look like at the end of the plan. Starting off with the best situation or scenario stops people from killing good ideas before they ever get off the ground. It is also good to remember that it is much easier to tone down an exciting idea than it is to enhance one that is not exciting or interesting.

In planning, the group can write as many ideal goals as necessary but should cover all aspects of the situation. An example of an ideal goal for a school would be that there will be full enrollment for the coming year, or that there will be no deficit for the coming year.

B. Identify and describe the influences and constraints

Once the ideal picture has been established, then the group can come back to earth and deal with constraints. These could be technical, financial, legal, moral, political, social or demographic limitations. The key during this stage is to concentrate on what is and not what should be.

For example, to have no deficit for next year, the school would have to raise $100,000 through either tuition or third-source funding.

C. Set attainable goals

Attainable goals are the result of adjusting the ideal goals in light of the influences and constraints.

Once the new goals have been written, it is important to see whether or not they have maintained their exciting nature.

An example for an attainable goal might be to have no school deficit three years in the future.

D. Develop alternatives for reaching the goals

There is never just one way to do anything. Creativity and imagination are the key factors here. Even the most outlandish ideas must not be dismissed too quickly. The key to success is brainstorming and a ban on all comments like "That's not practical," "We've never done it that way before," "We don't have the time." Just the fact that there is a backup plan increases confidence and the chances that the preferred plan will be successful.

For example, if the group locks in on only tuition as a solution, the goal may not be attained; they should look at all aspects of raising funds and cutting expenses.

E. Do a cost-effective analysis

After the alternatives have been identified and established, it is important for the group to decide on the most effective alternative. The choice is between a) what are the costs, and b) what are the benefits. Cost does not just mean money; it can refer to money, time, space, morale, public relations.

For example, it may be possible to raise tuition to eliminate the deficit, but the school may lose 30 students.

It is always necessary to have a detailed written time schedule for each plan. Without it, there is no accountability.

F. Establish fallback positions for failed plans

No group is infallible. It is always possible that the best plans will not succeed. The future is not predictable, no matter how good the plan. Thus, it is important to plan for contingencies, that is, to have fallback positions in the event that the future does not turn out the way it is projected. For example, suppose the pastor who is very supportive of the school is transferred and the new pastor is not as supportive; what happens then?

G. Implement and evaluate the plan

Use the timetable previously established to begin implementation of the plan. The group itself should monitor the plan closely to see that there is constant evaluation. Usually the principal and the board chairperson have the responsibility for seeing that evaluation takes place. On a yearly basis, there should be a more in-depth and formal evaluation of the long-range plan.

Roles and Responsibilities in Planning

As the canonical administrator of the parish which includes the parish school, the pastor's primary responsibility in planning is to commission the preparation of a formal long-range plan. This commission is usually done in writing to the school board and principal, and when the process is under way, the pastor provides information to the board regarding parish finances, attendance trends, and parish goals and directions. At the beginning, it is helpful if the pastor communicates any "non-negotiables" that the board should keep in mind.

As the educational leader of the school, the principal is responsible for working with the chair to initiate the planning process and guide it to completion.

The primary role of the school board is to receive information from the faculty and administration to develop assumptions that will be included in the long-range plan, and to place these assumptions within a policy framework. It is important that the board not become involved in the administration of the school.

Plan Format

This suggested long-range plan appears in the NCEA publication *Elementary School Finance Manual*. It is designed not only to provide a direction for the school, but also as an historical perspective for that direction. As a result, the narrative section of the long-range plan should be completed in such a way that each major topic area discusses the historical perspective, the current situation, and the assumptions which have been adopted for the future. In short, the narrative should attempt to answer these questions:
- Where have we been?
- What factors have influenced our historical development?
- Where are we today and why?
- Where are we going and why?
- How are we going to get there?

Each of these questions should be related to the philosophy of Catholic education generally and to the individual school in particular. In addition, the narrative should support the projections made in each section of the plan (enrollment, curriculum, staffing, facilities, finance and development).

Again, it should be emphasized that care should be taken during each phase of the plan's creation, to involve various individuals who have particular interest in, and responsibility for, that section of the plan.

Developing the Long-Range Plan

The following suggested chronology may be used by individual school boards and principals for developing a comprehensive long-range plan.

MONTH	PERSON RESPONSIBLE—TASK
July	**Principal**—Set aside time for dreaming and goal setting. What problems and opportunities exist for the school? What should it be doing better? What ought it to emphasize now to be more faithful to its philosophy?
August	**Principal/Board Chairperson**—Issue recommitment invitation to board members. Make committee assignments. Note: During initial

year, provide board members with *To Teach As Jesus Did, The Catholic School, Teach Them, Religious Dimensions of Education in the Catholic School,* and the school's philosophy.

Arrange and conduct board preservice program—include discussion of:
- Philosophy
- Roles and Responsibilities
- Distinction between policy making and administration

Pastor/Principal—Issue letter to board commissioning long-range plan.

September

Principal/Board Chairperson/School Board—Convene long-range planning committee. Review basic assumptions, constraints and timetable. Administrator shares dreams, problems and possibilities for school with board. Board reviews school position in light of documents listed above, diocesan goals and school philosophy.

October

Principal with Committee—Review enrollment history and enrollment mix. Begins creation of narrative, citing reasons for enrollment changes.

Enrollment and/or Data Committee
- Collect and study prior five-year enrollments by grade and by religious category (Catholic parishioners, Catholic non-parishioners, non-Catholics).
- Collect and study baptismal records for parish(es) for last five years. (High schools will need to study feeder school trends.)
- Compare baptismal records to "parishioner enrollment" for appropriate years.
- Study grade-to-grade attrition over five-year period.
- Secure pertinent data from local public school officials concerning population trends in public school enrollment projections.
- Secure population trend information from Census Bureau, Chamber of Commerce and telephone company.
- Build a five-year enrollment projection based on all of the above. The projection should list enrollments first by grade and then by religious mix. Be sure to consider current demographics, trends, health and fire codes as well as class size.
- Outline plans for market research as required.

November

Principal with Committee—Prepare enrollment projections for five years by grade level with accompanying narrative. A marketing plan for school "image" and enrollment should accompany enrollment projections in order to insure ability to achieve projections.

December   **Principal/Faculty** — Complete curriculum section of five-year plan and present for review by board through committee.
- Review and revise the school philosophy in light of *To Teach As Jesus Did, The Catholic School, Religious Dimensions of Education in the Catholic School,* and other documents cited including diocesan guidelines.
- Review current curriculum in light of diocesan guidelines and build a five-year plan for curriculum, updating as necessary.
- Include assumptions concerning textbooks (purchasing and replacement), library books, workbooks, equipment, teaching aids, audio-visual equipment, laboratory supplies, guidance, campus ministry, cafeteria, etc.
- Build a catalog of investment opportunities based on the dreams of the principal and staff.
- Evaluate program offerings including specialized areas, e.g. Physical Education, Music, Art, etc.

January   **Principal**—By reviewing current personnel records on all teachers, prepare an historical perspective and overview of current staffing situations, including qualifications, experience, salary, benefits, etc. This perspective is reviewed by the board.

Review staffing assumptions for next five years and prepare a summary for the board.

Principal/Pastor/Committee—Based on enrollment and staffing assumptions, prepare a five-year projection for staffing by grade and/or department. Assumptions should be made in the areas of salaries and fringe benefits.

February   **Principal/Pastor/Board Facilities Committee**—Complete initial plan for plant and facilities.
- Make a complete survey of all physical facilities available, including school buildings, residences and grounds. Based on current fire and health codes, list all necessary and desirable repairs and capital improvements.
- Develop a five-year plan to complete improvements. Include cost estimates. Survey should be specific as to the number of classrooms and specialized areas to be utilized.
- Build a catalog of investment opportunities based on capital improvements and repairs to buildings, grounds, furniture and equipment.

March   **Principal/Pastor/Board Finance Committee**—Review school costs for the last three years using annual reports.
- Insure that all line items are exclusively those of the school, and are not attributable to other parish or religious education programs.

- Develop an expenditure budget based on enrollment, curriculum, staffing, and plant and facility considerations. (Financial growth assumptions should be stated clearly in footnotes or in the assumptions section of the plan.) Include provision for some level of student assistance.

April

Principal/Pastor/Board Finance Committee—Develop a five-year income plan with realistic assumptions in the areas of tuition, subsidies, traditional fundraising, and investment opportunities.

- Create a five-year development plan.

May

Board—Review the completed five-year plan including projections and accompanying narrative in the areas of philosophy, enrollment, curriculum, staffing, plant and facilities, and finances and development.
- Approve five-year plan.

June

Principal/Board—Prepare summary "Case Statement" and Development Plan, based on five-year plan, to be used in promoting the school to various publics. (Note: may take more than one month.)
- Identify Case Statement. Summarize history, philosophy, vision and objectives of school, in a manner that invites credibility and investment. This statement should stress the unique and desirable characteristics of the total educational program, especially through elements related to the school's Catholic identity.
- Identify for past five years:
  —Alumni relations
  —Public relations
  —Special gifts
  —Publics being served
  —Endowments
  —Foundation grants
  —Business/industry participation
  —Estate planning (bequests)
  —Insurance gifts
  —Fundraising gifts.
- Identify priorities for next five years.
- Project realistic involvement and dollar increase to support Finance Committee projections.
- Establish appropriate committees to respond to five-year priority selections.

Note: It is assumed that in fulfillment of the planning role assigned to him/her above, the principal will involve the faculty, through frequent consultation and other appropriate ways.

Using the Long-Range Plan

When the five-year plan, including specific actions and strategies, is completed, it becomes the basic guideline document for the principal, pastor and board. The plan should be reviewed, refined and updated on an annual basis, so that it continually looks four years into the future.

It should be pointed out that the full five-year plan is not designed for general circulation. For that purpose, a "Case Statement" based on the five-year plan should be prepared which summarizes the assumptions made in each of the areas including enrollment, curriculum, staffing, plant finance, and development. The philosophy and mission statement of the school should also be clearly stated.

It is, of course, understood that every effort should be made during the planning process to insure that the curriculum and all aspects of the plan are reflective of the philosophy, and that the values of Catholic education are well integrated with the curriculum.

From the school board's point of view, the long-range plan becomes the guiding document from which annual budgets are developed. These budgets should, on an annual basis, be based on and reflective of the school's long-range plan.

Finally, five-year planning should be seen not as an end in itself, but as a prerequisite to and a part of good development, and as an important help to the school in attaining its goals.

Annual Update of Long-Range Plan

It is essential that the five-year plan be updated annually in each succeeding year. In order to simplify the annual update, all of the data used to prepare the plan must be carefully documented and available for future use.

In order to insure that the projections are updated annually, it is recommended that the school board formally adopt a policy requiring that the update take place. During the updating process, every effort should be made not only to develop an additional year's projection, but also to revise and to refine the assumptions used throughout the plan.

Chapter 3
POLICY FORMULATION AND ENACTMENT

While a school board engages in many activities, two are major ways for giving direction and advice. These are planning and formulating policies. Planning gives the board purpose and focuses its energy. It provides the board with a year-long (or multi-year) agenda. Policies convey to the school the mind of the board on critical or sensitive matters. Policies are intermediaries between the school's climate and its philosophy on the one hand, and its regulations and practices on the other hand.

Relationship: Law/Policy/Regulation

Before discussing policy formulation in some detail, it will be helpful to discuss the relationship between and among laws, policies and regulations.

Law

According to Canon Law, the ordinary is the sole legislator in a diocese. This authority may not be delegated. The canons go on to say that "a law comes into being when it is promulgated" (Canon 7), and "laws are authentically interpreted by the legislator, and by that person to whom the legislator entrusts the power of authentic interpretation" (Canon 16).

Policy

Policy is a guide to discretionary action by the administrator. It states what should be done, not how it should be done.

There are three aspects to policy. A policy must be formulated, enacted and implemented before it is accurate to say that policy exists. The formulation of policy is the responsibility of the diocesan or local school board or board of trustees. Enactment of policy is a function of authority. If the board is constituted with limited jurisdiction, then in those areas in which it has jurisdiction, the board legitimately enacts authority.

For consultative boards, policies must be enacted by either the ordinary of the diocese or the pastor of the parish before the policies may be implemented by the educational administrator.

Regulations

Regulations are administrative acts designed to assist in the implementation of policy and are the responsibility of the educational administrator.

Rev. James Mallet, writing about different boards and commissions, makes a proper distinction between law and policy:

> In my judgment, binding norms or law should be issued by the bishop only in special cases where it is necessary to protect rights and promote the common good. This understanding of the limited nature of law is incorporated in the revised code...Where it is a question of rights, laws may be necessary. To give one example: If a diocese instituted a retirement program for all school teachers, it would not suffice merely to exhort pastors and principals to cooperate with this program. The demands of justice would require the cooperation of all administrators so that equitable retirement benefits can be provided for all teachers.
>
> I understand a policy to be a statement which limits the administrative discretion proper to administrators. Arbitrariness in administration should be eliminated, but administrators need to exercise a certain flexibility in the application of standard criteria and procedures. Policies provide limitations to this administrative discretion. . . . I do not believe that policies should be understood as laws, since laws completely eliminate discretionary application unless the administrator obtains a dispensation from higher authority. Educational policies promulgated by competent diocesan authorities are often recognized as binding by civil courts. (cf. *A Primer on Educational Governance in the Catholic Church*, NCEA, 1987.)

The question arises: If policies are not laws in the strict canonical definition, then what is their binding force? According to Canon 27, "custom is the best interpreter of laws." The custom in recent years has been for the ordinary of the diocese to write the introductory letter to diocesan policy manuals, stating that the policies are to be operative in the parishes and schools in his diocese.

For example, in his introductory letter to the 1985 "Policy Manual for Elementary and Secondary Schools, Diocese of Little Rock," Bishop Andrew J. MacDonald states, "In presenting this handbook for use in our school system, I offer it with the full measure of my teaching authority as the bishop of the diocese."

In statutes for diocesan high schools promulgated by the Diocese of Nashville, the following statement is used: "These statutes are laws of the Roman Catholic Diocese of Nashville, promulgated by the Bishop of Nashville in his legislative capacity, and become effective on July 1, 1982."

Significance of Policies

Policies promulgated with an introductory letter from the ordinary of the diocese, indicating his intention that the policies be implemented in his parishes and schools, have the same force as "diocesan laws" in our understanding of civil law.

In preparing diocesan policy manuals, the diocesan educational administrator should clarify with the bishop his intentions, and make that known in the introductory letter to the manual.

In our civil system, law as it applies to private schools is basically contract law. What constitutes the contract between teachers, parents and Catholic schools is policy. Boards should be sure that the terms of the contract are clear by defining with accuracy diocesan law and diocesan and local policies and regulations.

Boards also need information regarding the civil incorporation under which they function (cf. Chapter 1). The agent(s) of the civil corporation or their delegates are those authorized to enter into contractual agreements. Agency creates liability.

Ordinarily, a consultative board is not liable except in cases of negligence, while a board with limited jurisdiction is liable in those areas where it has delegated authority.

The Board and Policy

A policy is "a guide for discretionary action." It tells people what the board expects, but not how to accomplish it. Formulating policy is a responsibility of the board. Determining how policy is to be implemented is a responsibility of the administration. The term "regulation" is used to describe the administrator's means for specifying how people are to act or how something is to be done. In addition to regulations, administrators also use programs, procedures, and organizational structures for getting the administrative job done.

In contrast to regulations, policies are broad, general, and direction-setting statements. Regulations are specific, concrete, and tightly written; ideally, they contain few loopholes. If you want to know whether you have a policy or a regulation, ask yourself: "Does this statement leave room for discretionary action on the part of the administrator?" If the answer is "yes," you have a policy. If it is "no," you have a regulation. There are few exceptions to this rule. Occasionally, however, overriding considerations will motivate the board to adopt a very specific policy (for example, the establishment of a tuition payment plan or a grievance procedure).

Some policies, by their nature, call for regulations to support them; other policies exist primarily to set a tone or to establish the school's position (for example, a personnel policy calling for nondiscrimination in hiring practices). By the same token, not every administrative regulation has to flow from policy. Some arise out of practical concerns or the need to implement applicable state or federal law; others are an outgrowth of the school's philosophy or tradition.

Some Things Policy Can Do

- **Give general direction to the administration**
  If the board does not give direction to the administrator, it has failed in its purpose for existing. However, the board must be careful not to tie the hands of the administrator with a collection of detailed demands and restrictions; it is the administrator's job to "run the school."

- **Anticipate and forestall crises**
  As the proverbial line goes, "An ounce of prevention is worth a pound of cure." While policy cannot prevent a lawsuit (or a catastrophe), it can guide the administrator to take reasonable precautions and reduce the possibility that rash judgment or negligence will rule in a crisis situation.

- **Clarify expectations for students, parents, teachers and others**
  A policy lets people know where the school stands and "what happens if..." they choose to disregard that position. Those associated with the school have a right and a duty to know what the school expects of them.

- **Codify and preserve the board's decisions**
  Board policies should not be a well-kept secret, nor should board members have to sift through piles of old minutes in order to trace the decisions of their predecessors. Once enacted, board policies should be promulgated (through the school's normal channels of communication), numbered, and placed in a folder or manual of school policies. A loose-leaf binder is a useful means for maintaining the school's policies. Reference to policies in handbooks for students, teachers, and parents can also help preserve the board's decisions and communicate them to those whom they affect.

- **Reduce subjectivity, inconsistency, and arbitrariness**
  Charges of unfairness and inconsistency are some of the most damaging accusations that can be made against a school or its administrators. As board members and administrators change, keeping track of prior decisions and the reasons behind them becomes even more difficult. Policies foster continuity and assist the school through periods of transition between administrators and board members.

Some Things Policy Can't Do

- **Control or supervise administration**
  The board should be able to trust its administrator to implement policy and to manage the day-to-day operations of the school. The principal is the school's professional leader — that

is the job he/she has been hired to do. If, after unsuccessful attempts to resolve differences, the board cannot put faith in the administrator, then the board's responsibility is to find a new administrator, not to try to administer the school.

- **Resolve specific problems after the fact**
  While surviving an unexpected or unavoidable disaster may suggest the need for new or changed policies, policies cannot be made to work retroactively. People cannot be held responsible for rules enacted after the fact.
- **Address isolated cases or petty items**
  To create a policy for the exceptional case is a mistake. It creates misunderstanding regarding the school's "norms;" it can cause bad will and poor public relations; it can backfire on the board by legitimizing (even glorifying) actions that are unacceptable or petty. Individual cases should be addressed individually — by the administrator, with those responsible for them.
- **Substitute for programs**
  Policies, by their nature, give general direction. They cannot educate. If students' standardized test scores are disturbingly low, a policy directing that they be higher probably will not help.

When Do Policies Get Developed?

In the natural cycle of board activity, formulating policy comes up at several times:

a. When the board does its annual goal-setting. As the board surfaces needs and wants and translates these into goals, specification of the goals usually calls for either projects/programs to be undertaken or policies to be developed.

b. When there is a problem to be resolved or a decision to be made, and there is neither a local guideline nor a guideline from a higher level of governance to which the school or school system can appeal.

c. As a third opportunity: the school or school system should review its manual of policies on a regular basis (every five years is not an unmanageable time frame). Ordinarily, such a review will surface areas in which new policies are needed, suggest points of clarification for existing policies, and lead to the discarding of policies which are no longer useful.

Getting to Policy

There are 10 steps in the life cycle of a policy proposal, from the idea state to formal approval to follow-up. The example which is used to illustrate these steps is one in which the board is working on a code of conduct for students (policy proposal on discipline).

1. **Determine the need**
   Suggestions for policy can come from numerous sources: the

administrator, parents, teachers, board members themselves, a generally recognized need arising from a unique set of circumstances. The board should ask itself whether policy really is the best way to respond to the need. Is the item petty? Is it likely to recur? Does it really require a *program* rather than a policy? One person on a policy committee should be appointed to research the need and draft a policy proposal. An example: A priest who is a board member of a local community agency serving abused children approached the bishop with a request for assurance that the local disciplinary policies of the Catholic schools respect the dignity of persons of all ages and follow generally accepted educational principles. He was particularly concerned about the number of Catholic schools which still permit corporal punishment. With the bishop's knowledge, the priest wrote to each Catholic school to urge schools to reassess their disciplinary policies and to prohibit corporal punishment where it is allowed. Specific policy formulation follows this assessment.

2. **Identify the issues involved and the facts surrounding them**
Ask: What do we know about this matter? Are there likely to be varying points of view on how to address it? What assumptions, beliefs, and values underlie these points of view? Who has vested interests? What authorities, principles, or laws need to be respected? In this example:
   a. State law allows corporal punishment.
   b. Recently enacted legislation (highly publicized) gives each district in the state the authority to prohibit corporal punishment. While this legislation does not bind Catholic schools, there is strong public pressure on the Catholic schools to conform to the law.
   c. The priest who brought the matter before the bishop is a well-known figure and considered a champion of causes involving human rights.
   d. The existing code of conduct in this school is written in negative language and includes a lengthy list of acceptable forms of punishment—including corporal punishment.
   e. Many parents in the school favor strictness. There rarely are complaints regarding measures used to discipline students.
   f. While corporal punishment almost never is used by the school, parents are known to brag that this Catholic school reminds them of the "good old days" when "if you didn't do what you were told, Sister gave you a good rap over the knuckles." Older sisters deny that hitting students was ever an approved disciplinary practice.
   g. The diocese has left to each school the right to determine its code of conduct for students.

3. **Gather data**
The identification of issues and the facts surrounding them will

lead to a search for further information to support one (or more) policy options. This information is used for formulating the policy, building the rationale for it, and projecting possible consequences for the position recommended. The board also may find it desirable to engage "experts" for a presentation to accompany the first reading of the policy proposal. This is particularly advantageous where the subject matter is complex or controversial. In this example, the following materials should be available:

a. Copies of current state law;

b. Documentation on the states which permit (and prohibit) corporal punishment; documentation on what other public and Catholic schools in the area have done regarding codes of conduct for students;

c. Position statements from relevant professional groups (medical, psychological, educational, etc.);

d. Articles on the effectiveness of various forms of school discipline.

The board invited the diocesan assistant superintendent of schools (who also teaches administration courses in a local college) to give an overview of the research on school disciplinary practices prior to the first reading of the policy proposal.

4. **Draft the policy**

Generally, one person is designated as the writer of a policy proposal. If the board uses a policy committee, the committee might serve as readers to critique the draft before its presentation to the entire board. If several options for policy have been considered, **one** is chosen for presentation to the board at the first reading. It is wise to seek legal counsel regarding the policy proposal before presenting it to the board. The recommended policy proposal should be briefly and clearly stated and supported by attached documentation. The person charged with presenting the proposal for the first reading should be prepared to explain the rationale behind the recommendation and to project possible consequences if the policy is adopted. In this example, a policy proposal was drafted by the principal with the aid of several teachers. It was submitted to the board with articles on discipline and a copy of the state law regarding corporal punishment.

5. **First reading**

At the first reading of a policy proposal, the policy is presented for understanding and clarification of what is being recommended. This is an opportunity for a "case" to be made (with or without the aid of experts) for the proposal and for questions to be answered. The proposal is **not** debated at this time, nor (as a rule) are changes made to it. In this example, the presentation by the assistant superintendent allowed board members to question disciplinary practices in other schools. It also took some of the pressure off the principal in explaining the rationale for the code of behavior recommended in the proposal.

6. **Consultation**

   Time allowed for consultation depends upon the school or school system's immediate need, the board's calendar, the desire for additional input from experts, and the board's decision as to whether a public hearing or open board meeting on the policy issue is in the best interests of those concerned. If other groups are affected by the policy, there should be sufficient time for these groups to meet and to submit their opinions to the board. In this example, a space of one meeting between first and second readings allowed board members time to talk with randomly selected parents (by phone). The faculty invited the board to a faculty meeting to discuss the proposed code of conduct; many board members were able to attend.

7. **Second reading**

   The second reading of a policy proposal affords formal opportunity for discussion and vote. At this time, the proposal can be accepted, amended and accepted, sent back to the writer(s) for reworking, or rejected. In this example, several parents attended the board meeting at which the vote took place. They had no quarrels with the proposal, but asked how it would be spelled out in specific rules for students. The principal invited several of these parents to serve on the faculty committee charged with revising the student handbook. The proposal passed with a consensus position of the entire board.

8. **Approval**

   If the policy has been altered from its original form, it should be reviewed by legal counsel before final action is taken. Once passed by the board, a policy then must be submitted to the appropriate authority for formal approval (e.g., the pastor in a parish school, selected pastor in an interparochial school, ordinary at the diocesan level). In this example, the pastor signed the policy and urged support for it.

9. **Promulgation**

   All of those affected by board policy should be informed when policies are added, deleted, and changed. Those who must use the policy should receive copies of it. Other channels of communication may include the school's newsletter, parish bulletin, diocesan newsletter, church bulletin boards, letters home to parents, school handbooks, and even presentations at meetings of teachers, clergy, parents, and students (should the issue require it). In this example, the policy was incorporated into the handbooks for students, parents and teachers. In each case, the policy preceded more detailed explanations of regulations for students. Immediately following the pastor's approval of the policy, it was reproduced in a letter sent to parents by the principal and accompanied by a brief history of the policy's development.

10. **Follow up**

It is the responsibility of the board to evaluate the effectiveness of its policies after they have had a reasonable time to be tried. This might be several months or a year, depending upon the circumstances. In addition, the board should have an internal mechanism for reviewing all policies on a regular basis (perhaps every five years). In this case, the board decided to evaluate the effectiveness of the policy by conducting a random survey of parents and asking the principal to conduct interviews of a similar nature with staff and selected students at the close of the following school year (one year away).

Areas Which Need Policies

Schools write policies where the need exists for them. That is why a "master list" of policy areas can be dangerous. If the school is part of a larger (diocesan) school system, many topics already may be covered by policy which supercedes that of the local school board. In those cases, the local board is usually free to make the policy more specific to its circumstances, as long as the resulting statement does not conflict with that of diocesan policy. For example, in one diocese where use of corporal punishment was strongly discouraged, many individual school boards formulated policies prohibiting the use of corporal punishment altogether. The following list contains topics which frequently become substance for local school policies:

- Relationships with public schools
- Financial reports to the school community
- Use of the school facilities
- Hiring, evaluating, and releasing personnel
- Job descriptions for nonprofessional staff members
- Personnel benefits
- Purchasing procedures
- School visitors
- Admissions criteria and priorities
- Discipline/suspension and dismissal
- Field trips
- Uniforms
- Tuition payments; penalties for non-payment
- Athletic eligibility
- Substance abuse
- Married students/pregnancy/single parents
- AIDS

Good Policies

Good policies achieve their purpose if they
- respond to or anticipate educational needs of the community
- are clear enough to give guidance, broad enough to give space

- are stated in language that is clear, simple, non-technical
- are communicated to all, but especially to those affected
- are written down
- are systematically indexed and placed in a loose-leaf manual
- are regularly evaluated

Codification Systems

The Davies-Brickle Codification System, adapted by many school boards, contains these categories:

1000 Community Relations
2000 Administration
3000 Business and Noninstructional Operations
4000 Personnel
5000 Students
6000 Instruction
7000 New Construction
8000 Internal Board Operations
9000 Bylaws of the Board

Local school boards should use the system in effect in their own diocese for the sake of consistency. For example, it is important that each local board have its own book of local policies which are codified in a way that is similar to the system used by the diocese.

Diocesan Policies

Subsidiarity is the guiding principle. This requires that "what can be accomplished by initiative and industry at one level should not be assigned to or assumed by a higher organization or authority." With that principle in mind, the following guidelines should be helpful.

Diocesan policies
- are developed and evaluated by the diocesan board
- are guides for the superintendent's and/or the principals' discretionary action
- govern all of the schools (elementary and/or secondary as approved by the diocesan board) in the diocese
- provide the framework within which local policies and regulations can be written
- are adopted where the overall good of the system is best served by common policy

Once passed by the diocesan board, proposed policies become policies subject to the approval of the bishop. Once signed and dated by the bishop, policies passed by the diocesan board become binding upon the superintendent, pastors, principals, and staffs of the schools in the diocese.

Chapter 4
THE ROLE OF THE BOARD IN FINANCES

How Schools are Funded

Before a Catholic school board can appreciate its role in the financial management of the school, it is important for the board to understand how Catholic schools are funded and the differences which exist between the funding of public and Catholic schools.

How Schools are Funded
Funding of Public Schools[1]
[1]Reference: Futrell, Mary Hatwood, NEA, "An educator's Opinion, Who Pays for America's Schools?" The Washington Post, p. B3, Sunday, June 7, 1987.

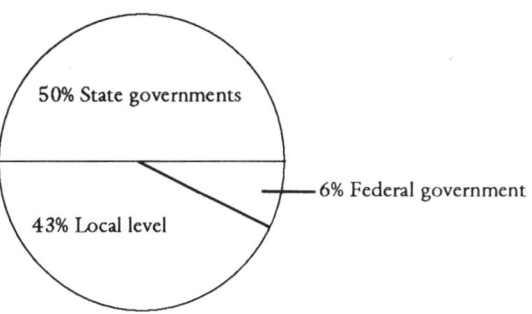

Funding of Catholic Elementary Schools
1986-87 U.S. Average[2]
[2]Reference: United States Catholic Elementary Schools & Their Finances, 1988 NCEA Data Bank Report.

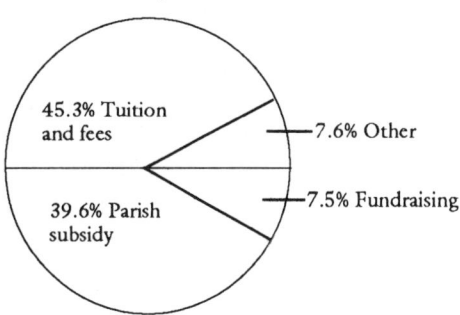

25

National Estimated Funding of Catholic Secondary Schools[3]
[3]Reference: Catholic High Schools & Their Finances 1986, page 13, NCEA Data Bank Publication.

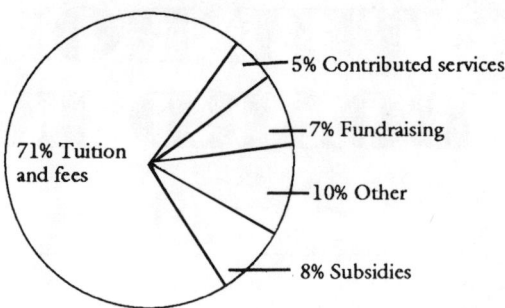

Catholic schools are funded from a combination of tuition, subsidies (parish, diocesan, religious congregation, and contributed services), fundraising, and development. Public schools on the other hand, are funded from state, local and federal taxes.

The current funding trend in the public schools is toward more state aid rather than local aid in order to equalize educational opportunities for all public school students in the state.

On the other hand, Catholic school funding remains dependent on tuition, with assistance from subsidy and increasing development efforts. However, several state conferences of Catholic bishops in pastoral letters have re-stated that the financing of Catholic schools is the responsibility of the total Catholic community — not just users and staff.

School boards should always include provisions for some financial aid in budgets so that Catholic schools remain available to students regardless of their family's socio-economic status.

The manner in which the board is constituted will certainly determine who has authority to make final decisions. Whether the board is constituted as consultative or one with limited jurisdiction, it is involved in two major areas of financial management: the annual budget and tuition.

Budget

The annual budget is the key to financial control and is based on the philosophy, mission statement and long-range plan of the school.

The expenditure budget is prepared by the finance committee of the board and the principal, and considers the total amount of money to be spent and the cost per pupil in relation to schools of similar size and situation, both on a diocesan and national level. The *Elementary School Finance Manual* and the *Self-Study Guide for Catholic High Schools*, both published by NCEA, are resources for this information.

The income budget is prepared by the finance committee of the board and the principal, in conjunction with the pastor and the finance council of the parish or parishes involved. At the diocesan school, or private Catholic school, appropriate diocesan and religious congregation personnel should be involved. The income budget considers the financial mixes and relationship among subsidies, tuition, fees and assessment, fundraising and development.

The amount of subsidy which the school receives is determined by the parish, diocese, or religious congregation. The finance committee of the parish school board should meet with the finance council of the parish and the pastor to determine the amount the total parish will invest in the school. The school subsidy is part of the parish budget and is approved with the total parish budget according to diocesan and parish policies and practices. The approval of the school budget is the responsibility of the school board according to its procedures and guidelines. Other schools' subsidy is determined by diocesan and religious congregation policies.

Budget Preparation Guidelines

1. Budget figures should be realistic and not "padded." A contingency account should be established to meet unanticipated expenses.

2. The budget makes realistic allowances for inflation.

3. The budget format should follow the standard "Chart of Accounts" (NCEA *Elementary School Finance Manual,* 1984 or other approved charts of accounts).

4. Projected expenses should have supporting documentation to justify the planned expenditure.

5. Projected income items should have a supporting plan to insure that the income can, in fact, be realized. Do not budget uncertain income.

6. The budget should reflect the priorities of the board and administration. New programs or expanded programs should not be forced into a pre-established budget.

7. The budget includes all expenditure items. Budgeted figures should be based on actual expectations using the most recent expenditure data. Avoid basing line item budgets on the prior year's budget.

8. The budget should include money for financial aid to families who cannot afford the tuition.

Budget Calendar

A regular, scheduled approach to budget preparation through the use of a calendar can provide the necessary structuring to the budget process for a school. In NCEA's *Elementary School Finance Manual,* the following calendar is suggested:

MONTH	RESPONSIBLE PARTY AND TASKS
July	Principal with monthly monitoring by school board—Begin implementation of current year's budget.
August	No budgeting activity.

September (and each succeeding month)	**Principal and school board**—Review monthly and year-to-date actual performance against budget
October	**School board's long-range plan committee**—Update five-year plan. Present new assumptions to the budget development committee no later than December.
	Principal/school board; school board budget or finance committee—Convene budget planning committee for review of basic assumptions set forth in the long-range plan.
December	**Principal/school board finance committee**—Begin actual preparation of annual budget based on revised long-range plan.
	Principal—Present **school board finance committee** members with budget preparation forms and "Chart of Accounts." Assign responsibilities for various sections of the budget.
	Develop assumptions in the areas of enrollment and staffing presentation to the committee in January.
January	**Principal**—Finalize enrollment and staffing assumptions, including salary schedules and fringe benefits.
	Use back-up forms detailing faculty by name, grade taught, salary base, and additional information.
	Distribute budget request information to faculty for use in preparing textbook, supply, and departmental requests.
February	**Principal and school board finance committee**—Develop line-by-line expenditure budget using faculty and departmental requests, as well as assumptions built into long-range plan.
	List all salary costs, including fixed charges and fringe benefits. This will be the largest single expenditure in the operating budget. It should be refined and finalized at this point.
	Detail building repairs and improvements for the operating budget from the five-year plan. The **finance committee** should review the priorities established by the board for repairs and maintenance.
March	**Principal and school board finance committee**—Develop line-by-line income assumptions including tuitions, fundraising, subsidies, and development income.
April	**Principal and school board finance committee**—Present tentative budget to the school board for approval.

Provide back-up information on specific income to the board, particularly in the areas of tuition and fund raising.

May — **Principal**—Calendarize budget for control purposes and develop a monthly cash flow. (See Appendix C of *Elementary School Finance Manual.*)

June — **Principal**—Publish budget in annual report.

Budget Approval

Ordinarily, a board with limited jurisdiction has authority to approve the annual budget. A consultative board will need the enactment of the pastor or comparable diocesan or religious congregation person before the budget can be implemented by the principal.

The process for approval should be determined in the operating procedures of the board. It is appropriate that the pastor and parish finance and pastoral councils be involved in determining the amount of parish subsidy to the school. This is also an appropriate role for the diocesan education office or religious congregation in the case of many diocesan and private Catholic schools. The school board should be responsible for factoring the subsidy into the total balanced budget and submitting that for the approval of the pastor, diocesan office, or religious congregation.

Budget Reporting

Usually, the budget is presented in the annual report, which includes—in addition to the approved budget - the school's goals and objectives which were established for the preceding year and the activities which took place in meeting those objectives. It also should include plans for the following year and resources needed to accomplish them. A final item is the financial statement which compares actual income and expenses with the projected budget.

The annual report is made available to those persons and groups who are involved in the school: for example, the pastor or pastors who subsidize the school, members of the parish pastoral council(s), diocesan office, bishop and religious congregations for diocesan and private schools, parents, parishioners, and donors. It is also important to note there should be a monthly financial report to the board so that the budget can be monitored responsibly.

Tuition

The questions which need to be addressed regarding Catholic school tuition are: What share of the actual cost per pupil is to be borne by parents who choose Catholic schools for their children, and who makes this determination?

Traditional Approach

The most traditional approach to tuition used by over 90 percent of Catholic elementary schools defines tuition in the following way: The tuition charge is the cost per pupil, less the subsidy, less operating revenue per pupil (fundraising, interest earned, etc.). That figure equals the per-pupil user cost or the traditional tuition charged. The advantage of this system is its simplicity. The two major disadvantages are that this approach usually ignores capital costs and provides the same subsidy to each student whether the subsidy is needed or wanted.

Alternative Methods

There are several alternative methods of determining tuition and financing schools that are being used in some dioceses. All of these seem to fall into the category of negotiated or fair share tuition charges. In these methods, the actual per-pupil cost is presented to parents who are asked to consider seriously how much of this amount they can pay as tuition. Persons selected to meet with parents should be known in the community for their commitment to the school and their ability to maintain confidences. These approaches are based on the following assumptions:

1. Communication is necessary. When people totally understand the financial facts, they are more likely to respond.

2. People have a need to give. When they have an ever so slight amount of discretionary funds, they will support the self-perceived needs and good causes.

3. The preservation of Catholic education for all. Catholic schools should not be available only to those who can afford increasing costs.

Strategies

If a group is considering an alternative means of determining tuition, such as negotiated or fair share, there are certain strategies which should be considered for implementation.

This is also true if a parish is considering instituting a program of sacrificial giving and operating a tuition-free school.

The first point to remember is the good will of people and their need to give. Parents should be informed and involved in this new approach from the beginning. The second important strategy is the essential component of leadership, that is, the principal and pastor(s) **must** be behind this effort. The third strategy involves the importance of presenting the actual per-pupil cost and marketing the effort and determining the time relationship between marketing and the actual implementation. The fourth strategy includes the selection and training of a limited number of negotiators who ought to be known for prudence and discretion. And the last strategy is the significance of communicating the changed approach with parents.

Tuition Collection

Another consideration of the board is determining when tuition should be collected. The traditional practice requires that tuition and fees be paid by the end of the academic year. This is called a post-paid plan. More schools are moving toward some type of prepaid tuition plan or variations to this approach. For example, some schools use the entirely prepaid and discounted approach while others use the prepaid and discounted approach with commercial or credit union borrowing available. Some schools are allowing parents to prepay tuition by using a major credit card, while others are assisting parents through arrangements with a local bank to assume low-interest loans to repay tuition. Additional information concerning some alternative plans can be found in the appendix.

Daily Financial Management

Although the board is not engaged in the daily financial management of the school, it is essential that this phase of the school's operation is organized and functioning adequately; therefore the board may want to develop adequate policies which will ensure such an efficient operation.

Principles:

1. The system should be clear, concise, and repetitive.

2. The procedures should be governed by the policies of the diocese, religious congregation, or parish. This would include bonding of all persons who handle money. All school savings and checking accounts should require more than one person's signature for issuing checks and withdrawing money; and the actual daily financial "set-up" should be designed to allow for the preparation of the following types of information:
    a. cost per pupil;
    b. revenues and expenses incurred for a given time-period; and
    c. comparison of actual revenues and expenses with budgeted amounts.

3. It is preferable that the school have a separate financial account. However, if school funds are mingled with parish, diocesan, or religious congregation funds, then the school should have a means of generating regular financial reports for its own operation.

4. The roles and responsibilities of those involved in financial management should be clearly stated (school bookkeeper, parish bookkeeper, pastor, principal, board and parish finance council).

Chapter 5
APPOINTMENT/ SELECTION OF THE PRINCIPAL

Ordinarily the person or group which has responsibility for hiring the administrator is also charged with the responsibility of initiating a process to find a replacement. Policies and practices vary among dioceses and religious congregations; however, the use of a search committee which includes representatives from a number of interested parties is preferred by many.

Clarifying the Charge

Whether looking for a parish director of religious education, a diocesan superintendent of schools, or a Catholic school principal, the responsibilities of the search committee should be clearly stated. It is essential that the members know such things as who is responsible for hiring the administrator (offering the contract), who must be consulted in the process, and who should serve on the committee.

Diocesan and local policies, bylaws of corporations of private secondary schools, and directives of the sponsoring group are sources of information regarding these issues.

The following sample statements from several dioceses illustrate different charges to the search committee for a superintendent and may be modified for use in local situations.

"The diocesan board submits applicants to the bishop to screen. The board selects the finalist."

"Nominees are submitted by the board to the bishop who appoints the superintendent."

"The superintendent is appointed by the board, subject to the approval of the bishop."

"The bishop appoints the superintendent."

The bylaws of the corporation of a private secondary school give a clear mandate to both the chair of the board and the search committee:

"In the event of a vacancy in the office of President of the Corporation and Principal either by death, resignation, or disqualification, the Chairman of the Board of Trustees, with the approval of Board members, shall appoint a Search Committee to seek a duly qualified person as principal.

"The following groups shall be represented on this committee:
- Board of Trustees
- Administration of Religious Congregation
- Local corporation of Religious Congregation
- Faculty and staff of the school
- Parents of the school

"The search committee shall present its findings to the administration of the religious congregation who will approve a list of suggested candidates, all of whom must be members of the Catholic faith, from which the Board of Trustees will appoint a principal."

In addition to providing direction concerning membership, this charge also provides information concerning other important issues such as the reserved power of the religious congregation to approve the list of suggested candidates before the board of trustees hires and the fact that the principal must be a Catholic.

Laying the Foundation for the Search

The first order of business for the search committee is to answer the following questions:
- What does the school community want in an administrator?
- How to announce and market the job opening?
- How to conduct the interview?

Job Description

The search committee should check that the job description for the position is current and accurate. Roles, relationships, expectations and lines of accountability should be stated.

Searching

Most dioceses and religious congregations make provisions for assisting educational institutions in their search for personnel by sending notices to parishes, schools, and community members. The search committee should also contact the director of personnel for the religious congregations serving in the area as well as place advertisements in the diocesan newspaper, those of neighboring dioceses, and publications such as the *National Catholic Reporter, Sisters Today*, and *NCEA Notes*.

Information should be prepared for all inquiries. The packet should include such items as the following:

1. application and request for at least three references and an official transcript;
2. job description, including requirements for certification,

salary expectations, responsibilities and expectations;
3. history and mission of the school and parish;
4. search committee process including time line;
5. cover letter from the chair of the search committee indicating that additional information may be requested from some applicants (these may include a statement of health from a physician and a letter from one's pastor/major superior).

Screening of Responses

Since it is not unusual to receive many applications for the administrative position, the committee should determine a process for rating the applications to determine who will be interviewed. One approach could be for the committee to use the "A Portrait of the Catholic School Principal: Qualities and Competencies — Self-Evaluation," which appears in the appendix. Many committees also use the telephone to interview candidates and check references in completing a rating scale.

Conducting the Interview Visit

After the search committee has determined which applicants will be invited for an on-site interview, there are many details which should be handled in order to make the time profitable for all.

Hospitality

Either a member of the search committee or a board member should be the person responsible for local arrangements, such as details of travel, accommodations, and hospitality. Expenses should be paid by the institution.

Consideration should be given to having other members of the board and school community meet serious candidates in an informal manner.

Interview

The chair of the search committee assumes responsibility for the interview procedures to be followed with each candidate. Uniform questions should be prepared so that each candidate can be rated on the same material. The chair need not ask all of the questions, but should check to see if each question has been handled.

Questions should invite and encourage expression. They should provide an opportunity for quality responses by allowing the person being interviewed to spend a period of time elaborating an answer. In most instances, questions which are quantitative or lead to a simple yes or no answer should be avoided. Some interview questions appear in the appendix.

Weighing Personal Qualities

Usually, specific questions regarding personal qualities of the person being interviewed are not appropriate. Personal qualities can be inferred from the way the applicant responds to interview questions and from reference letters. They can also be deduced from records or written exercises (e.g., writing a school philosophy) the applicant is required to submit.

The person should be thanked at the end of the interview. Committee members should then share their impressions and feelings and the reasons for them after individually completing a prepared rating scale.

Arriving at Decisions

In a prayerful context, the search committee is then ready to make some serious judgments and decisions. Each member should complete an individual rating scale for each candidate and be asked to rank the interviewees with reasons for the ranking. This information should be discussed among the members and every effort should be made to reach consensus on the order in which the candidates will be recommended to the person or group who will hire. When consensus is not possible and a vote is taken, the report from the search committee should note the differing views.

Pursuing Follow-up Obligations

The chair of the search committee has the responsibility to communicate with each of the candidates in a timely fashion after the person selected has been notified and accepted the position.

The chair should also remind search committee members of their mutual responsibility to maintain confidentiality even after the search has been completed and should see to it that appropriate materials are filed and others destroyed.

Chapter 6
DEVELOPMENT/PUBLIC RELATIONS/MARKETING

In considering the role of the board in the development function of the school, it may be helpful to review the general responsibilities of a board. The board exists primarily to formulate policy and give direction to the school. Some of the areas in which this is accomplished are:
- participates in the formulation of the philosophy and mission statement of the school
- formulates goals and objectives for the school
- formulates policies which guide the administrative staff in working toward these objectives
- evaluates the effects of the board's policy decisions in achieving the objectives
- approves the budget
- participates in the selection and retention of the principal
- provides for development, including public relations and marketing

It is essential to keep these responsibilities in mind when considering the proper role of the board in school development programs, because it is through them that the board shapes the school development program.

The development officer for the school is hired by the principal and often staffs the appropriate board committee(s).

What Is Development?

Gonser, Gerber, Tinker, Stuhr, a Chicago consulting firm, defines development as follows:

The overall concept of development holds that the highest destiny of an institution can be realized only by a total effort on the part of the institution to analyze its educational or programmatic philosophy and activities, to crystalize its objectives, project them into the future,

and take the steps necessary to realize them.
Development:
a. is not simply an attempt to raise dollars through more or varied fundraising techniques;
b. is a systematic effort to attract friends for the school and build confidence in it for the long term;
c. requires common understandings on the part of all involved in the leadership of the school:
   1. Understand basic concept of development, i.e., "friendraising"
   2. Understand the philosophy and mission of the school
d. assumes long-term effort and involvement of people.

Four Initial Steps in Establishing a Development Program

1. Statement of the Philosophy
   The role of the board is to participate in the approval of the philosophy as developed by the school community under the leadership of the principal. The philosophy is the **WHY** of the school—what the school is called to **BE**. In a very real sense, all of the Catholic schools in a given diocese share a common philosophy of education.
   The common elements of a Catholic school philosophy are:
   a. Integrate faith and learning—primary component.
   b. Educate the total person.
   c. Establish a caring environment.
   d. Educate for justice.
   e. Educate for global awareness.
2. Statement of Mission
   The board participates in the approval of the mission statement developed by the school community under the leadership of the principal. The mission is the **WHAT** of the school—what the school is called to **DO**. In that sense, each Catholic school has a unique mission.
   The common elements of such a mission statement are:
   a. Responds to question: if the school burned down tonight, would it reopen in September? Why?
   b. Tailors the work of the school: nature of program, description of students, constraints on operation.
   c. Opportunity to state what is important about the school to students and to all the school's publics.
3. Development Commitment
   Everybody connected with the school, especially school board members, should internalize the development concept. Development is a long-term process which requires broad-based commitment.
4. Involvement
   Involvement in the development process is cultivated by educating

all involved to what development is. It is important to stress that development is not simply fundraising, although that is an important component. It is also necessary for those involved in development to have an understanding of why they need to talk about the school's successes.

Outline of a Development Program

After these four initial steps, the board should direct administrative efforts into more detailed planning and work on behalf of a development program.

A long-range or strategic plan should be developed. The plan should look ahead and make projections, not only about finances, but also about the philosophy and mission, enrollment, staffing, curriculum, facilities, and the development program. (Appendix includes forms to assist with five-year development plans.)

Next, a Case Statement should be developed. A compelling Case Statement is one of the most important tools for the success of a major development program. An effective Case Statement is more than a brochure for prospective donors. It is the rationale for the very existence of the institution as well as for its growth and strengthening. It shows the institution's productivity and how it benefits society. It presents clearly the ways the school wants to improve its service to society and the resources required. The board is actively involved in this process and recognizes the importance of consensus around the approval of this significant document.

An effective development program depends on thorough and comprehensive communications with various constituents and publics to create awareness and understanding about an institution's mission and goals. The Case Statement is the foundation for all successful communication. It is a narrative developed by the school's key leaders, first for internal and ultimately for external use. The document serves as a basis for the preparation of communications materials to meet other needs, such as annual reports, promotional brochures, state of the school reports as well as general publicity. In a word, it states the institution's rationale for existence.

The Case Statement should consider the institution in terms of philosophy, mission, long-range plans, programs, effects on the broader community and resources necessary to achieve the goals. Under no circumstances should the Case Statement simply present needs. It should present primarily the school's opportunities for growth, expansion and involvement of people.

A Case Statement makes straightforward comments about the following:
- The institution's programs and objectives, what it must do to improve or change its activities or aims, and why the institution is valuable to society.
- The goals of the fundraising program to support the institution. What are the funds to be used for? How will the success of the

program strengthen the institution? Why is reaching the goals vital to society and particularly to the special publics of the particular institution?

- Ways in which the institution will remain significantly productive in the next decade—both through the generosity of its supporters and through its own efforts to operate more efficiently.

A variety of funding programs can then be developed. Some of these include annual giving, capital campaigns, trusts and endowments, and deferred giving.

For additional information regarding a development program, the reader should consult the NCEA series of publications on development and the elementary and secondary department directors of development.

Public Relations

The role of the board in public relations is primarily to provide direction; that is, the board should be involved in determining what should be done, not the specifics of how public relations should be accomplished. Public relations is both an art and a science. As an art, it enables people to understand the school, and to stimulate their support of it in its mission. It is the science of selecting the appropriate media, materials and events to connect effectively with audiences with which the school wishes to establish goodwill. One can characterize public relations as the sum of all that a school or person does or does not do which affects how it is perceived and supported by various groups or publics in a community.

Handling Crisis Moments

The school board has a responsibility to be sure that appropriate plans and procedures are in place to handle the public relations aspects of the various crisis moments which develop in school communities. How such events are reported can result in positive or negative publicity for the school. Some examples of crisis moments for which the board ought to have policies and procedures in place are:

1. Emergencies involving suspected cases of child abuse, serious injury or student death
2. Announcements of program cutbacks, school closings, mergings
3. Response to parent concerns about curriculum, discipline

Careful planning, reflection, formulation of positions, and determining who will speak with confidence and clarity are the keys to handling such crisis situations.

Everyday Public Relation Opportunities—How Do You Use Them?

Every school community has a personality which it reveals by how it handles everyday occurrences with its publics. Recognizing that administration is the responsibility of the principal, a public relations committee could reflect with the principal on the following questions in light of present practices and the impact they have on parents, students, parishioners, neighbors, and inquirers.

- How are telephones answered?
- How are visitors welcomed to the building? Do signs point the way to the school office?
- How are halls decorated? Do they communicate something about the Catholic education happening there? What is their message?
- How do office staff respond to visitors? When are parents welcome in the building? How are they involved in the school's life?
- How are students recognized for achievements?
- What kinds of orientation programs exist for new students, for new staff?
- How many opportunities do you offer for neighbors, parishioners, and other members of the community to participate in the school's life?
- How are concerns of parents handled by teachers and administrators?
- How are concerns of neighbors voiced about students' behavior handled?
- In what ways does the school secretary see him/herself as an important part of the school's public relations effort?
- In what ways are students, parents, and faculty encouraged to be goodwill ambassadors for the school?
- How would you rate parent-teacher conferences in terms of creating goodwill?
- How are schedule changes communicated to parents and faculty?
- How do you gather the advice of experts in your community to improve instruction and other school activities?
- What kind of image do your school handbooks and publications convey?
- How do you provide for feedback in your building? from parents? from graduates?

Marketing

Marketing is an important function in the overall development of the school. By some, marketing is equated with sales, and so student recruiting and public relations are assumed to be marketing. In reality, these are strategies of the marketing program, and marketing is a strategy of the development program.

Marketing begins with the notion that people have needs which they must meet. The school is meeting a need people have to educate their children. If, however, the school is to succeed, it must analyze whose needs it serves, what service these people are looking for, and how the school can meet that particular need.

Thus marketing starts from an exchange relationship, where something of value is traded between at least two parties. Marketing, then, is the managing of these exchange relationships. The program begins outside the school with external needs. Only if the school is in tune with external needs will its marketing program succeed.

Beginning a Marketing Effort

The following are the first four steps to begin a marketing program.

1. **Establish a Marketing Committee.** Whether this committee is a formal or an ad hoc board committee, it is important that it has high-level support and involvement, that it has broad representation, that it be chaired by someone influential in the school who has had some marketing knowledge, and that someone be responsible for carrying out the decisions of the committee as approved by the board. At least the chair of the marketing committee should be a board member.

2. **Develop a Good Data Base.** Conduct a marketing audit of the school. Remember to be as objective, systematic and comprehensive as possible, but also remember to be realistic. Everything cannot be identified in a single audit. In fact, some schools will simply not have answers to many of the questions asked. Don't worry about it now, but do remember that these unanswered questions are areas in which the school needs to do additional work.

The following marketing audit for a Catholic school will be helpful.

The Marketing Environment

1. What effect will the short-term economic situation have on the school, and its ability to achieve its mission and objectives?
2. What effect will trends in the size, age, distribution, birth rate and religious preference in the local area have on the school?
3. What are the public's attitudes toward the school and its present (curriculum)?
4. What changes are occurring in the market size and demographic distribution of the school's student market?
5. How do current and prospective students and their parents rate the school and its competitors with respect to each element of the school's offerings? What are the needs, wants and benefits desired from the school? How do these market segments (potential clients) reach a decision on which school a student will attend?
6. Who are the school's competitors in attracting these stu-

dents? What are the school's perceived strengths and weaknesses? What are the competition's perceived strengths and weaknesses?

Marketing Strategy

1. Are the mission and objectives of the school clearly stated, and do they logically lead to the marketing objectives for the school?
2. Are the marketing objectives for students/parents/donors and other markets clearly stated in order to guide marketing, planning, implementation and control?
3. Are the marketing objectives appropriate, given what is known about the market, competition and the school's resources?
4. What are the school's marketing strategies?
5. Are the school's resources adequate to carry out these strategies and achieve the desired objectives?
6. Are these resources optimally allocated to different market segments and the different elements of the marketing mix?

Marketing Activities

1. How does the marketing process work at the school? Are there ways to increase its effectiveness and/or efficiency?
2. What is the marketing approach like, and what marketing activities of the school are occurring at each stage of the process?
3. How are the marketing efforts organized and staffed at the school? Why? Is there a high level marketing individual with adequate authority and responsibility over all marketing activities that affect parent/student satisfaction?
4. Is there a marketing research, or marketing information, system at the school? Is the system providing accurate and timely information on the market, and present and prospective parents/students/donors? Is the system measuring the effectiveness and efficiency of the school's marketing efforts?
5. Is there an annual planning process adequate to direct the school's marketing efforts? Is it tied to a control system to measure if annual objectives are being met?
6. Have specific objectives and strategies been established for each of the school's marketing efforts, and is the effectiveness of the each being measured?
7. Are the school's various marketing efforts, and especially the promotion effort, being integrated into a unified effort to project a clear, attractive and realistic image of the school? Are any of these efforts in conflict with any of the others?

3. **Identify Opportunities and Problems.** As a result of the marketing audit, the marketing committee will be able to identify a number of opportunities and problems facing the school, develop a prioritized list of these opportunities and problems related to market-

ing and identify those that need to be addressed immediately.

4. **Develop Prioritized Marketing Objectives.** Develop a list of prioritized marketing objectives that address the opportunities and problems identified. Make these specific and measurable. For example, if declining enrollment is a problem, a marketing objective might be to identify specific cause(s) of the decline within 90 days through a survey of student families. These objectives should focus the efforts of the marketing committee, and should be in accord with the overall planning efforts of the board. How many objectives can be dealt with in a given year will depend on the magnitude of the objectives, the time and funding available.

Chapter 7
EVALUATION

The key to knowing how to evaluate is knowing what to evaluate. The two major areas in which Catholic education boards are involved in evaluation are: the board's relationship with the administrator and the boards's internal and external effectiveness.

The Role of the Board in the Evaluation of the Administrator

Since the majority of existing Catholic education boards are constituted as **consultative** by diocesan policy, they are not the employers of administrators, and therefore do not have the responsibility for a total evaluation of performance. The agent of the civil corporation, the pastor, superintendent, or religious congregation administrator is the one responsible for ensuring that the administrators are evaluated according to an appropriate process. If, however, the board is constituted as one with **limited jurisdiction** with the delegated authority to hire the administrator, then the board has the responsibility to provide for a complete evaluation and may want to adapt the diocesan process for its own use. Some religious congregations provide a formal evaluation process for use by their boards.

Most dioceses provide an evaluation or appraisal process for principals. This type of process presents a philosophy of evaluation and a job description for the principal, together with evaluative materials for the individuals and groups involved in the appraisal. The principal receives the materials from the diocesan education officer and is responsible for circulating them to the pastor, faculty and school board. These responses, together with the principal's self-appraisal, are returned to the diocesan office for summarization, or a summary is presented to the principal by an outside facilitator. In either case, the principal is expected to use the results of this process to develop a professional growth or job target plan for the following year.

What follows will apply to consultative boards and their responsibilities in the evaluation of a principal. It may be adapted for use by a board with limited jurisdiction and for administrators of religious education programs, as well as those of diocesan education offices.

Evaluation is Difficult

Evaluation is one of the most difficult and challenging tasks. It is also one of the most important. If it is not done with care, concern, compassion, and a sense of honesty, evaluation can be destructive of the trust that has to exist among the people who work in any school. Ideally, the diocesan education office has developed a prescribed evaluation process that includes both of the following kinds of evaluation.

Types of Evaluation

The first type of evaluation looks primarily at the **professional growth** of the person being evaluated. This is intended to confirm the principal's strong points and help the principal to identify and make improvements in any areas of weakness.

The second type of evaluation is more difficult. It evaluates the **competency** of the principal and the results are used in making judgments about continuing employment or the termination of a contract. (It is important to remember that only an agent of the corporation, that is, the person who signed the contract for the church corporation, has the responsibility to evaluate in this sense.) However, often the first type of evaluation provides information which may lead to the second.

A Consultative Board is Limited in What It Evaluates

This board speaks to the principal's service to the board and the implementation of policy. Evaluation of the principal's performance in other professional responsibilities, such as the supervision of teachers, must come from people with the expertise to assess those responsibilities—usually the diocesan education office or the religious community in a community-owned school.

A committee of the local school board should prepare a composite evaluation form based on the responses of each individual member. The committee meets with the principal to discuss the results and provides an opportunity for the principal to respond. The entire board receives the composite evaluation together with the principal's response, which may be either verbal or written. A copy of this composite should be forwarded to the person designated according to the diocesan process, e.g., the principal, an outside facilitator, or the diocesan office.

If the issue arises regarding the principal's competency, the board contacts the hiring agent (pastor, superintendent, religious community) for information regarding the prescribed process. For example, if at one of the board meetings a member says that the principal has trouble with teacher morale, the principal should try to determine the nature of the problem and offer information about how the building-up of teacher morale is handled. If the issue cannot be solved at the local level, the board should go to the hiring agent for resolution. The principal should talk with the diocesan education office as well as with the employer.

The consultative board has the right and responsibility to participate in the evaluation of the principal's leadership and service to the board. Information shared and received in the board's evaluation of the principal must be handled in aconfidential manner. Only the summary of the board's evaluative responses should be presented to the full board in closed executive sessions. The evaluation form in the appendix is a sample which can be modified for local use.

A Board with Limited Jurisdiction and Evaluation of the Administrator

In those instances where a board with limited jurisdiction hires the principal, it is ultimately responsible for the principal's evaluation.

Using diocesan and religious congregation resources, the chair usually appoints a board committee to develop an evaluation process and to present a summary report to the full board. This formal evaluation occurs during the year prior to the last year of the principal's contract and includes input from all board members, faculty and staff, and some parents. Some processes provide for limited student participation.

Ordinarily the ad hoc evaluation committee circulates, receives and collates responses from individuals and discusses the summary results with the principal, who is always given the opportunity to respond. A written summary of the participants' ratings and the principal's response is prepared for presentation to the full board in a closed/executive session.

Pitfalls to Avoid in Evaluation

Mutual trust and respect are essential components for the good relationship between the board and principal. This understanding will provide the climate in which all can work together on behalf of an excellent Catholic school. Certain pitfalls common in poor evaluations should be avoided. Some of these are:

- Not establishing standards
  Unfortunately, some boards evaluate principals without any kind of criteria for the evaluation. Parents make judgments about how the principal has treated their child or the child of a friend, or whether or not the principal made a proper fuss over them at some social event. In any kind of evaluation, all board members should be furnished with the same instruments and have, as much as possible, the same understandings about the evaluation.
- Posturing as psychologists
  There is no room in an evaluation for such comments as "He is just too uptight; he needs to relax more." Or "If her marriage

were happier, she would be different." The board should make judgments about those things it is capable of judging.
- **Not providing a forum for response**
There should be a forum for the principal to respond to any evaluation. Some boards are so uncomfortable with the very act of evaluation that they try to avoid discussing the results with the principal at any cost. It is not sufficient to send one person with the good or bad news, and it is never acceptable simply to send a letter. Evaluation should be dialogic, that is, the board and principal talking together, preferably through a subcommittee.
- **Not allowing time**
Evaluations take time. They take time because they take reflection, because they are important. No worthwhile and profitable evaluation can be done hastily.
- **Taking longer than necessary**
At the same time, there is another pitfall that also should be avoided, and that is the assumption that longer is automatically better. Sometimes it is necessary to take a long time for evaluations; other times it is not. If there are no serious problems between principal and board, there is no reason to dwell on minor issues.

Non-Renewal and Termination of the Principal

To this point, evaluation has been addressed mainly in terms of commendations and recommendations for the principal. The second type of evaluation looks to that of actual job performance.

While the formal acts of non-renewal or termination are not the responsibility of a consultative board, sometimes the board finds itself in the position of being involved in such a process. The following guidelines should be followed:

1. No board should begin an evaluation that could possibly lead to the firing of a principal without notifying the superintendent, pastor, and/or religious congregation.

2. Except in unusual circumstances (public scandal, moral turpitude), no principal can be fired without a formal evaluation. Even in the absence of such an unusual circumstance, the principal should not be non-renewed without a formal evaluation.

3. Any termination procedure must include the agent of the corporation who hired. The only person who can fire another person is the agent of the corporation (pastor, superintendent, or religious congregation) who hired that person.

4. Any termination procedure should consider
   a. the long-term nature of the problems;
   b. evaluations (warnings) and offers of assistance; and
   c. supervision by the principal's employer.

5. The agent of the corporation should include a subcommittee of the board in the process with the understanding that strict confi-

dentiality will be observed.

6. The termination should be done in person by the agent with at least one other person present. A formal written statement should be given to the person fired or whose contract is not renewed.

7. The agent and the person fired may wish to agree on a public statement.

8. The board must maintain absolute silence on the whole question of the firing. The board can only act as a board and not as individual members. Therefore, individuals should not give out board information. The agent only should assume the position of speaking for the corporation and the board.

9. All diocesan policies as well as state and local laws must be followed. It is always prudent to consult the diocesan education office where one can get advice regarding legal counsel.

The Board and Its Own Evaluation

A Catholic board of education has responsibilities to evaluate its own internal and external performance. The **internal** functions of a board relate to how the board operates as a group: leadership, membership, level of participation, agenda, preparation for meetings, board committee structure.

Its **external** functions are concerned with how the board fulfills its areas of responsibilities: strategic planning (including development, marketing, and public relations), as well as finance, policy formulation, and buildings and grounds. Its external functions also concern how well it maintains good relationships with others: pastor, parish pastoral council and finance council, parishioners, parents, civic community, faculty, alumnae(i), diocesan education office, and others.

There are many different approaches to self-evaluation — from the very formal, highly structured to the informal and structureless one. The materials presented in the appendix represent a middle position and are based on the conviction that a board should have a sense of purpose and direction if it is going to serve the needs of Catholic education effectively and efficaciously. The forms presented highlight some issues which should be evaluated and offer different types of rating scales which can be adapted according to the needs and preferences of the board itself.

Evaluating the Instructional Program

Although the actual evaluation of the school's instructional program is the responsibility of the professional educators in accordance with diocesan policies, it is important that the board be kept informed.

The board should know what the diocesan policies are regarding evaluations, when the evaluations are occurring, and the results in a summary fashion.

As part of the regular administrator's report to the board, the principal should report on national and diocesan student testing results and faculty evaluations in summary fashion. Names are not used but the composite results are reported. For example, regarding faculty evaluations, the principal should report that they are occurring with some general remarks about the process.

A good way to involve the faculty is to invite them to report to the board on a regular basis the results of curriculum evaluations. This type of report could include such issues as:
- the goals and objectives of the specific subject or level;
- the materials used;
- the strengths of the program;
- the problems being encountered; and
- the efforts being made to overcome the problems.

When some outside evaluative process is called for, the board is often involved. For example, most dioceses invite schools to participate in an accreditation process which involves self-study and evaluation. The board should encourage the principal and staff in this worthwhile process by providing the necessary resources and support.

CHAPTER 8
ROLES AND RELATIONSHIPS

The role of the board in a Catholic school is to provide opportunities for representative members of the community to come together to work with staffs of dioceses, parishes and private schools to provide direction for education programs. Such groups provide unity, direction and stability for educational efforts, and the opportunity for dedicated people, lay religious, and clergy, to participate in the church's educational ministry.

Church governance can be understood as a ministry. It is a ministry that serves the people of God, by helping them maintain order. It promotes and protects the rights and obligations needed to carry out the mission Jesus gave to his church. Those who serve as ministers of governance have a distinct and unique responsibility to see that the rights and duties of individuals are affirmed within the institution and community of the church. Governance in itself is a means of exercising rights and responsibilities in the service of others, and in the service of one's own growth as a member of Christ (*Primer on Educational Governance*).

In order for these responsibilities to be adequately fulfilled, it is essential that participants understand their own roles and the roles of others with whom they collaborate.

Roles

Parish School Board

The school board fulfills its role by assuming responsibilities in the area of planning, policy formulation/enactment, finances, selection/appointment of principal, development including public relations and marketing, and evaluation. (Each of these responsibilities is discussed in detail in Chapter 2.)

Principal

The principal, with the authority delegated as specified in the employment contract or job description, is responsible for the operation of the school program. This responsibility includes the employment, supervision and evaluation of staff, the establishment of education programming, and the evaluation and management of student behavior. These responsibilities, of course, are assumed in accord with diocesan and local policies.

In addition to these administrative responsibilities, the principal has serious responsibilities as spiritual leader of the school. The principal is the one who assumes responsibility for understanding and accepting the unique role that Catholic schools serve in the educational mission of the Church. The principal serves as the chief spokesperson in articulating this mission, and in calling the faculty and students to participate in a significant way in the liturgical life of the church.

Pastor

The pastor is the canonical administrator of the parish. He is usually the agent of the civil corporation, and the enactor of local policy. The pastor hires, supervises and, with the assistance of the diocesan education office, evaluates the principal.

Bishop

The Code of Canon Law highlights the role of the bishop in regard to Catholic schools. The bishop has a special responsibility and authority over Catholic schools within his diocese. As Provost (1985) writes: "The bishop is to set the direction for education in the diocese within general norms that may or may not be established by the Conference of Bishops. He is also to exercise vigilance over faith and morals, and have a quality over teachers of religion in all schools in his diocese. These include those that are run by religious. The only exception would be a school run by religious only for its own members, like a novitiate. But any school whatsoever that professes itself to be a Catholic school, is subject to the vigilance of the bishop."

Diocesan Education Office

The superintendent of schools is ordinarily that staff person of the bishop with whom Catholic schools relate most directly. The responsibility of the superintendent and staff are clearly delineated in each diocese's educational policy manual.

Relationships

In a parish, the school board relates to a number of other groups. Some of these include the parish pastoral council, the parish finance council, the religious education board, and the parent organization.

The Parish Pastoral Council

The parish pastoral council is responsible for assisting the pastor in providing the establishment of parish goals and programming. The consultative school board works in the context of the parish's mission statement, programs and parish policies, which are established by the pastor and the parish pastoral council. It is the responsibility of the board to bring to the attention of the parish pastoral council all those matters which are broader than the school program for which the board is responsible. The board should provide a regular means of communication with the parish pastoral council about educational programming, accomplishments and needs.

The Parish Finance Council

The parish finance council is responsible for assisting the pastor in administering the temporal goods of the parish. The consultative school board is governed by the financial policies which are recommended by the finance committee and the parish pastoral council. It provides information on both educational needs and programming to the parish finance committee, and requests parish funds through the mechanisms established by the parish finance committee. The school board does not have responsibility for determining the amount of parish funds to support school programs; however, it is the primary advocacy group for parish funding of the school program, and it has responsibility for the effective use of parish funds allocated for educational purposes. In general, the parish finance council is responsible for the total amount of money spent on education. The board is responsible for articulating the need and determining how the money is spent. It is recommended that the finance committee of the school board and the finance council of the parish meet together to negotiate the parish's financial investment in the school, which is then presented by the finance council as part of the overall parish budget to the parish pastoral council.

Religious Education Board

A religious education board serves in a consultative role to the parish director of religious education and pastor in much the same way that the parish school board relates to the principal. It is important that appropriate lines of communication be established between the school board and the religious education board in order to accomplish a unified educational mission for the parish.

School-Parent Organization

The school-parent organization is responsible for maintaining good communications between the home and school, for providing a vehicle through which parents can provide service to the school (for example, volunteers and fundraising), for offering a mechanism for parent education, and for serving as a structure for political action when needed (for example, letter-writing, phone calls, visits to legislators). The school board works closely with the offices of the parent organization in order to understand more fully parent needs and concerns. It works with parent fundraising groups to coordinate the overall financing programs of the school. It uses the communication mechanisms of the parent organization to report to school families about board activities.

Other groups with which the board needs to establish and maintain good working relationships include the athletic association and various booster groups.

Boards for Interparish/ Regional School

1. **A Consultative Board**

The functions of the consultative board for an interparish school are the same as those for single parish schools, except for the role of the pastors, the composition of the membership, and the relationship to parish groups. From among the parishes sponsoring the school, one pastor should be selected/appointed to be the pastor for the school program. This pastor functions as a member of the administrative team as outlined for a single parish. Further, it is the responsibility of the selected pastor to provide information about board activities to the pastors of the other parishes and to secure their approval as may be necessary for major decisions (for example, the selection of the principal, the approval of the annual budget, the approval of sacramental preparation programs). Normally the selected pastor would be the pastor of the parish which houses the school. The members of the board are selected from the several parishes which sponsor the school. Membership should be proportionate to the services delivered to the parishes. The board must maintain a relationship with the parish pastoral councils of all the supporting parishes. This will require some formal recognition of communication between the board and the several parish pastoral councils.

2. **A Board with Limited Jurisdiction**

The role and function of a board with limited jurisdiction in an interparish/regional school is the same as that of a single parish, except for the role of pastors, the composition of members, and the relationship with parish pastoral councils.

The pastors of the parishes sponsoring the school should specify formally in accord with diocesan policy what authority is given to the board and what decisions are reserved to the pastors. Further, they should establish a mechanism through which the board may submit recommendations to the pastors, and a mechanism for arriving at agreement among the pastors on these recommendations.

The members of the board are representative of the sponsoring parishes. Membership is regionally proportionate to the services received by the parishes. The board meets to maintain formal communication with the parish pastoral councils of all of the parishes served.

A major concern with interparish programs is the possible separation of the program from the parishes. The pastors and other parish leaders must be kept involved and interested in the school. Although this concern applies to all education programs, schools have had the most experience in this area. The further a program gets away from the parish, the less ownership the parish has. Often the parish which physically houses the parish school looks on it as its own, while the other parishes have lesser feelings of ownership. It is especially important in these cases that there be a clear delineation of the rights and responsibilities of each of the parishes, a genuine means for each parish to enjoy the benefits of the school, an agreed upon way for each to participate in the governance and perceived financial equity. Too much independence can lead the people connected to the school to think of it as a private school.

The interparish school may be part of the juridic person of one of the sponsoring parishes. In this case the pastor of that parish has the canonical rights and obligations for the administration of the interparish school. In order to avoid the confusion that could result from such an arrangement, an interparish school could be established as a separate juridic person. The statutes establishing the separate juridic person would define the role of the pastor, the board (whether consultative or with limited jurisdiction), and of the principal, who has the canonical rights and obligations for administering the school program. Besides being a separate juridic person, an interparish school may be separately incorporated under the laws of the state and the policies of the diocese.

Boards for Diocesan Schools

1. **A Consultative Board**

    A consultative board is constituted by the diocesan bishop or his representative. The role and function of the board is the same as that for previous models. The board relates to the administrator of the diocesan school program, and to the principal of the school.

    The administrator for the diocesan school is the diocesan administrator to whom authority is delegated by the diocesan bishop for the governance of the program. This diocesan administrator may be the vicar for education, secretary for education, superintendent of schools, or some other diocesan administrator responsible for education programming.

2. **A Board with Limited Jurisdiction**

    A board with limited jurisdiction is constituted by the diocesan bishop and delegated the responsibility for the governance of the school, except for those matters and decisions which are reserved to the diocesan bishop or his representative. In all other ways, the function and role of the board with limited jurisdiction are similar to those of the preceding models.

    A diocesan school may be part of the juridic person which is the diocese. In this case the diocesan bishop or his representative has the canonical rights and obligations for administering the school. The diocesan school may also be established as a separate juridic person.

In this case, the statutes would define the role of the diocesan bishop, the board (whether consultative or with limited jurisdiction), and the administrator, who could also be the school principal, and who has the canonical rights and obligations for administering the school. A diocesan school may be separately incorporated under the civil laws of the various states.

Boards for Private Schools

1. **A Consultative Board**

    The board is constituted by the religious congregation which owns the school. The role and function of the board is the same as that for the single parish and interparish program. The board relates to the administrator of the religious congregation and to the school principal.

2. **A Board with Limited Jurisdiction**

    This kind of board is constituted by the religious congregation which owns the school. The board is delegated with the responsibility for the governance of the school, except for those matters and decisions which are reserved to the administrator of the religious congregation and to the diocesan bishop. The role and function of the board is the same as that for a single parish or interparish school.

3. **A Corporate Board**

    The corporate board is organized by individual persons desiring to operate the school under the laws of the state in which the school is located. The corporate charter and bylaws specify the authority and responsibilities of the board. To be identified as a Catholic school, the corporate board must seek the recognition of the school as Catholic by the diocesan bishop. The corporate board is the ultimate governing authority in all areas, with the exception of those reserved to the authority of the diocesan bishop by canon law.

    The corporate board hires, supervises and evaluates the principal, who is responsible for the administration of the school. Authority and responsibility are delegated by the corporate board to the school administrator.

    Like the other models, the corporate board exercises responsibility in the areas of planning, policy development, financing, appointment of the principal, development including public relations and marketing, and evaluation.

    The private school owned by a religious congregation may be part of the juridic person which is the religious congregation. In such a case, the administrator of the religious congregation has canonical rights and obligations for administering the school. The private school owned by a religious congregation can also be established as a separate juridic person. In such a case, the statutes establishing the separate juridic person would define the role of the administrator of the religious congregation, the diocesan bishop, the board (whether consultative or with limited jurisdiction), and the administrator (who could be the principal), who has the canonical rights and obligations for administering the school.

The independent Catholic school could be established by the diocesan bishop as a juridic person. In such a case, the statutes would specify the role of the diocesan bishop, the board and the principal.

A private school owned by a religious congregation may be separately incorporated under the civil laws of the various states. Normally, this incorporation takes the form of the two-tiered membership, board of directors corporation.

Diocesan Boards

1. **A Consultative Board**

    The consultative board is established by the diocesan bishop to assist him and his educational administrators in the governance of education programs. Diocesan educational policy is established through the activity of the board. The board is composed of the appropriate diocesan educational administrators and board members. This board formulates diocesan policy for the approval of the diocesan bishop. Each diocese has a clearly outlined procedure for the enactment of diocesan policies by the diocesan bishop. For example, the bishop may enact or reject suggested policy by signing the minutes of the board with appropriate comments. The authority to enact policy in the name of the bishop may be delegated to a diocesan education administrator as determined by a diocesan policy. The board members, apart from the authority of the diocesan bishop, cannot make policy binding on the diocese or its parishes.

    The diocesan board has responsibility in the following areas:
    a. Planning (establishing a mission statement, goals, future plans).
    b. Policy development (formulating policies which give general direction for administrative action).
    c. Financing (developing plans/means to finance the diocesan education program, including tuition and development and fundraising plans, to allocate resources according to a budget, and to monitor these plans).
    d. Development, including public relations and marketing (communicating with various publics about the diocesan education program and listening to their needs and concerns, and promoting the education program).
    e. Selection of the diocesan educational administrator (the diocesan board often serves as a search committee and interview group when a diocese is looking for a superintendent of schools. Information given regarding a principal search may be adapted).
    f. Evaluation (determining whether goals and plans are being met, not evaluating individual staff members and

administrators, and determining board's own effectiveness).

The board is related to other consultative bodies in diocesan administration. These are the diocesan finance council, the presbyteral council, the diocesan pastoral council. The diocesan school board is subject to diocesan policies which are formulated through these consultative bodies and approved by the diocesan bishop. It is the responsibility of the diocesan school board to keep other diocesan groups informed about diocesan education programming and needs. The board calls the attention of the appropriate diocesan consultative group to diocesan needs which are broader than those presented by school programming.

2. A Board with Limited Jurisdiction

The board with limited jurisdiction is constituted by the diocesan bishop to govern diocesan educational activities, subject to certain decisions which are reserved to the diocesan bishop. In constituting the board, the bishop clearly specifies in writing the areas in which the board has responsibility for governance. Normally, the board would have responsibility for all areas of educational governance, except those in religious education reserved to the bishop, and the stewardship of temporal goods specifically reserved to other groups by canon law.

The decisions of a board with limited jurisdiction are final and binding on all parties. However, its responsibility extends only to those clearly defined areas in its constitution. In those areas which are reserved for decision by the appropriate diocesan administrator, the board's role is consultative. The board prepares recommendations for consideration, but does not have final authority to make a decision.

The superintendent of schools is responsible for the administrative operation of education programs at the diocesan level. The superintendent may be an employee of the board with limited jurisdiction. In those cases, the superintendent is hired by the board, supervised and evaluated by the board. The superintendent, on the other hand, hires additional staff for the office of Catholic schools.

Unless the education program is separately incorporated from the diocese, the diocese is understood as the legal employer of the diocesan administrators. Accordingly, the bishop or some person clearly identified as having delegated authority must sign the employment contract with the diocesan administrator. Additionally, even when the bishop has established a board, he may want to reserve the final decision on the employment of the superintendent of schools to himself. In that instance, even though the bishop may give final approval to the employment of the superintendent, that person should be directly accountable to the board for all supervision and evaluation purposes.

The board's areas of responsibility are the same as those outlined for the diocesan consultative board. The board's relationship with other diocesan consultative bodies is also the same as those outlined for the consultative board.

Diocesan educational governance and its programs could be part of the juridic person which is the diocese. However, the diocesan bishop may decide to form a separate juridic person for educational purposes. The statutes establishing the separate juridic person would define the role of the diocesan bishop, the superintendent of schools, the board (whether consultative or with limited jurisdiction), and the individual possessing the canonical rights and obligations for administering the program. Diocesan education programs may be separately incorporated under the laws of the various states.

If there is a separate board for religious education in the diocese, it is recommended that this board and the diocesan school board work closely with one another for the good of the Church's educational ministry. For example, they could meet together twice a year, or their executive committees could meet several times each year. The diocesan bishop has the responsibility of insuring that the office personnel in schools and religious education model the kind of cooperation held up as ideal to boards. Only if diocesan officials model collaboration will separate boards cooperate effectively.

CHAPTER 9
MEMBERSHIP

The educational administrator (superintendent and principal) and the canonical administrator (bishop, pastor, religious congregation representative), in addition to elected and/or appointed individuals, are participating board members.

All contribute to discussions and consensus decision-making. If it is necessary to take a vote, it is probably better for the educational administrator, as the implementor, not to vote.

Boards in Catholic education need and deserve the most competent and dedicated members. Nominating committees work with eligibility and membership qualifications in preparing a slate of potential members.

Eligibility Requirements

Each diocese and religious congregation establishes its eligibility requirements for membership on diocesan and local boards.

The following issues should be among those considered in determining membership eligibility:
- membership in a parish/diocese
- eighteen years of age or older
- genuine interest in Catholic education/schools
- ability to work effectively with others in achieving consensus in decisions for the good of the entire school community
- ability and willingness to make necessary and substantial time commitment for thought and study as well as for meetings and related board activities, including development
- willingness to maintain high levels of integrity and confidentiality
- willingness to attend periodic inservice programs
- willingness to support school/diocesan philosophy and mission
- have a sense of future vision for the school
- be a credible witness of the Catholic faith to the school and beyond (in the case of those who are not Roman Catholic, the presumption is that the person is not opposed to the tenets of the Catholic faith)

- not a paid employee of any parish/diocesan education program (some also include and spouse, parent, or adult child of such an employee). The principal/superintendent of schools are non-voting board members.
- not a student

Membership Qualifications

The following is an example of membership qualifications used by several religious congregations when selecting members for boards of directors.

Nominees for appointment to membership of the board of directors shall be selected in light of the following qualifications:

Personal:
- A willingness to give the time to serve conscientiously
- A willingness to attend board functions regularly
- The highest level of honesty, integrity and prudence
- Ability to act without bias toward faculty and other employees of the school
- An inquiring mind—open to both sides of an issue
- The courage to face unpleasant tasks and decisions
- Ability to be very objective and free of personal, financial or operational interest in the school
- Willingness to disclose any existing or potential conflicts of interest

Professional:
- A commitment to the importance of service to the civic community
- A depth of experience with general management problems
- A position of respect in the community
- The ability to influence public opinion favorably in areas of importance to the school
- A willingness to balance a prudent concern for fiscal stability with a spirit of creative risktaking
- A willingness to learn while preparing for and serving as a board member
- A demonstrated professional competence and administrative ability in his/her chosen field

Board:
- A commitment to understand and support the mission of the congregation.
- A commitment to support the teachings of the church on education and directives of the local ordinary and the (arch)diocesan department of education.
- An acknowledgement of the powers retained by the members of the corporation.

- A willingness to exercise the delegated authority and control for conducting the business and affairs of the school.
- A willingness to serve within the philosophy, directives and corporate structures of the congregation.
- An appreciation for maintenance of confidentiality in matters pertaining to the board, the school and the congregation.
- A willingness to support board decisions even if he/she does not fully agree.

The director will not be considered a representative of any special interest group, such as the faculty, parents or donors. Employees of the school are not eligible for board membership (with the exception of the principal whose board appointment is *ex officio*).

Recruitment of Members

Each board has a nominating committee which includes the pastor and principal, charged with the responsibility of identifying potential members and present a slate of nominees for election or appointment. Vital, dynamic and productive board members can be recruited by:

- articulating clearly the purpose, direction and mission of the board
- maintaining key individuals on the board—quality attracts quality
- organizing well the member recruitment campaign
- providing professional orientation and inservice
- putting new recruits to work at once in areas of expertise
- never being satisfied with anything other than efficient board and committee meetings
- maintaining an enthusiastic, credible, and responsible position before the school, parish and civic communities

Information from Candidate

Using the approved eligibility criteria, the nominating committee actively solicits potential members. Either by means of personal interviews of written forms, the nominating committee gathers the following information about candidates:

- Biographical sketch
    name
    family
    parish membership
    diocesan/parish/civic involvement
    occupation

- Statement of candidacy
    vision for the school
    talents, expertise available to the board
    willingness to give time, talent, energy to membership

Orientation of New Members

One of the best ways to provide orientation for potential members is to have them serve on board committees. However, once a person assumes board membership, responsibilities and relationships change and therefore it is essential that new members participate in some formal inservice program. Some topics which should be addressed are: roles and relationships of board, principal, and pastor/superintendent/religious congregation; specific board responsibilities; meeting skills; expectations of members; differences between policy and administrative regulations and guidelines, diocesan policies.

When a member joins a board, the principal should prepare a packet of materials to include: church documents on education, school philosophy and mission statements, diocesan guidelines for boards, diocesan and local educational policies, parent/faculty/student handbooks.

The principal should maintain a current resource library for board members. One valuable source of current information is NCEA's National Association of Boards of Education.

Specific Issues Regarding Membership

Representative of the Community

Catholic school board members should recognize that their primary responsibility is providing quality Catholic education to the greatest number of children and youth and therefore they do not represent specific constituencies within the community. With that understanding, members are representative of the community in the sense that they come from the community and are accountable to the school community for actions taken. If, for example, the school enrolls a significant number of students who are not Roman Catholic, and/or who are members of ethnic minorities, then the board may want to insure some members from those groups. It would not be appropriate for the "non-Catholic parents" to elect a board representative, because that could connote constituency representation. For the same reason, it is a good idea to avoid too many "ex-officio" members.

Election or Appointment

Once eligibility qualifications have been established and promulgated and the nominating committee is functioning well, some board members could be elected according to local practice. However, it is recommended that provision be made for some appointees in order to insure that the composition of the board is balanced and meets the needs of the school.

Terms

The goal in establishing terms for board members is to maintain continuity and prevent lifetime membership. Ordinarily, members serve three-year terms and are eligible for an additional consecutive three-year term. With new boards, it is important to provide for staggered terms with those who initially draw a one-year term being eligible for two full three-year terms.

Size

The best size for a board depends on local circumstances. It should be large enough to fulfill its responsibilities but small enough to insure adequate dialogue and good group interaction.

Ex Officio but Non-voting

Preference should be given to having board members with both voice and vote even though consensus, rather than voting, is the preferred mode of decision-making. Presuming that the reason for having "ex officio" people present for board meetings is to insure both good communications and commitment, the practice of having these people serve as consultants to the board may be preferable to the ex officio but non-voting status. For example, the parents' club and the board may be better served if they appointed a consultant to the board. This would also be an appropriate way of handling faculty participation in the board. The consultants would attend and participate in regular board meetings, but would not be present for executive or closed sessions of the board. The pastor and principal are ex officio members and often do not vote, but do participate actively in discussion and consensus building.

Conflict of Interest

Potential conflict of interest should not be the sole factor in determining ineligibility for board membership. However, this is the primary reasoning behind the practice of not having teachers and other paid employees of the school or parish on the board. Some would include spouses and parents of paid employees among those not eligible for board membership.

Board members should be willing to disclose any existing or potential conflicts of interest and abstain from voting or other actions in those areas where a conflict exists. The board minutes should reflect this abstention.

Confidentiality

Board members should respect the confidential information they receive in closed/executive sessions. If principals are going to feel comfortable sharing significant facts regarding personnel, for example, then they must be confident that board members will not discuss these matters outside of the closed session with anyone, including other board members and spouses. Inability to keep confidences violates stated eligibility requirements and is sufficient reason to request a resignation.

Most Difficult Things for Board Members to Learn

Experienced board members from across the nation were asked to identify the most difficult lesson or fact they had to learn about board service. Here's what they said most often, as reported in *Becoming a Better Board Member*.

- Determining what your function is on the board and how to accomplish it effectively.
- That no matter what you **think** you know about board service when you first come on board, you still have a lot to learn.
- Learning to acknowledge publicly that you have no power and authority as an individual board member; that only the board as a whole can function.
- Recognizing the difference between formulating/enacting policy (the board's job) and administering the school (the principal's job).
- That you must represent **all** the parents/students. Your decision must be made in the interest of the total school and not made solely for special groups or interests.
- Learning how to respond to the complaints and concerns of parents, school administrators, and other staff.
- That change comes slowly.
- That you can't solve everyone's problems by yourself.
- That you must think deeply and sometimes accept a reality that is contrary to your own beliefs.
- That effective boardmanship means being able to hold the minority viewpoint when voting on a given issue; then openly supporting the majority vote or consensus position in your community.
- Discovering how the school is funded.

CHAPTER 10
BOARD MEETINGS

Meetings are critical to the success of any Catholic school board. Scheduled meetings are at the heart of the effectiveness of the board.

However, the challenge for Catholic boards of education, particularly board leadership, is to structure the meeting in such a way as to maximize productivity and accomplishment and to minimize unnecessary and deadly boredom and disorganization. Another challenge is to refute the oft-quoted statement of Peter Drucker that "one either meets or one works; one cannot do both at the same time" (*The Effective Executive*).

Effective and efficient board meetings can energize, focus, and provide significant opportunities, not only in the life of individual board members, but also in the life of the school itself. Unplanned and simply routine meetings can be an effective turn-off for all involved. Again, board leadership is critical here. The board chairperson and principal must be committed to planning and carrying out enriching and lively meetings, adhering to appropriate and efficient routines, while providing for creative input from board members.

Responsibility of Members

In accepting membership on a Catholic school board, individuals accept the responsibility to prepare for meetings, participate regularly in committee and board activities, and to participate actively in the work of the board. Members also understand that as individuals they have no authority. It is only when the board is meeting in formal session that it is authorized to act in accord with its constitution and bylaws.

Role of Officers

The officers of the board are clearly stated in the constitution and bylaws of the organization. In preparing a slate for election, the nominating committee should be cognizant of the specific responsibilities of each member, and determine fitness for office in that manner.

Since the role of the chair of the board is so significant to the board's success, the committee should spend adequate time in discerning who should fill this role.

Committees

The types of committees are usually referred to in a board constitution and bylaws. The usual distinction is between a standing committee and an ad hoc committee.

A standing committee provides a continuing function for ongoing operation of the board. Some examples of standing committees are membership, finance, executive, and development.

On the other hand, an ad hoc committee is established to meet a specific objective at a given time. Examples of ad hoc committees are a search committee for a new principal and a nominating committee for board members and offices.

The committee structure of a board is intended to contribute to the board's efficient operation. Committees also provide needed information to the whole board, and organize information for action. While it is true that the board as a whole is authorized to take action on most decisions, some committees are empowered to make decisions on particular isolated cases.

Committee members need not be board members. However, the chair of each committee should be a board member. Frequently, committee membership is a good way to recruit prospective board members. Committee members should be knowledgeable about or interested in the area of committee activity. They should know the committee's responsibilities, the responsibilities of the staff to the committee, and the history of the committee's work. It is also essential that committee members know the school's policies, practices and procedures.

Preparation for Board Meetings

Agenda Preparation

Normally, preparation of the agenda is the joint responsibility of the principal and the board chair.

Step 1: Some items that might be included in a school board agenda are:
- Items carried over from this meeting.
- Committee reports due.
- Future events or deadlines coming.
- Long range needs or plans.
- New programs or special events happening in the school.

Step 2: Identify the items on the list which require neither discussion nor action by the board, but are merely intended to inform. Since these can be taken care of by written reports, delete them from the agenda, and ask the appropriate person to prepare a written report.

Step 3: Make a judgment: Can the rest of the items reasonably be handled in one meeting of a decent length? If there are too many, delete some. Put them off until another meeting or take care of them in another way.

Step 4: Arrange the remaining items in some logical order. Here are a few norms:
- Schedule the most difficult item late enough so the group has developed some momentum but early enough so that people are not too tired to give their best to it.
- Avoid putting two difficult items back to back.
- If the same person is doing two lengthy items, separate them on the agenda. This gives the person and the group a rest.
- Put expendable (or postponable) items at or near the end so they can be dropped if the meeting is going too long.
- Vary the order from your usual pattern.

Step 5: Assign responsibility and time allotment for each item. Be certain the person assigned knows that he or she is responsible.

Step 6: Provide background information on each item which would be helpful for board members to have ahead of item so that they can make a wiser, more expeditious decision. Who will get it ready? How will it be sent? (Note that an agenda of this type, with supporting information, must be sent early so members will have time to read the materials.)

Committee Reports

All committees should be requested to prepare written reports to be circulated with the agenda. In these reports, the chair should indicate what action, if any, the committee is requesting from the board, and cite any budgetary implications regarding the report. In this way, the agenda can be prepared so that committee reports which are simply for information will have less time on the agenda than those reports which require lengthy discussion by the entire board.

Steps to More Successful Meetings

1. Before the meeting:
   - Plan the meeting carefully.
   - Prepare and send out an agenda in advance. Allow time for feedback on agenda items prior to meeting date
   - Someone should arrive early to set up the meeting room.
2. At the beginning of the meeting:

- Start on time!
- Review, revise, and order the agenda. This is extremely important.
- Set clear time limits. Set ending time, generally no longer than two hours.
- Review action items carried over from the previous meeting.

3. During the meeting:
   - Focus on the same problem in the same way at the same time.
   - Have someone take minutes.
4. At the end of the meeting:
   - Establish action items: who, what, when.
   - Set the date and place of the next meeting and develop a preliminary agenda.
   - Evaluate the meeting.
   - Close the meeting crisply and on a positive note.
   - Clean up and leave the room in the manner in which you found it.
5. After the meeting:
   - Prepare the minutes and distribute after approval.
   - Follow up on action items and begin to plan the next meeting.

Decision-Making

According to Peter Drucker, "a decision is a judgment: a choice between alternatives." As a judgment, a decision is the best possible choice under given conditions. It is not always the optimal choice, but one on which the group agrees to act at the given time. The decision may be incremental progress rather than a final or complete solution, because the "right solution" may be unknowable or illusory.

Step One

A problem-solving process usually has three phases. The first is defining the problem. This step assumes a recognition on the part of the leader or some members, and then subsequently the group, that there is a decision which must be made. However, the question should be asked, is a decision necessary, or should we do nothing? These are the first questions the group must consider before any definition can be achieved. The board may want to consider the consequences of these stands. If we act, we may be better off. If we do not act, we probably will survive. The board should compare the effort and risk of action to the risk of inaction. Act if, on the balance, the benefits outweigh the costs and risks. Act, or do not act, but do not hedge or compromise at this stage.

The goal, therefore, in problem definition, is finding the right question, not the right answer. The board must identify the real problem, not the symptoms.

Step Two

The second step in problem-solving is solving and deciding. Once the problem has been identified, then it should be analyzed. Facts should be gathered by asking the following questions: What information is needed? How valid is the information we have? What more do we need to know? What information can we not get? At this point it is also appropriate to ask who must make the decision, who must be consulted, and who must be informed.

After analyzing the problem, the board should generate alternative solutions. There are three reasons to consider alternatives: 1) to safeguard the decision-maker from being held captive by a single idea; 2) to provide fallback positions, should initial position not be successful; 3) to stimulate the imagination and provide new and different ways of perceiving and understanding. Discussion and dissent are means to consensus.

In deciding which of the alternatives to choose, the board should begin with the alternatives which most clearly meet objective elements of the situation, recognizing that the best decision involves approximation and risk, and the compromise will probably occur.

Step Three

The third step in the problem-solving process is action. The action plan should recognize that action must be effected through other people, and therefore the plan should consider who these people are and how they can be helped to understand actions/changes that are expected. The board should ask who must know what action should be taken, who must take it, and what does the action have to be, so that those who must do it can do it. The last step of the action plan outlines the steps to be followed.

After the action or implementation has occurred, adequate means for evaluation should be provided. The evaluation should test the actual events against the expected results.

Benefits and Costs of Group Decision-Making

Decisions here are being made by a group, not an individual. This brings some particular dynamics to bear on the process of deciding. Awareness of some of these pluses and minuses could help one be more effective in making decisions.

Benefits

- Pooling of resources, both cognitive and experiential—usually two heads are better than one, or at least they can be.
- Number of alternatives increases, which means greater ability to handle more complex issues.
- Opportunity to utilize special talents and devise tasks.
- Presence of others increases motivation levels.
- Potential for unique solutions emerges, which no one member had.

- Potential for synergy makes group solution better than any individual solution.
- All understand the decision better.
- Increase acceptance of the decision because of participation in its creation.
- Individual and group development is enhanced.

Potential Costs
- More time and energy of members required.
- Consensus is difficult to reach.
- Potential for domination by strong individual, reducing contribution of others.
- Potential for shifting attention from decision-making to social relations (may become embroiled in personalities or external concerns).

Ambiguities
- Disagreement is likely, but may be constructive depending on the leader's or group's skill in dealing with it.
- It takes longer to make a decision, but it may be a better one or a decision may be avoided altogether.

Ways Groups Make Decisions

Groups have the potential to make better decisions than individuals do. Some behaviors and decision modes, however, may not work well for groups, or may inhibit building a consensus decision. At times these modes may happen or may be useful in moving the group forward, but in general, it is presumed that consensus decision-making is preferable to any one of these.

Some decision modes which **may not always work** are:
- Majority Rule Voting

  This is useful in routine procedural decision, but in major policy decisions it may leave a minority who cannot agree and may have difficulty supporting the majority decision. This would impede the effectiveness of the decision.
- Polling the Membership

  This may be useful to determine a prevailing opinion, but is not definite, nor does it always indicate the group has decided. It is a technique on the road to decision-making at best.
- Averaging

  This is an attempt to bring together the least common denominators in all perspectives under the guise of consensus. It may, however, not allow members to heartily agree or buy into the decision.
- Railroading

  A sub-group with an organized, unified agenda and is able to maneuver the majority.
- Handclasping

One member supports the suggestion of another and these two make a decision before the group has considered the situation. Example: One, "I think we should appoint a committee to investigate the possibility of a new gym." Two, "I agree and will serve on the committee." A decision is made by less than the total group.
- **Self-authorization**
An individual makes a decision, may announce it, and carries it out without the consent of the group. The person may be a leader or well-respected member. The decision does not, however, represent the will of the group.
- **The Plop**
A member makes a contribution and receives no response or recognition. This may represent a lost opportunity or a disorganized group.
- **Satisfying**
The group makes a so-called acceptable decision, but avoids dealing with the real issue.

Decision modes which usually **do produce** better group decisions are:
- **Consensus**
All members understand the decision and recognize it as the best possible, given the group and the situation. Everyone is willing to accept the decision and at least go along with it and support it. It is best that each person in the group articulate aloud his/her positive consent to the decision.
- **Genuine Unanimity**
This is rare and should only be accepted after a complete review of the alternatives.

Group Decision Behaviors

Consensus is a decision process for making full use of available resources and for resolving conflicts creatively. Consensus is difficult to reach, so not every decision will meet with everyone's complete approval. Complete unanimity is not the goal—it is rarely achieved. But each individual should be able to accept the group judgment on the basis of logic and feasibility. When all group members feel this way, you have reached consensus as defined here and the judgment may be entered as a group decision. This means, in effect, that a single person can block the group if s/he thinks it necessary; at the same time, s/he should use this option in the best sense of reciprocity. Here are some guidelines to use in achieving consensus:
- Avoid arguing for your own rankings. Present your position as lucidly and logically as possible, but listen to the other members' reactions and consider them carefully before you press your point.
- Do not assume that someone must win and someone must lose

when discussion reaches a stalemate. Instead, look for the next-most-acceptable alternative for all parties.
- Do not change your mind simply to avoid conflict and to reach agreement and harmony. When agreement seems to come quickly and easily, be suspicious. Explore the reasons and be sure everyone accepts the solutions for basically similar or complementary reasons. Yield only to positions that have objective and logically sound foundations.
- Avoid conflict-reducing techniques such as majority vote, averages, coin-flips, and bargaining. When a dissenting member finally agrees, don't feel that s/he must be rewarded by having his/her own way on some later point.
- Differences of opinion are natural and expected. Seek them out and try to involve everyone in the decision process. Disagreement can help the group's decision because with a wide range of information and options, there is a greater chance that the group will hit upon more adequate solutions.
- Be willing to accept a decision which may not be its first choice, but may be the best the group can make after weighing alternatives and the concerns of members.
- If consensus is not achievable, the leader must determine whether to continue the discussion at the next meeting or bring the matter to majority vote.

Appendix A—Consultative Boards

Appendix A1
Parish School Board
(Consultative)

BY-LAWS OF ST. JOSEPH PARISH SCHOOL BOARD
(Burlington, VT)

INTRODUCTION AND RATIONALE

The Catholic school is an expression of the education mission of the parish with which it is associated and of the diocese. Therefore, the pastor is responsible to the bishop for the administration of the total parish, including the parish school. The principal functions as the chief administrator of the school and is a member of the parish staff. Regular and open communication between the pastor and the principal is essential.

Just as the parish council serves with the pastor on behalf of the total parish community, so the parish school board serves with the principal for the good of the school community. Today's Catholic principal, with the many demands which are made, needs assistance from a group of people who are committed to the Catholic school and are willing to work for the good of the school and parish.

ARTICLE I   NAME OF THE ORGANIZATION

The name of this body shall be St. Joseph School Board.

ARTICLE II   PURPOSES AND FUNCTIONS

The board is established by the pastor, in accord with diocesan policy, to assist him and the principal in the governance of the parish school. When the board meets as pastor, principal, and members and agrees on a policy matter, the decision is effective and binding on all. The board is consultative in the following sense: the members cannot act apart from the pastor and principal and cannot make decisions binding on the parish school without the approval of the pastor and principal.

Consultation (cf. Canons 495-501) also means that decisions will not be made in major matters until and unless the school board has been consulted. The areas in which the board has responsibility and will be consulted are:
- A. Planning
- B. Policy development and formulation
- C. Financing (including budgeting and policies for financial management)
- D. Public relations
- E. Selection of the principal
- F. Evaluation of the principal's relationship with the board
- G. Major curriculum changes, especially in the areas of education in human sexuality and religious education.

ARTICLE III   RELATIONSHIPS WITH OTHER GROUPS

A. Parish Pastoral Council

The school board and the parish council are both consultative to the pastor. Therefore, it is essential that good communication exists between the groups. The relationship which exists is one of information sharing and common planning for the benefit of the total parish community.

B. Parish Finance Committee

The finance committee of the school board and the parish finance committee meet to plan the financial contribution/subsidy from the parish to the school. The parish finance commission includes the financial contribution to the school as part of the total parish budget which is approved according to the practice of the parish.

C. Parent Organization

The president or an elected representative to the Home and School Association is a member of St. Joseph School Board.

D. Diocese

The relationship between the parish school board and the diocese is stated in diocesan education policies which are available for local school board members.

ARTICLE IV MEMBERSHIP

The membership of the parish school board will consist of seven to nine members in addition to the pastor and principal. Members are elected for a three-year term which begins in May after election.

Other members are:

President or an elected representative of the Home and School Association.

Two to four members may be selected/named by the administrator as the need of St. Joseph School and parish demands.

ARTICLE V NOMINATIONS AND ELECTIONS
ELIGIBILITY

An elections committee consisting of the administrator, the principal, and the chairperson of the board shall seek out and prepare a slate of prospective board member nominees who meet the following criteria:

- Are members of the parish and/or parents/guardians of students of St. Joseph School;
- Have interest in and commitment to Catholic education and to St. Joseph School's philosophy and mission;
- Are available to attend meetings and periodic in-service programs and to participate in committee work;
- Maintain high levels of integrity and confidentiality;
- Deal with situations as they relate to the good of the entire school community; and
- Be a credible witness of the Catholic faith (or to one's own religion) to the school community and beyond.

INELIGIBILITY

Paid employees of the school or parish are not eligible for Board membership.

ELECTIONS/APPOINTMENTS

During February, the elections committee will invite eligible parents to place their names in nomination for elected board positions. This committee will have ballots prepared with names of nominees listed in alphabetical order. Nominations from the floor may be made at the time of voting. Voting shall take place in April.

If some members are to be appointed, the elections committee should prepare a list of possible appointees according to the stated criteria and specific needs of the board. Appointments by the pastor should be made by March 1.

All new members are expected to attend the May and June school board or committee meetings for orientation purposes prior to beginning their term on July 1.

Members who miss three board meetings in a 12-month period and are unexcused may lose membership by action of the board. The following procedure will apply: the member will be notified by the chairperson or administrator; the member shall be given opportunity to respond; the board may act or not act as the case may indicate. The administrator shall appoint a replacement for the remainder of the school year.

ARTICLE VI OFFICERS

In May or June, officers are elected by the board and serve one-year renewable terms. Their duties are those ordinarily performed by such officers.

    A. The officers of the school board shall be as follows:
        1. Chairperson
        2. Secretary
        3. Director of Maintenance
        4. Director of Finance
    B. The Chairperson shall: preside at all meetings of the school board; conduct internal elections; call all regular and special meetings; assist in preparing the budget; direct the functions and goals

of the school board; enforce the by-laws and perform any and all duties incident to the office of Chairperson. The Chairperson shall automatically be a member of the Parish Bingo Committee.

C. The Secretary shall: record and maintain minutes of all regular and special meetings; be the custodian of the by-laws; present the minutes and other material as required at the meetings; answer correspondence; and perform all duties incident to the office of Secretary.

D. The Director of Maintenance shall assist in: the care of the physical plant of the school, its operational needs, custodial staffing, its repair and improvement, its cleanliness and needs, in directing the workload, and any other related matter that may be brought to his/her attention.

E. The Director of Finance shall assist: in the billing of tuition, in checking regularly for delinquent/late payments, in the determination of financial aid to families and in notifying such families of grants-in-aid. The Director of Finance shall also be a member of the Parish Bingo Committee.

ARTICLE VII   MEETINGS

The full board meets every month beginning in July. Standing committees meet as needed. Special board meetings can be called by the administrator, principal and/or chairperson. If board meetings are attended by non-members, the board will go into executive session whenever the issues involve personnel or other confidential matters. Six (6) members shall constitute a quorum for the transaction of business in any special or regular meeting.

ARTICLE VII   STANDING COMMITTEES

EXECUTIVE COMMITTEE—The members of the Executive Committee are the administrator, principal and chairperson of the board. The Executive Committee should meet regularly to plan the agenda for the regular board meetings. The agenda and written committee reports should be available to monitor the budget and present regular financial reports to the full board.

BUILDING AND GROUNDS COMMITTEE - The director of maintenance shall be the chairperson of this committee. The functions of this committee are to assist in developing and monitoring a maintenance and improvement plan for the building and grounds. Membership may consist of board or non-board members.

DEVELOPMENT AND PUBLIC RELATIONS COMMITTEE—The function of this committee is to plan the overall development of the school - case statement, marketing, fundraising, and public relations.

FINANCE COMMITTEE—This committee will consist of the administrator, the principal, director of finance, and chairperson of the board. This committee will prepare and present the budget, allocate financial aid, and perform other duties related to finance.

The Ad Hoc Committees are:

ELECTIONS COMMITTEE— The functions of the committee are to solicit nominees for the board and to conduct the election for board membership.

ARTICLE IX   AMENDMENTS

These by-laws may be amended by consensus of the board and/or by vote of 2/3 of the membership of the board and provided:
1. The amendment has been recorded and
2. The Home/School Association membership has been informed.

ARTICLE X   RULES OF ORDER

Ordinarily, decisions regarding policy matters and other major issues are not made at the "first reading" which is for information and clarification. The "second reading" of the policy occurs after additional consultation and clarification. At that time, the board begins its decision-making process.

In order to make the best decisions, the consensus method of decision-making should be used. When the board is unable to reach a consensus, a vote should be taken and the minutes should reflect the different positions and appropriate reasons. In cases involving voting and business procedures, Roberts Rules of Order, Revised should be used.

In those matters in which the board has jurisdiction, the vote of the majority carries and the decisions should be implemented. In those matters in which the pastor has reserved his decision, the board should present its recommendations and rationale. These decisions should be implemented when the pastor renders a decision in writing.

Adopted:_____
                (Date)

Revised:_____
                (Date)

Signatures: _____   _____

                      _____   _____

                      _____   _____

Appendix A2
Parish Board of Education
(Consultative Board)

CONSTITUTION FOR A PARISH BOARD OF EDUCATION
(EDUCATION COMMITTEE)
(Archdiocese of Dubuque—Required Components)

ARTICLE I
Title
    The name of this body shall be _____Parish Board of Education.

ARTICLE II
Nature and Function
    Section 1.   This Board is a governing body operating education programs at _____, subject to
                                  (parish)   (city)
policies and regulations that proceed from the Archdiocesan Board of Education and the Archdiocesan Office of Education. The Board of Education serves as a committee of the Parish Council according to the Archdiocesan Pastoral Guidelines.

    Section 2.   The Board shall be responsible for all aspects of formal educational programs in the primary areas of catechesis: adult catechesis, catechetical program for children, the Catholic school, family catechesis, youth catechesis, special catechesis, and catechesis for preschool children.

    Section 3.   The Board shall implement at the parish level the policies and regulations of the Archdiocesan Board of Education and the Office of Education.

    Section 4.   The Board is the voice of the parish community in educational planning, goal setting and policy development in accord with the intent and spirit of the Archdiocesan board.

    Section 5.   The Board shall have as an integral part of all its educational programs the four tasks of catechesis: a) to proclaim Christ's message; b) to develop community; c) to lead people to worship; and d) to motivate to service of others.

    Section 6.   Specific duties and functions include the following:
    a.   Coordinate parish educational programs and activities;
    b.   Build understanding and support for Catholic education in all its forms;
    c.   Develop the educational budget in collaboration with the Parish Council in accord with the Archdiocesan Pastoral Council Guidelines and Archdiocesan Board procedures;
    d.   Adopt and oversee the implementation of the annual educational budget;
    e.   Retain personnel according to established policies of the Archdiocesan and Parish Boards;
    f.   Consult with and support administrators who operate parish education programs.;
    g.   Work with the Parish Council
        —in planning, operating and maintaining facilities
        —in planning and building new educational facilities;
    h.   Serve as a liaison body with public authority as appropriate;
    i.   Insure that Archdiocesan Board and Parish Board policies are being implemented effectively;
    j.   Evaluate periodically
        —the accomplishment of goals and objectives
        —the effectiveness of internal functioning as a Board of Education.

ARTICLE III
Membership
    Section 1.   Members of the Parish Board of Education shall be the pastor (ex officio) and _____ elected representatives.

Section 2. Members of the Board shall be elected for a term of three years and may be reelected for a second term. A board members having served two consecutive terms may again be a candidate for board membership after a lapse of at least one year.

Section 3. A member of the Board who is absent from two consecutive regularly scheduled board meetings shall, unless excused by action of the Board, cease to be a member.
The Archdiocesan Board of Education, with the approval of the Archbishop, may remove a member(s) from the Parish Board.

Section 4. Election of new members shall be held annually on or before the third Sunday of May, according to procedures specified in Bylaws. New members take office at the first meeting of the Board in fall.
Vacancies on the Board shall be filled by appointment by the Board.

ARTICLE IV
Officers

Section 1. The officers of the Board shall consist of President, Vice-President and Secretary. They shall be elected annually by board members in the spring before June 30. Officers assume their responsibilities at the first fall meeting of the Board.

Section 2. All members of the Board are eligible for any office.

Section 3. The duties of the officers shall be as follows:
a. The President shall preside at all regular and special meetings of the Board; shall be executive head of the Board; shall appoint committees; and, in general, shall perform the duties relative to the office of President.
In accord with Archdiocesan Pastoral Council Guidelines, the President of the Board of Education or the designee shall be an ex officio member of the Parish Council.
b. The Vice-President shall perform the duties of the President at the request of or in the absence or incapacity of the President.
c. The Secretary shall be responsible for the minutes of board meetings; maintain a written record of all acts of the Board; conduct, receive and dispose of all correspondence as directed; preserve reports and documents; and, in general, shall perform all duties incident to the office of Secretary.
d. The Executive Officer shall be advisor to the Board and administrator of the Board's policies. The Executive Officer keeps the Board informed as to the condition of the educational system/programs and may propose the adoption of needed policies.
The Executive Officer is not a member of the board and does not have a vote.
An Executive Officer must be designated for the sake of coordination and unity though all administrative functions are not in the hands of one person. Administrative functions are jointly performed by the pastor, the principal, and the director of religious education (DRE). Though one is designated as Executive Officer, each administrator attends board meetings and takes responsibility for programs under his/her leadership. Administratively, all are accountable to the Archdiocesan Office of Education.

ARTICLE V
Meetings

Section 1. The Board shall meet regularly at a time and place specified in its Bylaws. Special meetings may be called by the President as needed, or by a majority of the members.

Section 2. A quorum, a majority of the entire Board, is necessary for the transactio of business at meetings; a majority vote of those present shall be sufficient for any decision or election.
Proxy voting is never permissible.

Section 3. All meetings of the Board are open unless designated as being executive. Decisions made in executive sessions must be presented and voted on at open sessions before becoming effective.

The right of non-members to address the Board shall be limited to those whose petition has been approved for the agenda in advance of the meeting.

Section 4. A written record of all acts of the Board, maintained by the Secretary, shall be preserved in the archives.

ARTICLE VI
Conduct of Meetings

Section 1. As a Christian community, the Board will endeavor to arrive at consensus in its deliberations. Formal decision-making will utilize parliamentary procedures as outlined in Robert's Rules of Order or another procedure of the Board's choice.

Section 2. The ordinary order of meeting shall be:
Call to Order
Prayer
Board Inservice/Study
Recommended Actions
—Routine matters
- Approval of minutes
- Approval of reports

—Old business
—New business
Information/Communications/Delegations
Future Business
—Meeting dates
—Preview of topics for future agendas
Adjournment

ARTICLE VII
Approval

This Constitution must have the approval of the Parish Council and the Archdiocesan Board of Education.

ARTICLE VIII
Amendments

Section 1. This constitution, excepting Required Components, may be amended by a vote of two-thirds of the total membership and approval by the Parish Council and the Archdiocesan Board of Education.

Section 2. Amendments must be presented to the Board at least one meeting prior to voting on such.

ARTICLE IX
Bylaws

   Section 1.   Bylaws in accord with this constitution may be developed to further specify the internal operation of the Board.

   Section 2.   Bylaws may be developed and amended by a vote of one more than a simple majority at any regular meeting with a quorum present.

   Section 3.   Bylaws and/or amendments to Bylaws must be presented at least one meeting prior to voting on such.

OFFICIAL SIGNATURES

_____
Pastor

_____
President of Parish Council

_____
President of Parish Board of Education

_____
Vice-President of Parish Board of Education

_____
Secretary of Parish Board of Education

Dated:_____

APPROVAL

   This Constitution is approved by the Archdiocesan Board of Education.

_____
President of the Archdiocesan Board of Education

Dated:_____

Appendix A3
Regional/Interparish School
(Consultative Board)

REGIONAL SCHOOLS AND BOARDS OF DIRECTORS
Office of Catholic Schools—Diocese of Richmond

Introduction
   In the Diocese of Richmond schools which are not parish or private are designated as regional to indicate that they are supported by more than one parish. The Bishop as the chief catechist of the diocese has final authority over these schools. He relies on the staff of the Office of Catholic Schools to exercise administrative jurisdiction in accord with diocesan policies, regional and state accreditation standards, and the laws of the Commonwealth of Virginia.
   The local regional school principal, together with the Board of Directors, is responsible for the operation of the regional school. Both the principal and the board are expected to function within the policies of the diocese and under the administrative jurisdiction of the Office of Catholic Schools.
   The selection of board members and their inservice as well as the selection, hiring, and evaluation of the principal are key to the effective and efficacious operation of the school The services of the diocese are available in these significant areas.
   While the hiring of the principal is the responsibility of the Superintendent of Schools, this responsibility is fulfilled in consultation with the local board which is responsible for establishing a search committee at the time a vacancy in the principalship occurs; a staff member of the Office of Catholic Schools is a member of this committee. It is the responsibility of the search committee to recommend to the Superintendent the name(s) of the individual(s) recommended for principal. The Superintendent of Schools will provide for adequate evaluations of the principal and will maintain lines of communication with the board to ensure that there is a good working relationship between the board and the principal. Termination of a principal's contract is the responsibility of the Superintendent of Schools in consultation with the Board of Directors.

Board of Directors
   Each regional school shall have a Board of Directors. The Board of Directors for regional schools shall prepare a constitution to submit for approval to the Diocesan School Board. This constitution stresses the accountability of the Board to the total community — the school, the participating parishes, and the diocese.
   Minutes of all Board meetings shall be submitted to the Bishop for his signature through the Superintendent of Schools. No decision may be implemented until the approval of the Bishop has been obtained.

Title
   The name of this organization shall be "The Board of Directors of
_____."

The participating parishes are:_____

_____

_____.

Purpose
   The purpose of the Board is to formulate policy consistent with diocesan and state guidelines and directives for the operation of _____, so that the largest possible number of students may be effectively educated in a Christian environment and encouraged to make a deep personal commitment to Jesus Christ.

Functions

The Board of Directors has the right and duty to concern itself with the public image of the school and its effect on the people in the nearby parishes and local community in general. The Board has the further right to have its views about these matters incorporated in the general school program. If a conflict arises between the Board and the administration, the matter should be referred to the Superintendent of Schools.

The Board of Directors has the right and duty to approve or veto projects related to school finances or the physical status of the school plant, including school operations, financial reports, major repairs, alterations, construction, and major curriculum changes.

The Board, and not individual members, has the right to determine the continuing status of any school employee whose presence in the school it considers to be detrimental to the welfare of the school.

The Board of Directors shall determine the manner in which the school may accept students; i.e., by means of the parish quota system or by another stated system. Admission policies must be racially non-discriminatory and every effort must be made to have an integrated school. Catholic students should be given preference, and provisions must be made to provide some financial assistance to deserving students. Admission policies will be established without prejudice to the school's right to pass final judgment upon the admission of an individual student in accordance with the school's academic and disciplinary admission standards.

The Board of Directors shall have a written agreement with the supporting parishes and the diocese concerning specific areas of responsibility for capital improvement and major repairs to the building.

Membership

While it is desirable that membership on the Board of Directors include representation from all of the parishes which support the regional school, this may not be possible due to size and number of parishes. What is essential is the recognition that membership on the Board presumes support for the school and a willingness to work to ensure the future of the school. It may be necessary to limit the size of the Board and provide for the local pastors to elect/select from among themselves one or several priests to represent them on the Board. Each participating parish should be given the opportunity to recommend lay members to the board. The ideal number of members for the Board of Directors is between eleven (11) and fifteen (15), excluding ex officio non-voting members. Members ordinarily serve for three years.

Officers

1. The officers of the Board of Directors shall be a chairperson, a vice chairperson, a secretary, and a treasurer.
2. The officers shall be elected by the Board and their term of office shall be one year.
3. The duties of the officers:
    a. The chairperson shall preside at meetings and perform other duties usually associated with this office.
    b. The vice chairperson shall preside and act as chairperson in the absence of the chairperson.
    c. The secretary shall record minutes of meetings of the Board that shall accurately reflect actions and decisions of the Board.
    d. The minutes of each meeting are sent to the Superintendent of Schools. Decisions are implemented on the approval of the Bishop.
    e. A copy of each set of approved minutes will be available at each parish house for parishioners.
    f. The treasurer shall serve as head of the budget committee. (It is advisable that each local Board agree on duties of the treasurer.)

Meetings and Quorum

1. The business of the new Board shall begin each year on July 1. The Board shall meet at least quarterly.
2. Emergency or special meetings may be called at the request of the chairperson, the Bishop or his representative, or by a majority of the Board members.
3. A written agenda should be available to all board members at least one week prior to each regularly scheduled board meeting. Copies of the agenda should also be available at each parish house for non-board members.
4. All regular and special meetings of the Board shall be opened to the community. Non-members

may address the Board with the approval of either the chairperson or a majority of the Board members. The Board has the right to go into closed session at any time to discuss personnel matters.
5. A quorum shall consist of a simple majority of voting members.
6. The rules of parliamentary procedure as contained in *Roberts' Rules of Order Revised* shall govern meetings of the Board except as otherwise provided.

Committees

Standing committees of the Board are:
1. Financial management, including budget preparation and tuition scales.
2. Long-range planning.
3. Public relations and publicity.
4. Others according to local needs.

Members of these standing committees shall be appointed by the chairperson of the Board in consultation with the Board of Directors. The chairperson of each of the standing committees must be a member of the Board. Members of the committees need not be members of the Board.

Ad hoc committees shall be appointed by the chairperson of the Board.

The duties and responsibilities of both standing and ad hoc committees shall be determined by the Board.

Amendments

This constitution and all subsequent amendments shall be effective upon approval of two-thirds of the members of the Board present and voting and the approval of the Bishop.

DIOCESAN POLICIES, REGIONAL SCHOOLS
Boards of Directors
February, 1982

INTRODUCTION:
Authority, Responsibility, Key Factors, Principals
- I. Authority
  - A. Bishop, as chief catechist, has final authority.
  - B. OCS exercises administrative jurisdiction.

- II. Responsibility for regional school operation
  - A. Principal together with Board of Directors.
  - B. Within diocesan policies and under the jurisdiction of OCS.

- III. Key factors in the effective and efficacious operation of regional schools.
  - A. Board members (selection and inservice)
  - B. Principals (selection, hiring and evaluation)

- IV. Principals
  - A. Hiring
    1. Responsibility of Superintendent in consultation with local Board
    2. Responsibility of Board
       a. Establish a search committee (one member from OCS)
       b. Recommend to Superintendent name(s) of individual(s)
  - B. Evaluation—responsibility of Superintendent
  - C. Termination
    1. Responsibility of Superintendent
    2. In consultation with Board

BOARD OF DIRECTORS:
- I. Required of each regional school

- II. A constitution
  - A. Prepared by Board
  - B. Approved by Diocesan School Board, then Bishop
  - C. Accountability stressed (school, participating parishes and the diocese).

- III. Minutes
  - A. Submitted to Bishop through Superintendent of Schools
  - B. No decision implemented until approved by Bishop

- IV. Title (name and participating parishes)

- V. Purpose: formulate policy
  - A. So that the largest possible number of students can be
    1. effectively educated in a Christian environment, and
    2. encouraged to make a deep personal commitment to Jesus Christ.
  - B. Consistent with diocesan and state guidelines and directives.

- VI. Functions
  - A. Rights and duties
    1. Public image and its effect on the people.
       a. Board views incorporated in the general school program.
       b. Conflict between Board and administration referred to Superintendent
    2. Approve or veto projects related to school finances or status of school, including:
       a. school operations
       b. financial reports

c. major repairs
d. alterations
e. construction
f. major curriculum changes
3. To determine the continuing status of any school employee whose presence is considered detrimental.

B. Other
1. Admission policies
a. racially non-discriminatory
b. every effort for an integrated school
c. Catholic students given preference
d. financial assistance to deserving students
e. manner of acceptance (e.g. parish quota system, or other)
f. cannot prejudice school's right to pass final judgment upon admission of an individual student.
2. Responsibility for capital improvement and major repairs—written agreement with the supporting parishes and the diocese.

VII. Membership
A. Essential Criteria
1. Support of school and
2. willingness to work to ensure its future
B. Composition and Size
1. Desirable, representation from all supporting parishes
2. Ideally, 11-15 members, excluding ex-officio non-voting members
3. Possible Limitation, local pastors elect/select 1 or 2 priests to represent them
C. Term—ordinarily serve for three years

VIII. Officers
A. Chairperson, vice chairperson, secretary and treasurer
B. Elected by Board for term of one year
C. Duties
1. Chairperson
a. preside at meetings
b. other duties usually associated with the office
2. Vice chairperson—preside and act as chairperson in his/her absence.
3. Secretary—record minutes of meeting
a. accurately reflect actions and decisions
b. send to Superintendent
c. approved minutes available at each parish house
4. Treasurer
a. head of the budget committee
b. advisable—duties agreed on by Board

IX. Meetings and Quorum
A. Business begins on July 1 for new Board
B. Meetings
1. Meet at least quarterly
2. Emergency or special meetings may be called
3. Written agenda —
a. one week in advance
b. available in each parish house
4. All meetings are open
a. non-members may address Board with approval of
(i) chairperson or
(ii) majority of Board

                b. closed session—to discuss personnel matters
            5. Quorum—simple majority of voting members
            6. Parliamentary procedure (Roberts' Rules except as otherwise provided)
X. Committees
    A. Standing committees
        1. Types: financial management, long-range planning, public relations and publicity, others according to local needs
        2. Membership
            a. appointed by board chairperson in consultation with Board
            b. chairperson of a standing committee must be member of Board
            c. other members need not be Board members
    B. Ad hoc committees—appointed by chairperson
    C. Duties and responsibilities—determined by Board

XI. Constitution and subsequent amendments effective upon approval
    A. of 2/3 of the members of Board present and voting
    B. of the Bishop

Appendix A4
Diocesan Secondary School
(Consultative Board)

THE CONSTITUTION
OF
BISHOP LUERS SCHOOL BOARD
(Diocese of Fort Wayne-South Bend, IN)

The Bishop Luers School Board is committed to the development of Bishop Luers High School as a unique Catholic educational institution in the Diocese of Fort Wayne-South Bend. The School Board will engage in long range planning to make Bishop Luers High School uniquely committed to the basic and comprehensive, and yet creative education, characterized by excellence in all areas, curricular and co-curricular; and the School Board will develop strategies for the implementation of its planning. It will strive to make Bishop Luers High School ever more faithful to its unique Franciscan heritage through affirmative action, committed to providing this education to all members of the community, regardless of race, color, creed, or economic background.

In cooperation with and subject to the Executive Board of Bishop Luers High School, the School Board will be responsible for recommending and generating policies in the following areas: the religious life of the school; the academic program; student life; budgetary matters and monetary policies; the maintenance and expansion of school facilities; recruitment and development; and the promotion of Bishop Luers High School to the larger community and other areas as requested by the Executive Board. The School Board will furthermore suggest strategies for the implementation of these policies.

The principal of Bishop Luers High School is appointed by the Bishop of the Fort Wayne-South Bend Diocese in conjunction with the Franciscan Provincial upon the recommendation of the School Board. The Principal shall have sole authority in the employment and direction of other school personnel.

Membership on the School Board shall consist of nine members elected by parents or guardians of Bishop Luers High School students. A majority of these School Board members must have students enrolled at Bishop Luers High School at the time of election. No employee of Bishop Luers High School may serve on the School Board. The term of office shall be three years; no member shall serve more than two consecutive three year terms.

The Bishop Luers School Board recognizes the Ordinary of the Diocese of Fort Wayne-South Bend as the proprietor of the total school enterprise and will therefore expect a continuation of substantial financial support. This School Board is committed to direct Bishop Luers High School in full conformity with principles and guidelines set forth in official documents of the Roman Catholic Church on faith, morals, and Catholic education, and welcomes the direction of the Ordinary in the implementation of this constitution.

BISHOP LUERS SCHOOL BOARD
BY-LAWS

ARTICLE I — Composition of School Board
- A. The name shall be Bishop Luers School Board.
- B. The Board shall be composed of nine (9) members.
    1. A majority of the Board (5) must have students enrolled at Bishop Luers High School at the time of election.
    2. The term of office shall be three (3) years.
    3. Members may serve no more than two (2) consecutive terms.
    4. No employee of Bishop Luers High School may serve on the Board.
- C. Election to membership on the Board shall be contingent upon a desire to serve Bishop Luers High School as evidenced by written consent (completion of the nominee form).
- D. Board members shall be elected by Parents/Guardians of Bishop Luers students in the following manner:
    1. Nominations will be opened by an announcement mailing to all Parents/Guardians of Bishop Luers students ten (10) days prior to the February Parents Association Meeting. All nominees must submit a signed nomination form.
    2. Nominations will be closed at a time selected by the board, not to exceed 10 days following the date of the February Parents Association meeting.
    3. Election of members will be by mailed ballot to all Parents/Guardians of Bishop Luers students. Each Parent/Guardian shall have one vote. Two (2) weeks will be allowed for the return of ballots. Those receiving the highest number of votes will be elected. The next in line will be notified that he/she will be asked to serve if a replacement on the Board becomes necessary. In case of a tie, the board President, Vice-President and School Principal will select the winner based on current board needs and credentials of the nominees.
    4. Newly elected members shall attend all Board meetings subsequent to their election in March and shall officially take office at the June Board meetings.
- E. Officers of the School Board shall be elected each year at the June meeting.
    1. Members of the School Board shall elect a President, Vice-President, and a Corresponding Secretary.
        a. The President will preside over the Board meetings and be held accountable for managing the meetings process on a timely basis. The President is also responsible for securing relevant input from members and administration and to minimize tendencies to wander from the issue at hand. The President shall appoint committees within the Board, i.e., Academic, Administrative, Building & Grounds, Finance, Fund Raising and Recruiting, but not limited to, or specifically, these committees. Roberts Rules of Order will be used in conducting meetings.
        b. The Vice-President will assume the responsibilities of the President in the absence of the President. The Vice-President shall be responsible for the implementation of the nomination and election process of new School Board members and for the implementation of the nomination and election process of School Board Officers.
        c. The Corresponding Secretary shall be responsible for all official correspondence transacted by the School Board.
    2. All members of the board are eligible to hold office.
        a. Nominations will be secured prior to the June meeting.
        b. All Board members will be notified of the nominees prior to the June meeting.
    3. The Recording Secretary of the School Board shall not be a member of the Board.
        a. The Recording Secretary shall be responsible for recording relevant transactions during the board meetings. Relevant transactions include all decisions, votes, commitments, and reasons for these transactions. The minutes of each meting will be submitted to the School Administration on a timely basis so as to be mailed to each Board member prior to the next meeting.
- F. Meetings of the School Board will be held monthly throughout the year. The day, time and location of the meetings will be established each year by a majority consent of board members present at the June meeting. These regular meetings are open to anyone who

wishes to attend. If an individual, or group of individuals, wishes to discuss an issue with the Board, they must first submit a written proposal to any member of the Board or to the Administration. They will then be notified, in writing, as to the date, time and place of the meeting. Special meetings may be called by the Principal, Assistant Principal, or the President of the Board. Attendance at these special meetings will be limited to Board members, the Principal, the Assistant Principal, and the School Pastor. Others may be included by invitation only.

ARTICLE II — Relationship to the Executive Board

There may arise the issue where the decision of the School Board is not acceptable to the Principal and/or the Executive Board. In such an instance, the Executive Board shall have the final decision. It is expected that the Executive Board will share with the School Board the reasons for the decision.

ARTICLE III — Qualifications for Principal

In the case of a vacancy in the position of Principal, the School Board will establish a Search Committee and enlist the assistance of the Diocesan School Administration Office to find and select suitable and qualified applicants for the position. Upon the recommendation of the School Board, the Principal is appointed by the Bishop of the Fort Wayne-South Bend Diocese in conjunction with the Franciscan Provincial.

ARTICLE IV — Amendments

The constitution of the School Board may be amended in the following manner:
1. Any parent or Board Member may propose an amendment to the Constitution.
2. The Administration shall be advised of the proposed amendment prior to its presentation to the School Board.
3. The proposed amendment must be submitted to the School Board and approved by a 2/3 vote of the School Board.
4. The approved proposed amendment must be submitted to the Parents Association for approval by these means:
    a. The approved proposed amendment must be submitted in its exact wording to all parents/guardians at least fourteen (14) days prior to a meeting of the Parents Association.
    b. The approved proposed amendment shall be placed on the agenda of the Parents Association meeting for discussion only.
    c. Within five (5) days of said Parents Association meeting, a ballot shall be mailed to parents/guardians.
    d. The approved proposed amendment shall be carried with a two-thirds (2/3) majority of votes cast. Less than two-thirds (2/3) majority of votes shall defeat the proposed amendment.

ARTICLE V — By-Laws

By-Laws may be enacted or amended by a vote of two-thirds (2/3) of the properly established Board Members present at any regular meeting provided there is a quorum and provided the amendment has been presented at the previous meeting of the Board and provided the exact wording of the amendment has been communicated through the minutes of the meeting to all Board Members

ARTICLE VI — Replacement of Board Members

If a School Board member decides that he/she can no longer serve on the board, the replacement shall be the next person in line based on the annual election votes of the parents/guardians.

ARTICLE VII — Displacement of Board Members

In the event a member of the Board has been absent from three regular meetings in one year, the remaining members of the Board may, at their discretion, determine and declare that a vacancy exists. Upon such declaration, such member shall be deemed to have resigned.

Initial Ratification:	4/19/79
Revised and Accepted by School Board:	12/16/82
Proposed Revision:	9/27/85
Revised draft #2:	10/24/85
Adopted:	12/17/85

Appendix A5
Diocesan School Board
(Consultative Board)

CONSTITUTION OF THE SCHOOL BOARD
(Diocese of Phoenix, Arizona)

Article I. Preamble

Section 1. Mission: It shall be the mission of the school board of the Diocese of Phoenix (hereinafter referred to as "diocese"), as established herein below, to promote a system of Catholic school to bring forth Christian virtues by transmitting and integrating Gospel teachings in an educative process which, within an excellent program of academics, directs the students toward a conscious choice of living a responsible Catholic life.

Section 2. Goals: To fulfill such mission, the school board of the diocese hereby sets the following goals for itself:

The Diocesan School Board shall formulate and propose policies to the ordinary of the diocese of Phoenix (hereinafter referred to as the "Bishop"), designed to:

A. Train young people to live knowingly and understandingly as children of God through a school environment which proclaims the Good News revealed in Christ, promotes fellowship in community, and encourages service to others.

B. Prepare students to practice the Good News and transfer it into action in order to accomplish the twin purposes of the educational effort of the church — personal sanctification and social reform.

C. Promote in students a deep concern for and skill in peacemaking and the achievement of justice, to help them learn and be sensitive to human needs, and to respond positively to such needs through individual and joint action.

D. Create and maintain in the school a living, conscious, active community of faith where teachers and staff, by work and by integration of faith in their own personal conduct, enable students to live a life in Christ.

E. Encourage a teaching and learning atmosphere permeated with the Gospel spirit of freedom and love.

F. Provide quality education in all areas of the school curriculum without regard to economic, cultural, ethnic or racial background of the students.

Article II. Creation and Name

There is hereby established an association of persons, which is organized under the name of "The Diocesan Catholic School Board of the Roman Catholic Diocese of Phoenix, Arizona" (hereinafter referred to as "board")

Article III. Purposes and Authority of the Board

Section I. The board shall be advisory to the Bishop in all diocesan school matters for which the Bishop seeks the board's advice and counsel including, but not limited to, preparing and submitting proposed goals and objectives of the diocesan school system.

Section 2. The board shall give advice to the Diocesan Department of Education (hereinafter referred to as the "department of education") and the Bishop on financial matters concerning all Catholic schools within the diocese.

Section 3. The board shall recommend to the department of education and the Bishop approval or disapproval of the annual budgets for diocesan high schools.

Section 4. The board shall formulate and propose written policies designed to further the goals specified in Article I of this constitution. Such policies shall be subject to the approval of the Bishop.

Section 5. The board shall continually monitor and evaluate the effectiveness of its policies and particularly the feasibility of application and enforcement by the Catholic schools within the diocese.

Article IV. Membership

Section 1. Number: The board shall consist of not less than twelve (12) nor more than fifteen (15) voting members. The Bishop, the Vicar for Christian Formation, and the Superintendent of Schools are ex-officio members of the board.

Section 2. General Eligibility: Any person who is eighteen years or older and who has shown a deep interest in and commitment to Catholic education and shall be willing to give time and energies for the betterment of Catholic education and who is a positive contributor to the parish in the diocese in which he/she participates is eligible to become a member of the board.

Section 3. Selection by Appointment: The members of the board shall be appointed by the Bishop in accordance with the bylaws of the board.

Section 4. Non-Eligibility: No employee of the department of education or of any Catholic school in the diocese may be a member of the board.

Section 5. Term of Membership: Each member shall serve a term of three years. No member may serve more than two consecutive terms unless requested to do so by the Bishop. Two or more years in filling a former member's unexpired term shall be considered a term of membership.

Article V. Officers

Section 1. Officers: The officers of the board shall consist of a president, a vice-president, and a secretary.

Section 2. Eligibility: Any voting member of the board is eligible for election as an officer of the board.

Section 3. Term: The terms of any officer of the board shall be for one year. No member of the board shall hold the same office for more than two (2) consecutive terms.

Section 4. Duties: The duties of the officers of the board shall be established in the board's bylaws.

Article VI. Meetings

The Board shall meet regularly and specially as provided in the board's bylaws.

Article VII. Amendments

This constitution may be amended by an affirmative vote of two-thirds of the authorized voting members of the board and upon approval by the Bishop; provided, however, that any proposed amendment shall have been presented in writing at the regular meeting of the board immediately preceding the meeting at which such a vote is taken.

Date:_____

Approval:

_____
President of the Board

Date:_____

Approval:

_____
Vicar of Christian Formation

Date:_____

Approval:

_____
Bishop of Phoenix

BYLAWS OF THE SCHOOL BOARD
OF THE DIOCESE OF PHOENIX, ARIZONA

Article I.   Appointment of Members

The nominating committee of the board shall have the responsibility of acquiring the nominees for appointment to the board in accordance with the board's constitution (Article IV). The names of the nominees shall be presented to the board at its regular meeting in January of each year. At that meeting, the board shall review and discuss the nominees. The nominating committee shall submit with each nominee's name a brief resume of his/her biographical data and a statement by the nominee of his/her willingness to serve.

The board, at is regular meeting in February of each year, shall select from the nominating committee's recommended list of nominees. The names of the nominees selected shall be delivered to the Bishop immediately after such meeting. From this list of names, the Bishop shall appoint members to fill existing vacancies on the board.

The Bishop shall make his appointment of members no later than the second Saturday in April of each year.

The appointees shall take office at the Board's regularly scheduled meeting in May.

Article II.   Removal of Members of the Board

A member of the board may be removed from office for cause only by the affirmative vote of two-thirds of the voting members of the board. Any action to remove a board member shall be written by secret ballot.

Any member of the board who misses three consecutive regular meetings of the board without having been excused by the president shall have his/her office declared vacant by the president.

A vacancy in the membership of any member of the board caused by death, resignation, disability or declaration of the president as provided above, shall be filled by the Bishop from the nominee(s) recommended by the board. A vacancy shall be filled by the board no later than the next nominating process. The appointee shall fill said vacancy for the unexpired term of the position he/she fills in accordance with the board's constitution (Article IV).

Article III.   Meetings

Section 1.   Regular Meetings of the Board: Regular meetings of the board shall ordinarily be held nine times a year at a place and time determined by the board through minute action.

Section 2.   Special Meetings: Special meetings of the board for any purpose may be called at any time by the president in conjunction with the Superintendent of Schools, or if he/she is unable or refuses to act, by a majority of the members of the board.

Section 3.   Quorum: A simple majority of the authorized members of the board shall constitute a quorum for the transaction of business.

Section 4.   The Board may fix its own rules of procedure, but in the absence of such rules, *Roberts' Rules of Order Revised* shall apply.

Section 5.   Open Meetings: All meetings of the board, both regular and special, shall be open to the public unless the president or the board by majority vote deems it necessary to go into executive session for discussion, deliberation, and vote. If any person other than a member of the board wishes to bring a matter before the board, such person must obtain the approval of the president to place such matter on the meeting agenda prior to the meeting. The president or a majority of the members of the board present at any meeting may waive this requirement.

Section 6.   Majority Vote: After agreement on the wording of t motion is reached through consensus, a simple majority of those voting on any particular motion shall constitute board action on any motion.

Article IV.   Officers

The officers of the board, as established in the board's constitution, shall have duties as stated in these bylaws including the following:

President: The president shall preside at all regular and special meetings of the board, shall vote on the motion, shall make appointments of chairpersons of all standing committees of the board, shall have the authority to create ad hoc committees of the board and appoint members thereto, shall plan and organize the agendas of the board meetings in consultation with the Superintendent of Schools, shall insure that board decisions are implemented, and shall see that the functions of the board committees are being properly performed.

Vice-President: The vice-president shall, in the absence or disability of the president, perform all the duties of the president. When so acting, he/she shall have all the powers of and be subject to the restrictions on the president.

Secretary: The secretary shall be responsible for the preparation and retention of the official minutes of all regular and special meetings of the board and shall perform such other duties as designated by the board.

Article V.   Election of Officers

The officers of the board shall be elected annually at the board's regular meeting in April and shall assume the office at the regular meeting of the board in May.

Each officer shall hold the office until he/she shall resign, be removed by the board or otherwise be disqualified to serve, or until his/her successor be elected, whichever event occurs first.

Article VI.   Removal or Resignation of Officers

Any officer may resign or may be removed for cause by simple majority vote of the board at any time. Any action to remove an officer shall be by secret written ballot. Any vacancy caused by the death, resignation, membership, vacancy, or removal of any officer shall be filled no later than the next nominating process.

Article VII.   Committees

Except as otherwise provided in these bylaws, the president, immediately after his/her election year, shall appoint from the members of the board a chairperson for each standing committee of the board specified in these bylaws. The chairperson shall appoint the members of the committee, subject to the approval of the board at the meeting in which the appointments are announced.

Except as provided in Article VIII of the bylaws, a minimum of two committee members shall be members of the board, when possible. The president and the Superintendent of Schools shall be ex officio members of each committee.

The members of each committee shall serve until their resignation, their removal or by a simple majority vote of the board, or the first regular meeting following the election of a new president of the board, whichever event occurs first.

Article VIII.   Standing Committees

The standing committees of the board shall be as follows.

Nominating Committee

(A nominee for election to the Board shall not be a member of the nominating committee.)

Executive Committee

The board may, by resolution adopted by a majority of the whole board, name three or more of its members as an executive committee. Such executive committee will have and may exercise the powers of the board while the board is not in session. A majority of those named to the executive committee will constitute a quorum, and the executive committee may at any time act by the written consent of a quorum thereof, although not formally convened.

Finance Committee

The finance committee shall (i) formulate financial policies and recommend them to the full board, (ii) recommend changes in financial procedures, (iii) monitor ongoing revenues and expenditures, and (iv) recommend to the full board approval or disapproval of the annual budgets for diocesan Catholic high schools.

Article IX.   Executive Officer

The diocesan Superintendent of Schools shall be the executive administrator of the board and shall be responsible for implementing the board's policies.

Article X.   Liability

Any person who serves as a member of the board or who serves in an advisory capacity to the board shall be immune from civil liability and shall not be subject to suit directly or by way of contribution for any act or omission resulting in damage or injury if such person was acting in good faith and within the scope of his official capacity, unless such damage or injury was caused by willful and wanton or grossly negligent conduct of such person.

Article XI.   Amendments to Bylaws

These bylaws may be amended by a vote of a two-thirds of the authorized voting members of the board and upon approval by the Bishop; provided, however, that any proposed amendments shall have been presented in writing to the board at the regular meeting immediately preceding the meeting at which such a vote is taken.

Date:_____

Approval:

_____
President of the Board

Date:_____

Approval:

_____
Vicar of Christian Formation

Date:_____

Approval:

_____
Bishop of Phoenix

Appendix A6
Archdiocesan Board of Education
(Consultative Board)

BOARD OF EDUCATION
(Archdiocese of Boston)

ARTICLE I
Name, Purposes and Duties

Section 1

The Board of Education for the Archdiocese of Boston, hereinafter referred to as the "Board," is established to assist the Archbishop of Boston by formulating policies for the School Office and the Office of Religious Education of the Archdiocese. Once approved by the Archbishop, the decisions of the Board shall be binding on the School Office, the Office of Religious Education-CCD, parish councils, parish school boards, pastors, principals and staffs of the schools and of the various religious education CCD programs within the parishes of the Archdiocese.

Section 2

All Board policies shall be considered final only after they have been approved in writing by the Archbishop.

Section 3

Pastors and parish councils and boards have the responsibility to establish parish education policy and to make decision consistent with the educational policies promulgated by the Board. Religious congregations have the responsibility and the right to direct their private schools in a manner consistent with the Archdiocesan policies for the general welfare of school pupils.

ARTICLE II
Membership of Board

Section 1 — Number and Composition

The Board shall be representative of the Catholic community of the Archdiocese of Boston and shall include in its membership the clergy, members of religious congregations, and laity. There shall be not more than seventeen members.

Section 2 — Election, Vacancies, Removal

Members of the Board shall be appointed by the Archbishop of Boston. Vacancies in the Board shall be filled in the same manner. Any member of the Board, other than an ex-officio member, who is absent from three consecutive meetings of the Board shall, unless excused by action of the Board, cease to be a member.

Section 3 — Tenure of Office

Each member shall hold office for the term of three years, provided however, that in order that the terms may be staggered, the initial appointments shall be divided so that one-third of the members have a term of five years, one-third of the members have a term of four years, and one-third of the members have a term of three years. The present and future members of the Board shall hold office until the Archbishop shall appoint successors, or until prior resignation or death, or until disqualification by absence from three consecutive Board meetings not excused by the Board.

Section 4 — Advisory Council

The Board annually shall name an Advisory Council of at least (6) staff persons representing the School Office and the Office of Religious Education. The Advisory Council may attend all meetings, but shall not have voting powers and shall not hold office.

ARTICLE III
Officers

Section 1 — The Officers

The Archbishop of Boston shall be the ex-officio President of the Board. (The Vicar for Religious and a representative of the Chancery Finance Department shall be ex-officio members.) The Superintendent of Schools, the Director of Religious Education and the Director of Education shall serve as ex-officio but non-voting members.

Section 2 — Ex-Officio Members
The Archbishop of Boston shall be the ex-officio President of the Board. (The Vicar for Religious and a representative of the Chancery Finance Department shall be ex-officio members.) The Superintendent of Schools, the Director of Religious Education and the Director of Education shall serve as ex-officio but non-voting members.

Section 3 — President
As President of the Board, the Archbishop of Boston has the final approval of all actions of the Board.

Section 5 — The Chairman
In the absence of the President, the Chairman will preside over the meetings of the Board. He acts as the executive head of the Board, appoints all committees unless otherwise specified in the Constitution, reports the actions of the Board through the Secretary of the board to the Archbishop of Boston, and in general performs all duties incident to the office of Chairman and such other duties as from time to time may be assigned to him by the Board.

Section 6 — The Vice-Chairman
The Vice-Chairman at the request of the Chairman or in his absence shall perform the duties and exercise the functions of the Chairman.

Section 7 — The Secretary
The Secretary shall keep the minutes of the meetings of the Board; shall see that all notices are duly given in accordance with the provisions of this Constitution; shall be the custodian of the records of the Board; and in general, shall perform all duties incident to the office of the Secretary of the Board and such other duties as from time to time may be assigned to him by the Chairman of the Board.

ARTICLE IV
Meetings
Section 1 — Regular, Special and Annual Meetings
The Board shall meet at least every other month from September to June subject to change by the Board itself or by the postponement by the President, the Chairman or the majority of the board. The regular meeting held in the month of September each year, or if none is held in that month, then in the next month in which a regular meeting is held, shall be designated the Annual Meeting for the purpose of election of officers.

Section 2 — Time, Place and Notice
All meetings may be held at such time and place, within the Archdiocese, as may be fixed by the President or, in his absence, by the executive committee or by a majority of the Board, upon not less than three days notice. Notice of the place, the day and hour of all meetings must be delivered in writing. However, if an emergency matter arises, written notice may be waived and a telephone call will be considered sufficient notice.

Section 3 — Quorum
The presence of a majority of the voting members of the entire Board (more than half of the membership) shall be necessary for the transaction of business at meetings; and majority vote (more than half of those present with the right to vote) shall be sufficient for any decision or election.

Section 4 - Rules of Procedure
The Board may fix its own rules of procedure, but in the absence of such rules Roberts' *Rules of Order,* Revised Edition, shall apply.

ARTICLE V
Committees
Section 1 — Executive Committee

The Board will provide for an Executive Committee of five (5) members. The President, the Chairman and the Secretary will be ex-officio members, and two other members will be elected annually, one by the School Committee of the Board and one by the Religious Education Committee of the Board. All committee members are voting members. The President, or in his absence the Chairman, will preside at meetings of the Executive Committee. Between meetings of the Board, the Executive Committee shall possess and exercise all the powers of the Board conferred in this Constitution, to the extent authorized by the resolution providing for the Executive or by subsequent resolution. The Executive Committee shall meet at the call of the President or Chairman and shall fix its own rules of procedure and notice to be given of its meeting. A majority shall constitute a quorum.

Section 2 — School Committee

The Board will provide for a School Committee which shall have seven members and which will include the Superintendent of Schools and the Director of Education. The School Committee will concern itself with all school related matters and will regularly make reports and recommendations to the Board. This committee will meet monthly from September to June.

Section 3 — Religious Education Committee

The Board will provide for a Religious Education Committee which will have seven members and which will include the Director of Religious Education. The Religious Education Committee will concern itself with all matters related to religious education and will regularly make reports and recommendations to the Board. This committee will meet monthly from September to June.

Section 4 — Other Committees

The Board may, by resolution, provide for such other committees as it deems advisable and may discontinue the same at its pleasure. Each committee shall have such powers and shall perform such duties as may be assigned to it by the Board and shall be appointed, and vacancies filled, in the same manner determined by the Board. In the absence of other direction, the Chairman shall appoint the members of committees.

ARTICLE VI
Amendment of the Constitution
Section 1 — Amendment

This constitution may be amended, supplemented, suspended, or repealed, in whole or in part, at any time by a two-thirds vote of the total voting membership of the Board, subject to the approval of the Archbishop of Boston; provided that notice of the proposed amendment shall be given to the Board at a prior meeting of the Board.

ARCHDIOCESE OF BOSTON
BOARD OF EDUCATION
BY-LAWS
ARTICLE I
Section 1

No person or group shall be granted the right to address a meeting of the Board or participate in its deliberations unless prior approval to do so has been granted by the Board.

Section 2

Any person or group desiring to address a meeting of the Board in circumstances in which the entire Board cannot act on the request shall notify the Chairman prior to the next meeting of the Board. Upon receipt of such request the Chairman shall contact individually or collectively the President and the Secretary of the Board. It shall require an affirmative vote of two of the three officers to approve such a request and, granting such a request, a majority of these officers shall set forth the amount of time and nature of the participation in the deliberations of the Board to be granted each separate request.

ARTICLE II
Section 1

Upon agreement of the majority, the total voting membership of its duly authorized Committee may hold public hearings. The time, place, date or dates, the subject matter to be discussed and the manner in which the public hearings will be conducted, shall be decided by the Board in each instance.

Section 2

The information gained from public hearings shall be considered by the appropriate committee of the Board, which committee shall report its findings to the Board for its consideration.

ARTICLE III
Section 1

Any committee desiring to have any of its reports considered by the Board shall submit a request for inclusion in the agenda through the Secretary. If the Secretary receives such a request from any committee chairman at least ten (10) days before a meeting of the Board, the Secretary shall place the committee's report on the agenda for the next meeting.

ARTICLE IV
Section 1

These By-laws may be amended, supplemented, suspended, or repealed, in whole or in part, at any time by the two-thirds vote of all the voting members of the Board, with the approval of the Archbishop of Boston; provided that notice of the proposed changes in the By-laws shall be given to the Board at a prior meeting.

Appendix B—Boards with Limited Jurisdiction

Appendix B1
Central School System
(Board with Limited Jurisdiction:
two-tiered — members/director)

CONSTITUTION
FOR THE
CATHOLIC CENTRAL SCHOOL
(Diocese of Buffalo)

The twelve parishes of the Central City of the Diocese of Buffalo established the Catholic Central School. Sponsoring parishes are as follows:

ST. ANN ROMAN CATHOLIC CHURCH SOCIETY OF BUFFALO, N.Y.
Broadway and Emslie, Buffalo, N.Y. 14212

ST. BARTHOLOMEW ROMAN CATHOLIC CHURCH SOCIETY OF BUFFALO, N.Y.
335 Grider Street, Buffalo, N.Y. 14215

ST. BENEDICT THE MOOR ROMAN CATHOLIC CHURCH SOCIETY OF BUFFALO, N.Y.
18 Welker Street, Buffalo, N.Y. 14208

BLESSED TRINITY ROMAN CATHOLIC CHURCH SOCIETY OF BUFFALO, N.Y.
323 Leroy Avenue, Buffalo, N.Y. 14214

ST. BONIFACE ROMAN CATHOLIC CHURCH SOCIETY OF BUFFALO, N.Y.
18 Welker Street, Buffalo, N.Y. 14209

SS. COLUMBA & BRIGID ROMAN CATHOLIC CHURCH SOCIETY OF BUFFALO, N.Y.
418 North Division Street, Buffalo, N.Y. 14204

ST. JAMES ROMAN CATHOLIC CHURCH SOCIETY OF BUFFALO, N.Y.
3021 Bailey Avenue, Buffalo, N.Y. 14215

ST. MARY OF SORROWS ROMAN CATHOLIC CHURCH SOCIETY OF BUFFALO, N.Y.
333 Guilford Street, Buffalo, N.Y. 14211

ST. MATTHEW ROMAN CATHOLIC CHURCH SOCIETY OF BUFFALO, N.Y.
26 Wyoming Avenue, Buffalo, N.Y. 14215

OUR LADY OF LOURDES ROMAN CATHOLIC CHURCH SOCIETY OF BUFFALO, N.Y.
1107 Main Street, Buffalo, N.Y. 14209

SS. RITA & PATRICK ROMAN CATHOLIC CHURCH SOCIETY OF BUFFALO, N.Y.
Fillmore Avenue & Eagle Street, Buffalo, N.Y. 14210

ST. VINCENT DE PAUL ROMAN CATHOLIC CHURCH SOCIETY OF BUFFALO, N.Y.
15 Eastwood Place, Buffalo, N.Y. 14208

MISSION STATEMENT
of the
CATHOLIC CENTRAL SCHOOL

I. The Mission of the Catholic Church in the Central City includes the preservation and propagation of the Faith. The Diocese of Buffalo is committed to a concept of social justice which requires providing students of the Central City with basic, quality education.

II. To a great extent, the Mission of the Church in general, and the Diocese in particular, is effectively implemented through the Catholic Educational Apostolate. Students whose parents desire a Catholic value-oriented education are welcome in Catholic Schools regardless of race, color or creed.

III. The Catholic Central School exists with and for the families of the students and the Catholic Community. The families shall, therefore, participate in the financial support of the school and have the responsibility for its assets.

IV. In light of this Mission Statement, all constituencies of the school (students and families, faculty, school administration and board) shall make every effort to bring to life the following:
1. A deep reverence for the uniqueness giftedness of each student as a person and as a member in the community of families.
2. An appreciation of the traditions of each ethnic culture and encouragement for unity in the diversity of these cultures.
3. An environment that provides character development and responsible citizenship.
4. An effective social action program which is intended to bring about peace and justice in the larger community.
5. A sign of stability for families in an environment of chaos and flux.

GOAL AND OBJECTIVES
of the
CATHOLIC CENTRAL SCHOOL BOARD

Goal:
To serve the educational needs of the children and to promote the well being of the families within the Catholic tradition.

Objectives:
1. To acquire by lease, gift or purchase, or to construct one or more school buildings to be operated as the Regional Catholic School.
2. To remodel, repair and maintain the school buildings which come under its control.
3. To acquire by lease or purchase, furniture, furnishings, educational equipment and materials and items needed in conducting educational programs.
4. To hire the Supervising Principal and approve salaries for necessary personnel.
5. To prepare annual budgets to plan for the fiscal needs of the Catholic Central school.
6. To generate income in order to operate the educational programs through payments to be made in the form of tuition and parent fund raising, payments by individual parishes and funds collected through other fund raising events and any other means available.
7. To work with the Board of Catholic Education and the Department of Catholic Education to develop Catholic Central School programs and generate necessary income.
8. To encourage, support and cooperate with the Home School Association, which benefits students and parents of the Catholic Central School.
9. To borrow money to meet the needs of the Catholic Central School provided the approval of the Bishop of Buffalo has been given.

BY-LAWS
Article I　　　　　Address
　Section 1.　　　The office of the Supervising Principal of the Catholic Central School will be at
　　　　　　　　　_____.

　Section 2.　　　The two sites are:
　　　　　　　　　Msgr. David Herlihy Campus
　　　　　　　　　476 Emslie Street, Buffalo, NY 14212

　　　　　　　　　Fr. Joseph Bissonette Campus
　　　　　　　　　21 Davidson Avenue, Buffalo, NY 14215

Article II　　　　The structure of the Catholic Central School Board will be composed of the Members, the Board of Directors and representatives of the Pastoral Board.

Section 1.　　　Members
　A. The Members of the Catholic Central School shall be ex officio: the Bishop of Buffalo, the Vicars General of the Diocese of Buffalo, the Chancellor of the Diocese of Buffalo and the Superintendent of Catholic Education.
　B. The responsibility of the Members shall include the review and approval of the slate of the Board of Directors of the Catholic Central School.
　C. Amendments of these Articles shall be subject to the approval of the Members.
　D. The annual meeting of the Members shall be held in a timely fashion with the annual Board of Directors Meeting. Special meetings can be held after twenty-four hours notice. A quorum shall consist of a majority of members.

Section 2　　　　Board of Directors
　A. The Board of Directors (Directors) shall consist of no fewer than 21 members or no more than 27 voting members.
　B. The Board of Directors shall be made up of no fewer than 4 members of the Pastoral Board elected by that Board; no fewer than 6 parents of students enrolled in the Catholic Central School (3 from each site), no fewer than eleven other persons with expertise in areas designated in Article IV. The Principal(s) will serve as ex officio, non-voting members.
　C. Directors will serve for a term of three years with one third of the membership changing each year.
　D. A Director may not serve for more than two full consecutive terms.
　E. The Nominating Committee of Directors shall be Ad Hoc and shall present the slate of candidates to the Board of Directors for review and acceptance. The Board then presents it to the Members for final review and acceptance.
　F. Any Director may resign at any time by submitting a written notice to the Chairperson of the Board of Directors.
　G. A Director who has three unexcused absences within a twelve month period will be automatically removed from the Board. A Director can also be removed by a vote of the majority of the Board.
　H. Vacancies can be filled by a majority vote of the Board at any regular or special meeting of the Board of Directors. New Members will hold the position for the unexpired term of their predecessors.
　I. A quorum shall consist of a majority of the Directors.
　J. The annual meeting of the Directors shall be held in January. Regular monthly meetings will be held. Special meetings may be called by any officers on three (3) days written notice.
　K. The responsibilities of the Board of Directors include educational planning/ development, formulation of policy and management procedures of the school.
　L. The Board of Directors shall adopt the budget, which was previously submitted to the Pastoral Board for review and input (Article II, Section 3D), at the Board of Directors Annual meeting.
　M. The actions of the Board of Directors shall be valid unless vetoed by the Members.

Section 3.   Pastoral Board
   A. The primary responsibility for coordinating Pastoral Programs for Catholic Education belongs to the Bishop. He, in turn, shares this responsibility.
   B. The Pastors, and/or Pastoral Team Members of the supporting parishes, constitute membership on the Pastoral Board.
   C. The Pastoral Board is concerned not only with the Catholic identity of the school but is primarily concerned with the spiritual growth of all families and the extension of that spiritual life into the parishes.
   D. The Pastoral Board will be responsible for fiscal review and recommendations.
   E. The Pastoral Board at its annual meeting shall elect at least four members from their membership to serve on the Board of Directors (Article IV).

Article III   Officers
Section 1.
   A. The officers of the Board of Directors shall be the President, Vice-President, Secretary and Treasurer.
   B. The officers shall be elected by the Directors at the annual meeting for a term of two years. Officers shall be members of the Board.
   C. The President shall preside at all meetings of the Directors and perform all duties usually appropriate to the office of the President.
   D. The Vice-President shall, in the absence or disability of the President, perform the duties and exercise the powers of the President. The Vice-President shall have such powers and perform such duties as may be delegated to him or her by the President or prescribed by the Board of Directors.
   E. The Secretary shall keep the minutes of all meetings of the Board of Directors and shall, in general, perform all the duties appropriate to the office of Secretary.
   F. The Treasurer shall be the chief fiscal officer of the Catholic Central School who shall be responsible for all funds paid to the Catholic Central School, and for depositing them in such bank or banks as the Directors shall designate. He/she shall pay all bills approved by the Directors or their designee. The Treasurer will require a co-signer of checks. The Treasurer shall oversee the keeping of detailed accounts of the assets, liabilities, receipts and disbursements of the Catholic Central School. The books shall be open during business hours for examination or audit by the Members, Board of Directors and Officers or their representatives and the Controller of the Diocese.
   The Treasurer shall render an annual report to the Members and Directors, and the books of the Catholic Central School shall be audited annually by the Controller of the Diocese, or an auditor designated by the Controller. The Directors shall bond the Treasurer and/or the Financial Manager.
   G. The Board of Directors shall indemnify and hold its members harmless from liability incurred while serving the Catholic Central School.

Article IV   Committees
Section 1.
   A. There shall be an Executive Committee of at least five members made up of the President and Treasurer and at least three Directors, appointed by the President for staggered two year terms. The Executive Committee shall be authorized to conduct the affairs of the Catholic Central School referred to it by the President between meetings of the Board of Directors.
   B. There shall be a Finance Committee of at least seven Directors made up of the President, the Treasurer and at least two members selected by the Pastoral Board and such additional members as may be appointed by the President for a term of two years. The Finance Committee shall plan for the financing of the Catholic Central School and shall prepare a preliminary budget after receiving recommendations from the Pastoral Board. The budget will then be forwarded to the Board of Directors.
   C. The Administration and Policy Committee will handle all matters pertaining to personnel.
   D. The Spiritual Formation Committee will be concerned with the Catholic Identity of the

school, the Religious Education of the students and the spiritual growth of the total school family as reflected in a continual conversion to the Lord. Two members of the Pastoral Board shall be on this Committee.

E. The Buildings and Properties Committee will be concerned with the leasing and/or the purchase of the buildings and furnishings, the general upkeep and long range maintenance planning.

F. The Public Relations and Fund Development Committee, working with the Diocesan Development Department for long-term development, will be responsible for making the school known in the parishes and in the community.

G. The Education Program Planning Committee is responsible for overseeing the implementation of the curriculum, professional growth of the staff, to review with the Principal and staff the development and tailoring of Education Programs to help our students achieve excellence, intercultural awareness and become responsible citizens.

H. The President may from time to time create other committees as the need arises which shall not be limited to members of the Board of Directors except the Chair thereof. The President shall be an ex officio member of all committees.

Section 2. Membership on these Committees will include at least one Director and other members of the Community.

Article V Miscellaneous

Section 1. Fiscal Year:

The fiscal year of the Catholic Central School shall begin September 1 and end August 31 of the following year.

Section 2. Remuneration:

No member of the Catholic Central School may receive remuneration for services rendered on the Pastoral Board or on the Board of Directors.

Section 3. In the event of dissolution of the school, all assets will become the property of the participating parishes according to the current lease agreement.

Section 4. The Supervising Principal shall be directly responsible to the Board of Directors.

Section 5. The Board of Directors shall hire a Financial Manager who shall be directly responsible to the Treasurer of the Board of Directors and the Supervising Principal.

Article VI Amendments

Section 1. Articles to be amended should be proposed at any duly called meeting and voted on at a subsequent meeting. Approval requires a majority vote of the Board of Directors.

Signature_____
May 20, 1988

Appendix B2
Interparish School Board
(Board with Limited Jurisdiction:
separately incorporated — members/directors)

INTERPARISH SCHOOL BOARDS
(Archdiocese of Baltimore)
ARTICLES OF INCORPORATION
OF
_____, INC.

We, the undersigned, being at least eighteen years of age, hereby form a corporation under and by virtue of the General Laws of the State of Maryland.

SECOND: The name of the Corporation (which is hereafter called the "Corporation" or "School") is _____, INC.

THIRD: The Corporation is formed for religious and educational purposes as follows:

To establish and maintain an educational institution and program in accordance with and subject to the standards, guidelines, and discipline of the Roman Catholic Archdiocese of Baltimore.

FOURTH: (A) The Corporation is organized exclusively for religious and educational purposes, including, for such purposes, the making of distributions to organizations that qualify as exempt organizations under Section 501(c)(3) of the Internal Revenue Code of 1986 (or the corresponding provision of any future United States Internal Revenue Law), and, more specifically, to receive and administer funds for such religious and educational purposes, all for the public welfare, and for no other purposes, and all subject to the standards, guidelines, and disciplines of the Roman Catholic Archdiocese of Baltimore, and to that end:

1. to take and hold, by bequest, devise, gift, purchase, or lease, either absolutely or in trust for such objects and purposes or any of them, any property, real, personal, or mixed, without limitation as to amount or value, except such limitations, if any, as may be imposed by law;

2. to sell, convey, and dispose of any such property and to invest and reinvest the principal thereof, and to deal with and expend the income therefrom for any of the before-mentioned purposes, without limitation, except such limitations, if any, as may be contained in the instrument under which such property is received;

3. to receive any property, real, personal, or mixed, in trust, under the terms of any will, deed of trust, or other trust instrument for the foregoing purposes or any of them, and in administering the same to carry out the directions, and exercise the power contained in the trust instrument under which the property is received, including the expenditure of the principal as well as the income, for one or more of such purposes, if authorized or directed in the trust instrument under which it is received, but no gift, bequest or devise of any such property shall be received and accepted if it is conditioned or limited in such manner as shall require the disposition of the income or its principal to any person or organization other than a "charitable organization" or for other than "charitable purposes" within the meaning of such terms as defined in Article ELEVENTH of these Articles of Incorporation or as shall in the opinion of the Board of directors, jeopardize the federal income tax exemption of the Corporation pursuant to Section 501(c)(3) of the Internal Revenue Code of 1986, as now in force or afterward amended;

4. to receive, take title to, hold, and use the proceeds and income of stocks, bonds, obligations, or other securities of any corporation or corporations, domestic or foreign, but only for the purposes as set forth in Article THIRD, or some of them;

5. in general to have, enjoy, and exercise all of the rights, powers, and privileges which are now or which hereafter may be conferred by the laws of Maryland upon a non-stock corporation organized for educational and religious purposes, all for the public welfare, but only to the extent the exercise of such powers are in furtherance of exempt purposes.

(B) No part of the net earnings of the Corporation shall inure to the benefit of, or be distributable to, its members, directors, officers, or other private persons, to pay reasonable compensation for services rendered and to make payments and distributions in furtherance of the purposes set forth in Article THIRD hereof.

(C) No substantial part of the activities of the Corporation shall consist of the carrying on of propaganda, or otherwise attempting to influence legislation, and the corporation shall not participate in, or intervene in (including the publishing or distribution of statements) any political campaign on behalf of any candidate for public office.

(D) Notwithstanding any other provision of these Articles, the Corporation shall neither have nor exercise any power, nor shall engage directly or indirectly in activities that would adversely affect its tax exempt status as an organization described in Section 501(c)(3) of the Internal Revenue Code of 1986 (or the corresponding provision of any future United States Internal Revenue Law) or as an organization to which contributions are deductible under Section 170(c)(2) of the Internal Revenue Code of 1986 (or the corresponding provision of any future United States Revenue Law).

(E) The Corporation may not at any time be controlled directly or indirectly by one or more disqualified persons as defined in Section 4946(a) of the Internal Revenue Code.

FIFTH: The powers of the Corporation shall be exercised, its property controlled, and its affairs conducted by the board of Directors; provided, however, that the following powers shall be reserved to the Roman Catholic Archbishop of Baltimore, a corporation sole, in accordance with the discipline and governance of the Roman Catholic Church, and shall require specific authorization, in writing, by the Archbishop of Baltimore, or his appointed designee:
1. Sale, mortgage, or long-term leasing of the real property;
2. Any significant change in character or size or nature of the School;
3. Closing of the School;
4. Any significant change in the physical structure of the School;
5. Dissolution, liquidation, winding up, or abandonment of the Corporation.

SIXTH: The post office address of the principal office of the Corporation in this State is _____. The name and post office address of the Resident Agent of the Corporation in this State is _____. Said Resident Agent is an individual actually residing in this State.

SEVENTH: The Corporation shall have no capital stock and shall not be authorized to issue capital stock. The Corporation shall not operate for the purpose of carrying on business for profit.

EIGHTH: The Corporation shall have _____ Corporate Members:
_____
_____.
All of the Corporate Members are Maryland religious corporations organized pursuant to MD. CORPS. & ASS'NS. CODE ANN., Sections 5-31 to 5-320. There shall be a written agreement between the School and the Corporate Members which delineates their respective rights and responsibilities with respect to such matters as financial support for the School and use, maintenance, utilities, repairs, and capital improvements with respect to the School.

NINTH: The Corporation's Board of Directors shall consist of not less than _____ and not more than ____ members, which number may be increased or decreased pursuant to the Corporation's Bylaws. The Directors shall be appointed by the Corporate Members in the manner specified in the corporate bylaws. The names of the Directors, who shall act until the first annual meeting or until their successors are duly chosen and qualified, are: _____
_____.

TENTH: All of the property and assets of the Corporation of every kind whatsoever are irrevocably dedicated to religious and educational purposes. Upon the liquidation, dissolution, or winding up of the Corporation's affairs, or upon the abandonment of the Corporation's activities due to its impracticable or inexpedient nature, after paying or adequately providing for the debts or obligations of the Corporation, the assets of the Corporation then remaining in the hands of the Corporation shall be distributed, transferred, conveyed, delivered, and paid over to the Corporate Members, all of which are charitable organizations, in such manner as determined by the Board and in accordance with the canons and regulations of the Roman Catholic Church.

ELEVENTH: The Corporation may by its Bylaws make any other provisions or requirements for the arrangement or conduct of the business of the Corporation, provided the same be not inconsistent with these Articles of Incorporation nor contrary tot he laws of the State of Maryland or of the United States.

TWELFTH: In these Articles of Incorporation,
(a) References to "charitable organizations" or "charitable organization" mean corporations, trust funds, foundations, or community chests created or organized in the United States or

any of its possessions, whether under the laws of the United States, any state or territory, the District of Columbia, or any possession of the United States, described in Section 170(b)(1)(A) of the Internal Revenue Code of 1986 or the corresponding provision of any subsequent federal tax laws, qualified as an exempt organization under Section 501(c)(3) of the Internal Revenue Code of 1986 or the corresponding provision of any subsequent federal tax laws.

(b) The term "charitable purposes" shall be limited to and shall include only religious, charitable, scientific testing for public safety, literary, or educational purposes within the meaning of the terms used in Section 501(c)(3) of the Internal Revenue Code of 1986 but only such purposes as also constitute public charitable purposes under the laws of the United States, any state or territory, the District of Columbia, or any possession of the United States, including, but not limited to, the granting of scholarships to young men and women to enable them to attend educational institutions.

IN WITNESS WHEREOF, we have signed these Articles of Incorporation this _____ day of _____, 1989, and acknowledge the same to be our acts.

ATTEST:

_____ _____
William H. Keeler
Archbishop of Baltimore
(SIGNATURES OF PASTORS OF SPONSORING PARISHES)

AGREEMENT

This Agreement, dated this _____ day of _____, 1989, is between
_____
_____
_____
_____ SCHOOL, INC. (hereinafter called SCHOOL).

WHEREAS, through a joint effort of the ARCHDIOCESE OF BALTIMORE,
_____
the concept of the SCHOOL has been formed to promote the overall educational mission and witness of the Catholic Church in the Archdiocese of Baltimore; and

WHEREAS, it is the intention of _____
_____, and SCHOOL to set forth a Mission Statement for the School, to set policies regarding admission of students and tuition assistance, and to delineate their respective responsibilities regarding the operation, use, maintenance, repairs, capital repairs/replacements/ improvements, fiscal responsibility, etc., relating to [the _____ campuses] of SCHOOL;

THAT in consideration of the benefits to the members of
_____
parishes and the mutual covenants and agreements contained herein, the parties have agreed as follows:

1. **Term.** The initial term of this Agreement shall be _____, 19__ to _____, 19__. The Agreement shall be renewed each year, following the review and adjustments described in section _____.
2. Mission Statement.
3. Admission to School.
4. Tuition Assistance.
   a) Eligibility.
   b) Criteria.
5. Use of Buildings.
   a) The SCHOOL will have the right of use of the physical plant at each campus during the hours of _____ A.M. to _____ P.M., Monday through Friday, _____, 19__ through _____, 19__, exclusive of Holidays or Holy days on which no classes are scheduled, for the conduct of all activities associated with the SCHOOL. The SCHOOL will assume all responsibility associated with the

use of the physical plant [at each campus] during these hours.
   b) The "host parish" [of each campus location, as specified below] will have the right of use of said physical plant at all times other than those specified in section 5(a). The host parish will assume all responsibility associated with the use of the physical plant during these times. The host parish will coordinate its use of the physical plant and other disruption of the orderly day to day operation of the SCHOOL. [The host parishes of each campus of SCHOOL are as follows:]
   c) The SCHOOL will be allowed use of the physical plant [of each campus] at times other than those specified in section 5(a) above, as long as such use does not interfere with the functions of the host parish [for that campus], and the SCHOOL will assume all responsibility during such times. Such use shall be arranged and scheduled in advance by and through the pastor of the host parish or his designee, and permission for such use will not be unreasonably withheld, subject to the needs of the host parish.
   d) The host parish will be allowed use of the physical plant during the times specified in section 5(a) above, as long as such use does not interfere with the functions of SCHOOL, and the host parish will assume all responsibility during such times. Such use shall be arranged and scheduled in advance by and through the Principal [at the campus], and permission for such use will not be unreasonably withheld, subject to the needs of [each campus of] the SCHOOL.
6. **Scheduling.** Designated representatives of [each] host parish and the SCHOOL will meet at least once annually (on or before June 1 of each year) to coordinate scheduling of use of the physical plant(s), in order to avoid duplication and conflicts.
7. **Maintenance.** The host parish and the SCHOOL will be jointly responsible for the maintenance and leaning of the physical plant [at each campus location], as follows:
   a. With respect to those maintenance personnel who perform duties and responsibilities for both the host parish and school, employment of such maintenance personnel will be jointly agreed upon by the host parish and SCHOOL. Salary, payroll additives, and benefits will be prorated as follows:
   A time study will be done during the _____ school year to determine an appropriate allocation of these costs for subsequent years.
   b. Maintenance personnel who perform duties and responsibilities only for the SCHOOL will be employed by the SCHOOL, and salary, payroll additives, and benefits, if any, will be the responsibility of the SCHOOL.
   c. Physical plant services (examples of which are shown below) will be shared as follows:

SERVICES		SCHOOL
Electricity	___%	___%
Gas	___%	___%
Water	___%	___%
Sewer	___%	___%
Service Contracts:		
Water Treatment and Boiler Maintenance	___%	___%
Trash Removal	___%	___%
Snow Removal	___%	___%

   On the fifteenth of each month, [each] host parish will invoice the SCHOOL for the previous month, and SCHOOL will invoice the host parish [at each campus location] for the previous month for reimbursement of physical plant services for that location in accordance with the percentages delineated above. [Each] host parish and SCHOOL will be responsible for payment of said invoices within 15 days after receipt.
8. **Escrow Fund.** The parishes which sponsor the School (_____) shall collectively establish and fund an escrow account to provide for capital expenses, extraordinary repairs, [emergency shortfalls,] and other agreed-upon expenses. The sponsoring parishes shall contribute the following amounts each year, until the account contains a minimum of $_____:

When the account balance reaches $_____, each parish need only contribute additional funds, in the proportions set forth above, in order to replenish the account as expenditures occur.

Actual expenses which are intended to be paid by funds from this account, but which exceed the funds which are actually in the account, as well as any other expenses of School such as operating deficits or other emergencies, will be paid by the parishes as follows:

Contracts for capital repairs, etc., to be paid for out of the escrow fund will be competitively bid, with the host parish responsible for contract administration.

9. _____ recognize that they each have a good faith commitment to and fiscal responsibility for the continuation of the School. The division of responsibilities regarding operation, use, maintenance repairs, capital repairs/replacements/ improvements, fiscal responsibility, etc., will be reviewed annually, and will be adjusted, if required, as agreed to by parties to this Agreement.

(SIGNATURES)

Appendix B3
Private Secondary School
sponsored by Religious Congregation
(Board with Limited Jurisdiction:
two tiered — members/directors)

MERCY HIGH SCHOOL
(Sisters of Mercy, Province of Detroit)
BYLAWS

ARTICLE I
Name and Location

The legal name of this corporation is Mercy High School (hereinafter referred to as the "School"), a Michigan non-profit educational Corporation. The principal office is in the City of Farmington Hills in the State of Michigan situated at the northeast corner of the intersection of Middlebelt and Eleven Mile Roads.

ARTICLE II
Purpose and Mission

The legal purposes of the Corporation shall be as set forth in its Articles of Incorporation, as amended from time to time. In pursuance of its legal purpose, the mission of the Corporation shall be the operation of a Catholic high school for young women, where the arts and sciences are taught and diplomas and honors are conferred in furtherance of and consonant with the system of motivating beliefs, concepts and principles as set forth in the Statement of Philosophy.

ARTICLE III
Membership

Section 1: **Members.** The members of the Corporation shall consist of the Provincial Administrator and elected Members of the Provincial Administration of the Religious Sisters of Mercy of the Union of the Province of Detroit and other such individuals as appointed by the Members. The terms of the Members (elected and appointed) shall coincide with the elected terms of the Provincial Administration.

Section 2: **Meetings.**
  (a) Annual Meeting
  The Annual Meeting of the Members of the Corporation shall be held at such time and place as designated by the Members. At this meeting, the Members shall elect officers and appoint Members and transact such other business as may properly come before such meeting.
  (b) Special Meeting
  Special meetings of the Members may be called by the Presiding Member or at the request of any two or more Members.
  (c) Notice of Meetings
  Ordinarily, written notice, stating the date, time and place of the meeting and, in case of a special meeting, the purpose for which the meeting is called, shall be delivered to each Member.
  (d) Place of Meeting
  Meetings of the Members shall ordinarily be at the principal office of the Province unless a different location shall be designated.

Section 3: **Quorum.** At each meeting of the Members, two-thirds of the Members present in person or by proxy shall constitute a quorum for the transaction of business. A Member or Members may participate in a meeting of the Members (and for all purposes shall be regarded as present at the meeting) by means of a conference telephone or similar communications equipment so long as all Members participating in the meeting may effectively hear each other.

Section 4: **Officers.** Officers of the Members shall be the Chairperson (Provincial Administrator), a Vice-Chairperson and a Secretary-Treasurer, who shall each serve a term of one (1) year.

Section 5: **Voting.** Each Member elected and appointed, shall have one vote. Unless otherwise provided by law, and assuming that a quorum shall have been established, a simple majority of those

Members present in person or by proxy shall have full power to decide any question coming before such meeting. Any action required or permitted to be taken at a meeting of the Members may be taken without a meeting if, before or after the action, all of the Members shall consent thereto in writing. The consents of the Members shall be filed with the minutes of the Members.

Section 6: **Powers.** Final authority necessary to the carrying out of the purposes as described in Articles of Incorporation and any matter beyond the capacity of the Board of Trustees is vested in the Members of the Corporation.

The Members, in addition to any powers granted by laws, shall have the power to:
  (a) approve the Statement of Philosophy, Mission and Goals for the School,
  (b adopt and thereafter amend the Articles of Incorporation of the Corporation,
  (c) adopt and thereafter amend the Bylaws of the Corporation,
  (d) appoint and thereafter remove and/or replace the Board of Trustees or any one or more of the Trustees, with or without cause,
  (e) approve the recommendation of the Board of Trustees of the appointment or removal of the Principal of the School,
  (f) approve the purchase, sale, exchange, conveyance or transfer of real or liquid assets, the borrowing of money, the issuance of note(s) or bond(s) for the repayment thereof with interest and the granting of such pledge(s), mortgage(s) or other security interest(s) with respect to property as shall be required therewith, upon such terms and conditions as shall have been recommended to the Members by the Board of Trustees,
  (g) approve a deficit operating and a capital budget,
  (h) initiate in collaboration with the Board of Trustees a process for identification of candidates to be considered by the Members for appointment to the Board of Trustees.

Section 7: **Records.** Written records of all actions taken by the Members shall be maintained by the Secretary-Treasurer in th Corporate Offices of the Members. A copy thereof, certified as correct by a majority of the Members, shall be delivered to the Secretary of the Board of Trustees for filing in the Corporate Minute Book.

Section 8: **Compensation.** Members as such shall not receive any compensation for their services to the Corporation, except for reimbursement of such out-of-pocket expenditures as have been identified and approved in the operating budget for the School.

ARTICLE IV
Board of Trustees

Section 1: **Trustees.** The affairs and business of the Corporation shall be governed by a Board of Trustees which shall consist of not less than nine or more than fifteen persons, at least one-third of whom shall be Sisters of Mercy. The Principal of the School, <u>ex officio</u>, shall be a Trustee with vote and shall hold the title of President of the Corporation.

Section 2: **Terms of Trustees.** The terms of appointment for Trustees shall ordinarily be for three years. A Trustee may be appointed to two consecutive terms, but cannot thereafter be appointed until the expiration of two years occurs. A Trustee may resign at any time by giving written notice of his or her resignation to the Secretary-Treasure of the Corporation. Such notice or resignation shall be effective upon delivery. A Trustee may be involuntarily removed from office only by the Members.

Section 3: **Meetings.** The Board of Trustees shall meet as often and on such dates as it may specify in order to transact the business within its power. Meetings may be held at any place within or without the State of Michigan; provided, however, that no meeting shall be held outside of the City of Farmington Hills, Michigan, unless the date, time and location thereof shall have been approved by a majority of all of the Trustees.
  (a) The Annual Meeting of the Board of Trustees shall be designated as that meeting which follows the appointment of Trustees by the Members to fill terms which are expiring. The purpose of the Annual Meeting is to elect officers and transact such other business as is necessary.
  (b) Regular Meetings
    Regular Meetings of the Board of Trustees shall be held at least three times during the year.
  (c) Special Meetings
    Special Meetings of the Board of Trustees may be called at any time by the President or by the Chairperson or, upon receipt by him or her of the written request of three Trustees if

the request is received at least twelve days prior to the proposed date of the meeting.

Section 4: **Notice of Meeting.** Ordinarily, notice of the date, time and place of any regular or special meeting shall be given to each Trustee not less than ten days before the meeting by notice delivered in person or by mail. The notice of any special meeting shall state the purpose or purposes of the meeting.

Section 5: **Quorum and Valid Trustee Action.** Two-thirds of the Trustees present and voting shall constitute a quorum for a valid transaction of business at any meeting of the Board of Trustees. The resolution or action of two-thirds shall be the valid action of the Board of Trustees; provided, however, that no resolution or action shall become effective without the affirmative vote of at least one-half (1/2) of the Trustees present.

Each Trustee shall have one vote. Any action required or permitted to be taken without a meeting if, before or after the action, all the Trustees then in office shall consent thereto in writing. The consents of the Trustees shall be filed with the minutes of the Board of Trustees.

Section 6: **Powers.** The Board of Trustees shall assume all powers not reserved to the Members of the Corporation for conduct of the business and affairs of the School. These powers include initiating with the Members the process for:

(a) The recruitment, selection and recommendation of an eligible candidate to serve in the position of Principal for approval by the Members; conducting an annual appraisal of performance of the Principal, identifying mutual goals and arranging appropriate compensation and related benefits.

(b) Develop short and long range plans in keeping with the Statement of Philosophy, Mission and Goals for the School to insure the School's viability.

(c) Review, evaluate and revise the Statement of Philosophy, Mission and Goals for approval by the Members.

(d) Develop and approve major policies, including the setting of tuition and fees, which guide the direction of the School in accord with its purpose and the Statement of Philosophy, Mission and Goals.

(e) Provide through the Principal for the adequate maintenance upkeep, and supervision of the land, buildings and other assets of the Corporation.

(f) Insure sound fiscal management through implementation of good accounting principles and procedures; insure an annual audit and develop and approve an annual operating budget except where such operating and capital budgets require the approval of the Members.

(g) Bequests, Grants and Contracts
The Corporation shall have full power to accept gifts, devises or bequests, and to take, receive and hold any property to be used for the purposes for which this Corporation is created. The Board of Trustees, subject to the provisions of subsection (h) of this Section and this Article, shall have full power and right to authorize the President and/or other appropriate Officers, in its behalf, to make, execute, deliver and sign any and all deeds, grants, contracts and other instruments of the Corporation.

(h) Borrowing of Money
The Board of Trustees with the approval of the Members, shall have authority to borrow money and may authorize the proper Officers of this Corporation to make, execute and deliver in the name of and on behalf of this Corporation such notes, bonds and other evidence of indebtedness as the Board shall deem proper, and the Board shall have full power to mortgage the property of this Corporation or any part thereof as security for indebtedness, provided that any such mortgage shall also be approved by the Members of the Corporation.

(i) Elect Officers annuals with the exception of the Office of the President, fill vacancies in Office due to death, resignation or removal of an Officer for cause.

Section 7: **Compensation.** Trustees as such shall not receive any compensation for their services; provided, however, that nothing herein contained shall be construed to preclude any Trustee from serving the School in another capacity and receiving such compensation therefor as shall be approved by a quorum of disinterested Trustees, except for reimbursement of such out-of-pocket expenditures as shall be approved by the Board of Trustees.

ARTICLE V
Executive Committee

Section 1: **Membership.** The Board of Trustees may create from their own number an Executive Committee consisting of not less than three nor more than five trustees. The Chairperson, the Vice-Chairperson/Chairperson Elect and the President of the Corporation shall be Members of the Executive Committee, *ex officio*.

Section 2: **Powers.** The Executive Committee shall have and exercise between meetings of the Board of Trustees all of the powers and duties of the Board of Trustees except that it shall not have the power to

- (a) amend or repeal any resolution previously adopted by the Board of Trustees,
- (b) establish a budget,
- (c) approve any recommendation or report to the Board of Trustees made by any committee thereof,
- (d) appoint or remove from office any Officer of the Corporation.

Section 3: **Special Meetings.** Meetings of the Executive Committee may be called at any time by the Chairperson, by the Principal or by any two members thereof and shall be held, whenever possible, upon twenty-four hours written or telephonic notice to each member of the Executive Committee. In the event of an emergency, a meeting of the Executive Committee may be constituted without notice; provided, however, that a quorum shall be present; actions are valid and effective if a simple majority of the members vote affirmatively. A member of the Executive Committee may participate in a meeting thereof (and for all purposes shall be regarded as present at the meeting) by means of a conference telephone or similar communications equipment so long as all persons participating in the meeting may effectively hear each other.

Section 4: **Records and Reports.** The Executive Committee is responsible and accountable to the Board of Trustees. Minutes of meetings are to be recorded and fully reported at the next meeting of the Board of Trustees. Actions taken shall be ratified or they may be rescinded or modified as deemed necessary by the Board.

ARTICLE VI
Other Committees

The Board of Trustees may create such committees as it shall determine to be desirable. Committees report regularly to the Board of Trustees and present recommendation for action as necessary.

ARTICLE VII
Officers of the Corporation

Section 1: **Titles, number and qualification.** The "Officers" of the Corporation shall be a chairperson, a Vice-Chairperson/Chairperson elect, a President, a Secretary and a Treasurer, all of whom shall be Trustees, and such additional assistants to any of the foregoing or other corporate officers as may be appointed by the Board of Trustees.

The Officers shall be elected by the Trustees from among themselves with exception of the President (Principal) and each shall hold office until removed therefrom by the Board of Trustees or until he or she ceases to be a Trustee. To the extent permitted by law, any two corporate offices may be held by the same person with the exception of the Chairperson, Vice-Chairperson/Chairperson elect, and President, but neither the Chairperson nor the President may at the same time serve as Secretary or Treasurer of the School.

Section 2: **Responsibilities.**

(a) Chairperson

The Chairperson shall preside at all meetings of the Board of Trustees or of the Executive Committee at which he or she is present and shall perform such other duties and have such other powers as may be delegated to him or her from time to time by the Board of Trustees.

(b) Vice-Chairperson/Chairperson elect:

Upon expiration of the term of Chairperson, the Vice Chairperson/Chairperson elect assumes the responsibility of Chairperson. In the event of absence or incapacity of the Chairperson, the duties of the Chairperson shall be performed by the Vice Chairperson/ Chairperson Elect. Should both the Chairperson and the Vice Chairperson/Chairperson Elect be absent at a meeting of the Board of Trustees, the Trustees in attendance other than the President shall select a Trustee among their number to preside over the meeting. If such remaining Trustees cannot select a presiding Trustee by majority vote, the President shall cast the deciding vote.

(c) President:

In the absence of the Chairperson and Vice-Chairperson/Chairperson Elect, the President shall preside at the meetings of the Executive Committee. The President shall be the chief administrative officer of the Corporation and as such shall have the general and active, day-to-day administration control and direction of all secular and nonsecular affairs of the School and shall have general supervisory authority over all employees of the Corporation.

(d) Secretary:

The Secretary shall attend all meetings of the Board of Trustees and shall record all votes and prepare minutes of all proceedings of the Board of Trustees. These records shall be maintained in the offices of the School. A current list of the names and addresses of all Trustees shall be on file and available. Notice of meetings and such other duties as described in the By-laws or requested by the Board of Trustees shall be performed by the secretary with staff assistance from the office of the President.

(e) Treasurer:

The Treasurer shall have general charge of the financial affairs of the Corporation and the care and custody and disbursement of its funds and securities. The Treasurer shall deposit or cause to be deposited all funds and securities of the Corporation to the credit or in the name of the Corporation in such banks, trust companies or other depositories as may be selected from time to time by the Board of Trustees.

The Treasurer shall insure that accurate records of all financial accounts and transactions are maintained and available to any Trustee and the President. In collaboration with the President, financial statements shall be prepared and an annual audit conducted if designated by the Board of Trustees. The Treasurer shall also perform such other duties as may be assigned from time to time by the Board of Trustees.

Section 3: **Term of Officers.** The term of office for any Officer ordinarily is for one year with the exception of the President. Elections shall be held at the meeting closest to the beginning of the fiscal year.

Section 4: **Vacancies.** Any vacancy caused by death, incapacity, resignation or removal of an Officer with the exception of the President shall be filled by the Board of Trustees at a duly constituted meeting thereof.

ARTICLE VIII
Officers of the School

Section 1: **Principal.** The Principal, in addition to having all of the powers and performing all of the duties of the President, shall, subject to the direction of the Board of Trustees, prescribe the course of study, shall execute the academic policies and administer the academic programs of the School, and shall sign and award all diplomas and other academic honors conferred by the School.

Section 2: **Business Manager.** The Business Manager, under the general direction and supervision of the Principal, shall perform such duties and have such administrative powers as the Principal shall from time to time delegate to this office. Additionally, the Business Manager shall perform such day-to-day functions of the Treasurer as are delegated by the Treasurer and shall keep and maintain such financial records and shall prepare such reports with respect thereto as the Treasurer shall reasonably require.

ARTICLE IX
Execution of Documents

Except as the Board of Trustees may generally or in particular cases authorize the execution thereof in some other manner, contracts, leases, deeds and other assignments of interest, mortgages, pledge agreements, security agreements, financing statements, bonds, guaranties, notes and other corporate obligations or instruments, except checks, drafts, orders and other similar instruments for the payment of money, shall be executed by the President and by either the Secretary or the Treasurer.

Checks, drafts, orders and other similar instruments for the payment of money including the regular payroll shall be executed by any one of the following: the Treasurer, the President or the Business Manager.

No check or other instrument for the payment of money to the School shall be endorsed otherwise than for deposit to the general account of the School. All checks of the School shall be drawn to the order of the payee. Each bank account of the School shall be established and continued by resolution of the Board of Trustees.

ARTICLE X
Fiscal Year

The fiscal year of the School shall begin on July 1 and end on June 30.

ARTICLE XI
Corporate Seal

The Corporate Seal shall remain in the custody of the President. The Corporate seal may be affixed to all contracts, instruments and other documents executed and issued by authority of the Board of Trustees.

ARTICLE XII
Amendments

These By-laws may be revised, in whole or in part and new By-laws may be recommended, by the affirmative vote of two-thirds of the Trustees present at a duly constituted meeting thereof; provided, however, that no amendment to or repeal of any provision of ARTICLES I, II, III or IV hereof shall be made. All recommended revisions shall become effective upon approval of the Members.

ARTICLE XIII
Indemnification of Members, Trustees, Officers, and Staff

The Corporation shall indemnify any person who was or is a party to or is threatened to be made a party to any threatened, pending or completed action, suit or proceeding, whether civil, criminal, administrative or investigative (other than an action by or in the right of the Corporation) by reason of the fact that he or she is or was a Member, Trustee, Officer or Staff member of the Corporation, against expenses (including attorneys' fees), judgments, fines and amounts paid in settlement actually and reasonably incurred by him or her to the fullest extent permitted by law from time to time in connection with such action, suit or proceeding if he or she acted in good faith and in a manner he or she reasonably believed to be in or not opposed to the best interest of the Corporation, and, with respect to any criminal action or proceeding, had no reasonable cause to believe his or conduct was unlawful.

ARTICLE XIV
Conflict of Interest

Any possible conflict of interest on the part of any member of the Board of Trustees should be disclosed to the other Trustees and made a matter of record when the possible conflict relates to a matter of Board action. Any Trustee having a possible conflict on a matter before the Board of Trustees should not vote or use his/her personal influence in the matter, and that Trustee should not be counted in determining the quorum for the meeting at which action is taken on the matter, even when permitted by law. The minutes of the meeting should reflect that disclosure of the possible conflict of interest was made, that the interested Trustee abstained from voting and that his/her presence was not counted in determining a quorum. These requirements should not be construed as preventing a Trustee from stating his/her position on the matter on which he/she may have possible conflict of interest, nor from answering questions of other Trustees, recognizing that the Trustee's knowledge may be of great assistance to the Board of Trustees.

ARTICLE XV
Dissolution

The Corporation may be dissolved only by action of the Members in conformity with the laws applicable to Michigan nonprofit corporations in effect at the time of dissolution. Upon dissolution, the assets of the Corporation shall be applied and distributed as and to the extent required by such laws and otherwise in conformity with the plan of distribution which shall be adopted by the Members. Any provision in the Articles of Incorporation regarding distribution of assets following dissolution shall have precedence over the plan of dissolution to the extent of any inconsistency therewith.

    Approved
    Provincial Administrative Team
    Voting Members, Sisters of Mercy, Province of Detroit, Inc.
    June, 1983

Appendix B4
Private Secondary School
(owned by parents)

BY-LAWS OF MARIAN CHRISTIAN HIGH SCHOOL
(Houston, Texas)

ARTICLE I.
NAME, LOCATION, AND PURPOSE
  1.1 Name:
        The name of the corporation is Marian Christian High School.
  1.2 Location:
        The principal office of the corporation and location of the school shall be 11101 South Gessner, Houston, Harris County, Texas.
  1.3 Purpose:
        This corporation is organized exclusively for purely public charity and strictly educational purposes, that is, for charitable and educational purposes to operate a Catholic denominational school dedicated to Christian principles and ideals. More specifically the corporation is created solely as an organization described in Section 501 (c) (3) and exempt from taxation under Section 501 (2) of the Internal Revenue Code of 1954 or corresponding provisions thereafter in effect. The corporation shall be operated exclusively for such purposes; no part of its net earnings shall inure to the benefit of any private member, director (trustee) or individual; no part of its activities shall be carrying on propaganda, or otherwise attempting to influence legislation, and it shall not participate in, or intervene in (including the publishing or distributing of statements) any political campaign on behalf of or in opposition to any candidate for public office. The corporation has a policy of non-discrimination with respect to admission of pupils to the school operated by the corporation, and with respect to employment of teachers and other employees. In other words, no pupil will be excluded from admission to the school because of race, color, nationality, religion, or creed, and the corporation shall be an "equal opportunity employer" with respect to all employees, including teachers and administrative personnel.

ARTICLE II
MEMBERSHIP IN THE CORPORATION
    The corporation membership shall consist of a parent or guardian of each household having one or more students enrolled in Marian Christian High School and shall have no capital stock. It shall be a non-share, non-profit corporation.

ARTICLE III
THE BOARD OF TRUSTEES: ELECTION, MEETINGS, AGENDA
  3.1 Number, Tenure, Election, and Vacancies:
        The direction and management of the affairs of the corporation and the control and disposition of its properties and funds shall be vested in a Board of Trustees (the "Board") which shall consist of not less than three (3) persons. The term for which the trustees shall serve as trustees shall be two (2) years beginning on July 1 of their initial year except as noted in paragraphs B and D below. No trustee shall serve more than four (4) consecutive years, except as noted in paragraphs A, B, and D below. Until changed by amendment to these By-laws, the number of trustees shall be fourteen (14).
        Each trustee shall serve for this term of office and until his successor is duly elected and qualified. A vacancy shall be declared in any seat of the Board upon the death or resignation of the occupant thereof, or upon the disability of any occupant rendering him permanently incapable of participating in the management and affairs of the corporation. In case of election to fill a vacancy, the term of the successor shall be for the unexpired term for which the former occupant thereof was elected. The manner of electing successors to the trustees and filling vacancies shall be as follows: At the regular monthly meeting immediately prior to the expiration of the respective terms of trustees, and at every succeeding election, successors to trustees whose terms shall have expired shall be elected as set forth in these By-Laws. The positions of trustees who have submitted their resignation, or shall have died, or shall have been removed from office as stet forth in these By-Laws, shall be filled for the remaining unexpired terms by the Board of Trustees at the next regular meeting or at a special meeting called for such purpose. The nomination for such unexpired term shall be made among the members present by

secret ballot. A simple majority vote shall elect the new trustee. The trustee shall immediately take office.

The voting members of the Board of Trustees shall be adults who have consented, prior to their nomination and election, to serve on the Board. The following shall not be considered candidates for membership on the Board: salaried employees of the school, whether teaching or non-teaching personnel (except as noted in paragraph D below) and/or their spouses. Furthermore, spouses shall not serve concurrently.

The fourteen (14) trustees shall be elected in the following method:
(A) Five (5) trustees shall be appointed by the bishop of the Diocese from a list of candidates offered by the president of the school. Their terms shall be for two years. Appointments shall be made at least ninety (90) days before the expiration of the Board term. There shall be no limit to the number of terms that may be served by trustees appointed in this manner.
(B) Three (3) trustees shall be elected by all the parents from among parents who have a child attending the school and who are members in good standing of the Roman Catholic Church. The chairman of the Board of Trustees shall appoint a three-person nominating committee in ample time to give the committee full opportunity to (1) seek qualified nominees and (2) ascertain that each nominee will serve as trustee for the term elected. Trustees shall be elected ninety (90) days before the end of the Board term and shall be invited to attend but not vote on matters coming before the sitting Board until their term begins. These three trustees shall be elected at the annual meeting of the corporation. Only one vote per household shall be allowed. Election shall be by simple majority of those present and voting. Proxy votes shall be valid. Election shall be by secret ballot. The term of each of these three trustees shall be one (1) year. There shall be no limit to the number of terms that may be served by trustees elected in this manner.
(C) Five (5) trustees shall be elected by the Board of Trustees from among parents of students attending the school or from persons who have demonstrated an interest in the school and a willingness to serve as trustees. The nominating committee appointed by the chairman to seek nominees fore election by the parents shall have the responsibility of seeking nominees to be elected by the Board. The election shall be held at a Board meeting at least thirty days before the expiration of the incumbent trustees' terms. The election shall be by secret ballot and by simple majority of trustees present and voting.
(D) The president of the school shall be a trustee by right of office, with the same rights and privileges as other trustees. The length of the president's term shall be stated in his/her contract of employment.
(E) At any election of trustees, either by parents at the annual meeting or by trustees at other meetings, nominations shall be taken from the floor. The person nominated shall meet the qualifications stated in paragraphs B and/or C above and shall express a willingness to serve if elected.
(F) The membership of the Board of Trustees shall at all times include a minimum of seven (7) Roman Catholics in good standing with the Church.

3.2a Annual Meeting:

The annual meeting of the corporation shall be held on the fourth Tuesday in April of each year (beginning in 1980) at 7:30 p.m. o'clock, if not a legal holiday, and if a legal holiday then on the next day following at such time, for the election of trustees and the transaction of such other business as may lawfully come before the meeting. It shall be the duty of the secretary of the corporation to give ten (10) days notice of such meeting in person to each member, or by mail or telegraph to each member not personally notified.

3.2b Semi-annual Meeting:

A semi-annual meeting of the corporation shall be held the first semester of each school year, beginning in 1985-86, in conjunction with the distribution of student report cards, and each year thereafter, for the solicitation of nominees to the Board of Trustees, for reports by the officers of the Board to the parents, and for any other school matters that the Board of Trustees may designate.

3.3 Regular Monthly Meetings:

Regular monthly meetings of the Board will be held on a mutually agreeable date and time, for the transaction of such business as may lawfully come before the meeting. An agenda of meetings shall be prepared and the secretary shall distribute by mailing or otherwise delivering same, to each member so as to insure receipt of the agenda and prior Board minutes one week preceding a regular monthly meeting. The Board meetings shall be open unless designated as executive sessions.

3.4 Special Meetings:

Special meetings of the Board shall be held whenever called by the secretary of the corporation upon the direction of the chairman of the corporation or upon written request of any two trustees; and it shall be the duty of the secretary to give sufficient notice of such meetings in person or by mail or telegraph to enable the trustees so notified to attend such meetings. The agenda, or purpose, of the special meetings shall be set forth in writing by the secretary.

3.5 Agenda for Meetings:

Matters may be placed on the agenda for any annual meeting or regular monthly meeting by any trustee by notifying the secretary by telephone or in writing of the matter to be placed on the agenda no later than ten (10) days preceding the annual meeting or the regular monthly meeting. No matter shall be considered by the Board unless it has been placed on the agenda or unless it is declared an "emergency matter" as hereinafter provided for in paragraph 3.7.

3.6 Order of Business:

3.6.1 Annual Meetings:

The order of business at each annual meeting shall be as follows:
1. Roll call.
2. Reading of notice of meeting.
3. Reading of the minutes of the preceding meeting and action thereon.
4. Report of the president.
5. Reports of officers.
6. Election of trustees.
7. Old business.
8. New business.

3.6.2 Regular Monthly Meetings:

The order of business at each regular monthly meeting shall be as follows:
1. Roll call.
2. Reading of the minutes of the preceding meeting and action thereon.
3. Election of trustees or officers (when applicable).
4. Report of the president.
5. Report of the chairman.
6. Reports of the committees.
7. Old business.
8. New business.

3.6.3 Special Meetings:

The order of business for special meetings shall be that for which the meeting was called.

3.6.4 All meetings, whether regular, special or annual, shall [**text missing**] parliamentarian may be appointed by the chairman.

3.7 Emergency Matters:

The Board may declare that any item of business required to be set forth in writing on the agenda of an anual meeting or regular monthly meeting, or any item coming before the Board at a special meeting, constitutes and "emergency matter" and the Board can thereby waive the requirement that such a matter be included on the agenda or in the notice of a special meeting. To declare a matter an "emergency" shall require a two-thirds vote of the members present, as long as a quorum is present.

3.8 Quorum for Meetings:

A majority of the trustees shall constitute a quorum for the transaction of business at all meetings convened according to these By-Laws. No business shall be conducted by the Board unless a quorum is present. The act of the majority of the trustees present at a meeting at which a quorum is present shall be an act of the Board.

3.9 Trustee Emeritus:

The Board of Trustees may from time to time at any Board meeting elect by majority vote one or more persons to the position of trustee emeritus. The term for which a trustee emeritus shall serve shall be for life. A trustee emeritus must be a former member of the Board of Trustees of Marian Christian High School. Any trustee emeritus may attend any regular or special meeting of the Board of Trustees as the guest of the Board of Trustees of Marian Christian High School and will be entitled to speak to any subject or question appropriate to the agenda, subject to the will of the Board members in attendance. Any trustee emeritus is eligible for appointment to full membership on standing or special committees of the Board of Trustees.

3.10 Removal of Trustees and Board Disagreements:

3.10.1   Absence, Leave of Absence, Resignation:

Unexcused absences from three (3) meetings shall constitute a resignation. The Board shall notify the absent member and replace him or her with nomination from the executive committee presented for Board approval at the next regular meeting. For sufficient reason, such as illness or vacation, a member may request a leave of absence. A written resignation shall be acted upon at the next regular meeting of the Board.

3.10.2   Disagreements:

In any case where a Board member, the school staff, pastor, parent or standing committee interprets an actin of the Board or the administration as being contrary to faith or morals or diocesan policy, he should point out in writing such interpretations to the chairman of the Board and ask appropriate action to reconsider.

Any cases where an action to reconsider has failed to resolve the problem or bring about the harmony necessary to the well-being of the school, the administration and the chairman of the Board should take action for resolution to the diocesan council or to the Bishop, depending upon the policies and structures available within the Diocese. Such matters shall be submitted in writing.

ARTICLE IV
GENERAL OFFICERS

4.1 Election:

The officers of this corporation shall be chairman, first vice-chairman, second vice-chairman, secretary, treasurer and such other officers as may be determined and selected by the Board. Officers of the Board shall be elected at the regular monthly meeting in July from the membership of the Board of Trustees. Nominations will be accepted from the floor. The officers so elected shall hold office for a period of one year and until their successors are elected and qualify.

4.2 Attendance at Meetings:

The chairman, or in his absence the first vice-chairman, shall call meetings of the Board to order, and shall act as chairperson of such meetings, and the secretary of the corporation shall insure that a recording secretary be present at all such meetings, but in the absence of the secretary the chairman may appoint any person present to act as secretary of the meeting.

4.3 Duties:

The principal duties of the several officers are as follows:

(A) Chairman: The chairman shall preside at all meetings of the Board. He shall be the chief executive officer of the corporation and, subject to the control of the Board, shall have general charge and supervision of the administration of the affairs and business of the corporation. He shall see that all orders and resolutions of the Board are carried into effect. He shall sign and execute all legal documents and instruments in the name of the corporation when authorized to do so by the Board and shall perform such other duties as may be assigned to him from time to time by the Board. The chairman shall submit to the Board plans and suggestions for the work of the corporation, shall direct its general correspondence, and shall present his recommendations in each case to the Board for decision. He shall also submit a report of the activities and business affairs of the corporation at each annual meeting of the Board and at each regular monthly meeting of the Board and at other times when called upon to do so by the Board.

(B) Vice-chairman: The first vice-chairman shall discharge the duties of the chairman in the event of his absence or disability for any cause whatever, and shall perform such additional duties as may be prescribed from time to time by the Board. The second vice-chairman shall perform such duties as may be prescribed by the Board.

(C) Secretary: The secretary shall have charge of the records and correspondence of the corporation under the direction of the chairman, and shall be the custodian of the seal of the corporation. He shall give notice of and attend all meetings of the Board. He shall discharge such other duties as shall be assigned to him by the chairman of the Board. In case of the absence or disability of the secretary, the Board may appoint an acting secretary to perform the duties of the secretary during such absence or disability.

(D) Treasurer: The treasurer shall keep account of all monies, credits, and property of the corporation which shall come into his hands, and keep an accurate account of all monies received and discharged. Except as otherwise ordered by the Board, he shall have custody of all the funds and securities of the corporation and shall deposit the same in such banks or depositories as the Board shall designate. He shall keep proper books of account and other books, showing at all times the amount of the funds and other property belonging to the corporation, all of which books shall be open at all times to the inspection of the Board. He shall also submit a report of the accounts and financial condition of the corporation at each annual meeting of the Board, at each regular monthly meeting of the Board, and at such other times as directed by the Board. The treasurer shall, under the direction of the Board, disburse all monies and sign all checks and other instruments drawn on or payable out of the funds of the corporation, which checks, however, may also be required by the Board to be signed by the chairman, vice-chairman, or such member of the Board or other appointive officer, as the Board shall designate. The treasurer shall also make such transfers and alterations in the securities of the corporation as may be ordered by the Board. In general, the treasurer shall perform all the duties which are incident to the office of treasurer, subject to directions of the Board, and shall perform such additional duties as may be prescribed from time to time by the Board. In case of absence or disability of the treasurer, the Board may appoint an acting treasurer to perform the duties of the treasurer during such absence or disability. The corporation shall purchase blanket fidelity bonds on all employees and trustees in an amount to be determined by the Board.

4.4 Vacancies:

Whenever a vacancy shall occur in any office of the corporation, such vacancy shall be filled by the Board by the election of a new officer who shall hold office until the next annual meeting and until his successor is elected and qualifies.

ARTICLE V
APPOINTIVE OFFICERS AND AGENTS

The Board may appoint such officers and agents in addition to those provided for in Article IV, as may be deemed necessary, who shall have authority and perform such duties as shall from time to time be prescribed by the board. All appointive officers and agents shall hold their respective offices or positions at the pleasure of the Board, and may be removed from office or discharged at any time with or without cause; provided that removal without cause shall not prejudice the contract rights, if any, of such officers and agents.

ARTICLE VI
COMMITTEES

6.1 Standing Committees:

The following shall be the standing committees of the Board:
1. Executive Committee (consisting of the chairman, vice-chairman, secretary, treasurer, and the president of the school).
2. Academic and Student Affairs Committee.
3. Physical Plant Committee.
4. Finance and Audit Committee.

Each standing committee shall consist of not less than one (1) member of the Board appointed by the chairman with the advice and consent of the Board. Each standing committee shall have a minimum of three (3) members. The standing committee shall select its own chairperson and shall keep minutes of its meetings and report its activities to the Board from time to time and when directed by the Board. Appointments to standing committees shall be for the duration of the fiscal year in which they are made or until such time as they are dissolved by the Board.

6.2 Special Committees:

The chairman shall appoint such special committees as are deemed necessary by the chairman of the board, and will appoint their chairperson. Special committees shall consist of such members of the Board as are selected by the chairman with the advice and consent of the Board. Special committee appointments and the life of the special committee shall be for the duration of time set forth in the appointment thereof, but in any event, not to extend beyond the end of the fiscal year in which such appointments are made or until such time as they are dissolved by the Board.

6.3 Recommendations of Committees:

Standing committees and special committees shall be advisory only and recommendations and actions of such committees shall not be binding upon the Board.

6.4 Financial Development Council:

The Board of Trustees on or before July, 1985, shall create a Financial Development Council ("FDC"). The FDC purpose shall be to provide or develop funds for those capital projects initiated and approved by the Board of Trustees of the school. The FDC shall report to the Executive Committee of the Board of Trustees and shall not have voting powers. No member of the FDC shall be a member of the Board of Trustees while serving as a member of the FDC. No employee of the school shall be a member of the FDC but may serve as a liaison to the Council.

The FDC shall have three (3) members appointed by the Executive Committee and approved by the Board. These three members are charged with the responsibility to determine the size and to select additional Council members. These members will serve until they resign or are removed by the majority vote of the Board of Trustees.

The school will provide staff support to the FDC as required.

The Council shall elect a chair and provide periodical reports to the Executive Committee.

The FDC will not take the place of the Board of Trustees and the Boards' responsibility of raising funds for operation of the school.

ARTICLE VII
FISCAL YEAR

The fiscal year of the corporation shall begin on the first day of August in each calendar year and end on the 31st day of July in the following calendar year.

ARTICLE VIII

The corporation shall have and use a corporate seal, and there is hereby adopted the seal, an impression of which is shown on the margin hereof.

ARTICLE IX
WAIVER OF NOTICE

Whenever any notice is required to be given to any member of the Board of Trustees of the corporation, a waiver thereof in writing, signed by the person or persons entitled to such notice, whether before or after the time stated therein, shall be deemed equivalent to the giving of such notice.

ARTICLE X

These By-Laws may be amended by the Board at any meeting of the Board by the affirmative vote of two-thirds majority of the trustees, provided that notice of the proposed amendment shall have been mailed to each trustee in writing at least ten (10) days prior to such meeting.

ARTICLE XI

In the event Marian Christian High School is dissolved for any reason and after all liabilities are paid, the remaining assets will be turned over to the Bishop of the Galveston-Houston Diocese, as trustee, to dispose of the assets as said trustee, in his sole discretion, deems proper.

_____
Chairman

_____
Secretary

_____
Date

Appendix B5
Diocesan Secondary School
(Board with Limited Jurisdiction)

ST. JOSEPH HIGH SCHOOL BOARD OF EDUCATION
(Omaha, NE)
BY-LAWS

ARTICLE I
TITLE

The name of this organization shall be St. Joseph HIgh School Board of Education of Omaha, Nebraska, and hereinafter referred to as the Board. St. Joseph High School shall hereinafter be referred to as the School.

ARTICLE II
Nature and Function

Section 1.   This Board is a participatory decision making body for policies of all matters pertaining to the School. All decisions of the Board shall be binding upon the Administration unless vetoed by the Ordinary or contrary to the rules and regulations of the Nebraska State Department of Education.

Section 2.   **Duties and Powers of the Board of Education.** The Board shall be responsible for all aspects of the formal educational program of the School. It shall have a most important duty implementing at the local level the policies of the Archdiocesan Board of Education. A partial list of other duties and functions follows:

1. Seeking a better understanding and wider support of the School within the local community.
2. Interpreting policies of the Diocesan Board for the local administrative officers and in matters wherein the Diocesan Board has not promulgated policies, creating such policies under which administration shall operate.
3. Having responsibility for evaluating the adequacy of its policies and the effectiveness of their implementation.
4. Determining local policies relating to the planning, expansion, operating and maintenance of facilities and equipment.
5. Being responsible for the approval of the annual budget, and for approving an economically sound fiscal program promoting the future welfare of the school.
6. Establishing Personnel Policies.
7. Reporting annually on all aspects of its responsibilities to its constituents.

ARTICLE III
Membership, Selection, Term

Section I. Membership

1. The St. Joseph Board of Education shall be comprised of ten (10) *voting* members. There shall be two (2) classifications of members:
    A. **Ex Officio: Voice-no vote**
        1. The Ordinary of the Archdiocese of Omaha.
        2. Archdiocesan Superintendent of Schools or his/her representative.
        3. Principal.
        4. President (Executive Secretary of Board).
        5. Campus Minister.
        6. Chairman of Development Committee.

Section II. Selection and Terms of Members

1. **Selection:**   Representatives are nominated by nomination committee from among membership of supporting parishes according to requirements in Article III, Section 1. Priest nominees are submitted to the Archbishop and the Archbishop will appoint.

2. **Term:**   Each member may serve two 3-year terms. Members may serve two (2) consecutive terms of 3 years, after which they must be off the Board for one year before being considered for re-election.

3. **Replacements:** If a member moves or resigns, a replacement is sought by the nominating committee. Priest nominees are submitted to the Archbishop and the Archbishop appoints. If a member has three unexcused absences, the Chairperson will contact the member about his/her interest in serving on the Board. If a replacement is necessary, he/she is sought by the nominating committee to begin a new term of 3 years.

Section III. Removal of Board Members
1. A Board member may be removed for any of the following reasons:
    1. Missing more than 3 consecutive regular Board meetings.
    2. Those who are considered to have a self-serving interest.
    3. Disloyalty or conduct considered to be inappropriate.
2. The membership is questioned; then the member may be removed by a 2/3 majority vote of the Board.

ARTICLE IV
Officers

Section 1. Creation of Officers. The officers of the Board shall consist of a Chairperson, Vice Chairperson, and such additional officers as the Board may elect.

Section 2. Election, Tenure, Vacancies and Removal. Officers shall be elected annually at the June meeting of the Board. They shall hold office for one year and may be re-elected for one year. All members of the Board are eligible for any position. Voting is done by secret ballot.

Section 3. The Chairperson. The Chairperson shall preside at all regular and special meetings of the Board, appoint all committees and is an ex-officio member of each committee. The Chairperson shall be responsible to meet with the Executive Secretary to prepare the agendas for mailings.

Section 4. Vice-Chairperson. The Vice-Chairperson in the absence of the Chairperson shall perform the duties and exercise the power of the Chairperson, and shall perform such other duties as delegated by the Chairperson. In case of the absence of both Chairperson and Vice-Chairperson, the remaining members shall select an acting Chairperson. Should the Chairperson be unable to complete the term, the Vice-Chairperson shall succeed to the office.

Section 5. Assistant Officers. The Assistant Officers shall have such duties as from time to time may be assigned to them by the Board or by the Chairperson.

ARTICLE V
Meetings

Section 1. Regular, Special and Annual Meetings. The Board shall meet in September, November, January, March and June subject to change by the Board itself or to postponement by the Chairperson with consent of Executive Secretary. Special or additional regular meetings shall be held whenever called by the Chairperson or by a majority of the Board. The nomination committee is to begin the nomination process in April and submit names for approval at the June meeting.

Section 2. Time, Place and Notice. Regular meetings shall be held at St. Joseph High School. Notice of the place, day and hour of regular meetings must be delivered in writing to all members. This is the responsibility of the Executive Secretary. Members must notify the Chairperson or the Executive Secretary if there are to additions to the agenda. Any additions to the agenda must be approved.

Section 3. All meetings are to be open meetings unless designated as being Executive Sessions. Policy decisions made in Executive Sessions must be presented and voted on at open sessions before becoming effective. In order for the Board to go into an executive session, a motion for executive session must be made, seconded and approved by the Board.

Section 4. The right of non-members to address the Board shall be limited to those whose petitions have been approved for the agenda in advance of the meeting. Petitions must be addressed to the chairperson of the Board and approved at least forty-eight (48) hours prior to the meeting.

Section 5. Quorum. A simple majority of the entire Board is necessary for the transaction of business at meetings; and a majority vote of those present shall be sufficient for any decision or election.

Section 6. Rules of Procedure. Roberts Rules of Order Newly Revised shall apply to all procedural matters.

Section 7. A written record of all acts of the Board, maintained by the Executive Secretary, shall be preserved in the archives.

ARTICLE VI

Section 1. Executive Committee. The Executive Committee is to be comprised of the President of the school, the Chairperson of the Board, and the Vice-Chairperson of the Board.

Section 2. Other Committees. The Board may, by resolution, provide for such other Committees as it deems advisable and may discontinue the same at its pleasure. Each entity shall have such powers and shall perform such duties as may be assigned to it by the Board and shall be appointed and vacancies filled in the manner determined by the Board. In the absence of other direction, the Chairperson shall appoint all Committees.

STANDING COMMITTEES:

a. **Educational Affairs.** The Educational Affairs Committee is comprised of the principal and/or president of the school and such other members as the Chairperson shall appoint. This committee is responsible:
   1) to receive, review and evaluate all relevant educational matters concerning the school and make related policy recommendations to the Board.
   2) to sustain quality education by study of the annual report and make recommendations for review and development.

b. **Religious Education.** The Religious Education Committee is to be comprised of the chairperson of the Religion Department and such other members as the Chairperson shall appoint.
   This committee is responsible to assist the Chairperson of the Religion Department in the planning, execution and evaluation of the total religious program.

c. **Financial Affairs.** The Financial Affairs Committee is comprised of the president and of such members as the Chairperson shall appoint.
   This committee is responsible to review all financial statements and budgets from all educational units and to make recommendations to the Board.

d. **Public Relations & Development.** The Public Relations & Development Committee is comprised of the president and of such members as the Chairperson shall appoint.
   This committee is responsible to study, review and recommend public relations policies and practices of the Board.

Section 3. All matters which are referred by the Board to Committees must be completed and ready for presentation at the next regularly scheduled Board meeting.

Section 4. Minutes are to be recorded for each committee meeting. These minutes are to be sent to each member of the Board before the Board meeting at which the minutes are to be considered.

Section 5. Committee Membership. Membership of committees need not be limited to members of the Board of Education. The chairperson of each committee must be a member of the Board. Membership for the Nominating Committee must include one priest.

ARTICLE VII

Amendment of By-Laws. These By-Laws may be amended by a vote of two-thirds of the Board Membership. Notice of proposed amendments must be mailed or hand delivered to the Board members no less than ten days prior to voting on such. Such notice shall also include the time and place when vote shall be held on such amendment.

(Approved 10/17/85)

Appendix C—Schools Constituted as Separate Juridic Persons

Appendix C1
Interparish Schools
(Separate Juridic Person)

DIOCESE OF LANSING

These statutes are a law constituting an official juridic act of the Roman Catholic Diocese of Lansing promulgated by the Bishop of Lansing and become effective on August 15, 1987.

1. Definition of the terms of art used in these statutes are as follows:
    1.1 "Principal" means the individual, designated as such by the Superintendent of Education of the Diocese of Lansing.
    1.2 "Church Law" means that body of law consisting of Canon Law and the laws of the Diocese of Lansing.
    1.3 "Superintendent of Education" means that person appointed by the Bishop of Lansing as Chairman of the Department of Education and Catechesis of the Diocese of Lansing.
    1.4 "Policy" means those acts issued by policy-making authorities within their limits of competence whereby guidelines are established for the discretionary authority of administrators.
    1.5 "Diocesan Policies" means those policies approved by the Bishop of Lansing as and expression of his expectations relative to the administration of schools that are subject to his jurisdiction.
    1.6 "Extraordinary Administration" means that aspect of administration that can be undertaken only after and in accordance with specific authorization from the Superintendent of Education and in the case of a school including: (a) fund raising, (b) civil litigation, (c) the acquisition, sale, lease or incumbrance of property, except as otherwise specifically allowed by the Diocese under ordinary administration, (d) the creation and administration of a trust or endowment, and (e) other matters specified by the Bishop of Lansing as extraordinary administration.
    1.7 "Interparochial Catholic School" means an educational institution that is:
        a) subject to the jurisdiction of the Bishop of Lansing;
        b) offering a formal program or instruction for students in any one or more of the grade levels ranging from early childhood through the fourth year of high school; and
        c) not subject to the administration of a particular parish.
    1.8 "Ordinary Administration" means that aspect of administration that can be undertaken in accordance with Church Law and the policies of the Diocese of Lansing without first obtaining any specific authorization from the Bishop and includes whatever is customarily required to:
        a) preserve and maintain the school's property;
        b) collect the school's income;
        c) pay the school's bills;
        d) keep the school's records; and
        e) transact the school's normal business.
    1.9 "Public Juridic Person" means an aggregate of persons or things so constituted by the Bishop of Lansing, within the limits set for them in the name of the Church, fulfilling a proper function entrusted to it in view of the common good, in accord with the prescripts of law.
2. Each Interparochial Catholic school is hereby constituted as a separate juridic person in accordance with the universal law of the Roman Catholic Church. The rights and duties of governance of an Interparochial Catholic school are shared by the principal and school board in accordance with the provisions and limitations of these statutes.
    2.1 All existing constitutions and by-laws now being used by Interparochial Catholic schools are hereby revoked. New by-laws consistent with these statutes must be developed and must have the approval of the Superintendent of Education (hereinafter "Superintendent"); such by-laws are binding as laws only insofar as they reflect the provisions of these statutes.
    2.2 Principals may request that the Superintendent grant a dispensation from a particular provision of these statutes. The request must be in writing and signed by the principal, and must contain the reasons for the request. The Superintendent must inform the Bishop of any dispensations granted.

2.3 The implementation of these statutes shall be without prejudice to legal rights acquired by written agreements between the Bishop and the trustees of restricted funds owned by schools.

2.4 Questions concerning the interpretation of these statutes should be referred to the Chancellor of the Diocese.

2.5 Each Interparochial Catholic school is juridically independent of parishes. The principals of such schools are expected to maintain relationships of effective communication with parishes, and to make responsible accommodations to the judgments of pastors and parish councils. Parishes are expected to support the Interparochial Catholic schools of their metropolitan area by subsidizing their operations and by otherwise promoting their welfare.

2.6 The principal is the administrator of the Interparochial Catholic school unless another provision is made by the Bishop of Lansing. The Bishop has the exclusive right to appoint and remove a principal or administrator, but he will consult with the Superintendent and the school board before doing so.

2.7 Interparochial Catholic school principals act on behalf of the juridic person except for specific rights and duties expressly given in these statutes to the school board, or, by virtue of written agreement with the Bishop, to a committee or subcommittee of the school board.

2.8 Robert's Rules of Order (revised) are to be used for all meetings of the school board and its committees.

3. Decisions of principals and school boards may be appealed to the Superintendent, and upon a showing of a violation of a law or directive, the Superintendent may intervene and reverse or amend such decisions. Principals may request a dispensation from a particular diocesan directive by submitting a written request to the Superintendent. Reasons for the request must be clearly stated. The Superintendent must inform the Bishop of all dispensations granted.

4. Neither Interparochial Catholic school boards nor principals may establish policies that are inconsistent with policies issued by the Bishop of Lansing. Exceptions to this rule may be granted only by the Superintendent upon written request from the presiding officer of the school board or principal. Reasons for the request must be clearly stated. The Superintendent must inform the Bishop of any exceptions granted.

4.1 Policies represent legitimate expectations of boards and administrators but they are not laws. Violation of policy does not ordinarily justify an appeal unless it can otherwise be shown that a right has been violated.

4.2 If a principal decides to take action which is contrary to a policy, he/she must notify the school board and the Superintendent, in writing, of the reasons for such action.

4.3 A violation of policy may occasion a complaint to the Superintendent and he/she may attempt to mediate such disputes, but the Superintendent cannot reverse or amend the administrative decision which occasions the complaint. Consequent disputes between the administrator and the Superintendent will be referred to the Bishop.

5. The school board is to be constituted as follows:

5.1 The school board will consist of two committees: the policy committee and the finance committee.

5.2 The policy committee should be representative of the community and its members should be elected or chosen in accordance with local by-laws. There should not be less than nine nor more than fifteen members of the policy committee.

5.3 The finance committee should consist of not less than three nor more than nine persons appointed in accordance with local by-laws. Those appointed should be experts in finance or management.

5.4 The finance committee elects its Chair from its own members. The Chair, in consultation with the other members, may appoint sub-committees for preparation of the budget, and for the promotion and management of endowment and development funds. The Chair may appoint persons other than the members of the finance committee to serve on the subcommittees, but at least one member of the finance committee must be appointed to each subcommittee. The implementation of this norm shall be without prejudice to the special provisions of the following norm.

5.5 The boards of trustees which presently exist in virtue of written agreements with the Bishop of Lansing will continue to operate in accordance with their approved by-laws. For the purpose of these statutes, however, they will be understood as subcommittees of the finance committee, even though their members are not appointed by the Chair of the finance committee. The trustees are encouraged to elect or appoint one member of the finance committee to their board.

    5.6 The Chair of the policy committee, elected by the members of the policy committee, also serves as the Chair of the school board. The administrator serves as Executive Secretary of the school board. Agenda for meetings of the school board are determined jointly by the Chair of the policy committee, the Chair of the finance committee, and the administrator.

    5.7 No committee or subcommittee is empowered to act independently of the entire school board unless otherwise provided in these statutes.

6. Each juridic person is capable of acquiring capital. Ownership of capital in church law belongs to the juridic person which acquired it. Internal questions of ownership are always adjudicated in the context of church law. Legal title to all church property in this diocese is held in the name of "N.N., Bishop of the Roman Catholic Diocese of Lansing and his successors in office." Ownership of real estate in the name of the Bishop and his successors in office is treated by the Bishop as a trust in state law, with the Bishop as legal owner and the juridic person as equitable owner. For purposes of protecting the diocese and its subsidiaries in questions of potential liability, the Bishop is presumed solely liable.

7. The equity or net assets of schools are the residual interest in the assets of the school that remain after deducting its liabilities. The net assets are divided into three classes: permanently restricted net assets, temporarily restricted net assets, and unrestricted net assets, based on the presence or absence of donor imposed restrictions and the nature of those restrictions.

    7.1 Permanently restricted net assets are the part of the net assets of a school resulting from contributions of assets whose use by the school is limited by donor imposed stipulations that neither expire by passage of time nor can be fulfilled or otherwise removed by actions of the school.

    7.2 Temporarily restricted net assets are the part of the net assets of a school resulting from contributions whose use by the school is limited by donor imposed stipulations that either expire by the passage of time or can be fulfilled and removed by actions of the school, pursuant to those stipulations.

    7.3 Unrestricted net assets are the part of net assets of a school that are neither permanently restricted nor temporarily restricted by donor imposed stipulations. That is the part of net assets resulting from: a) all revenues, expenses, gains and losses that are not changes in permanently or temporarily restricted net assets, and b) reclassification from (or to) other classes of net assets as a consequence of donor imposed stipulations, their expiration by passage of time or their fulfillment and removal by action of the school pursuant to those stipulations. The only limits on unrestricted net assets are broad limits resulting from the nature of the organization and the purposes specified in its by-laws, perhaps limits resulting from contractual agreements (i.e., loan covenants), diocesan policies and board policies.

    7.4 The school board has the right to designate a part of the unrestricted net assets for a specific purpose. This may be useful for the setting aside of funds, but since they are school board imposed restrictions, and can be later revised by the school board, they cannot be classified as either permanently restricted net assets or temporarily restricted net assets.

    7.5 Stable capital refers to the funds which are the essential financial basis of the high school. It can be comprised of: a) the permanent investment in real properties, plant and fixtures; b) funds set aside from restricted or unrestricted net assets for operation, replacement or renewal of plant and equipment or for the repayment of plant debt.

    7.6 All gifts or bequests to Interparochial Catholic schools are owned in church law exclusively by the Interparochial Catholic schools.

8. A budget must be prepared annually by the finance committee for all items of ordinary administration. The school board must approve the budget before it becomes effective; the principal must inform the Superintendent if this approval has not been granted before the beginning of the fiscal year.

    8.1 Diocesan policies concerning limitations on spending (1319), contracts binding on the diocese (1310), and fund raising (1321) are binding on principals of Interparochial Catholic schools.

    8.2 No school board or principal may approve a deficit budget. Any proposed deficit budget must be reviewed by the Diocesan Finance Committee and approved by the Bishop.

9. Principals act invalidly when the exceed the limits of ordinary administration without the written approval of the Bishop. Extraordinary administration includes such acts as do not occur at regular

intervals and are of their nature of greater importance. All acts of extraordinary administration can be divided into two categories: the destabilization of capital, and other major transactions.

    9.1 Since stable capital constitutes the essential financial base for the Interparochial Catholic school, any act whereby it is destabilized requires the written approval of the Bishop. Such acts would include the sale of operating property without stabilizing the proceeds in unexpended plant funds, and the transfer of plant funds or quasi-endowment funds to operating funds.

    9.2 Other major transactions, especially acts which would endanger stable capital, also require written permission of the Bishop. Such acts include, but are not limited to, the purchase of fixed assets or capital assets, the mortgaging or leasing of immovable property, the incurring of any indebtedness, the signing of any contract for the development of a capital project, the approval of any capital improvement or repair exceeding the figure established for public juridic persons in the Diocese of Lansing, initiation of any lawsuit or settlement, announcement of public fund drives, and the adoption of deficit budgets (Cf. 8.1, above).

    9.3 The Bishop will not accept a request from a principal for any act mentioned in these statutes unless the principal has obtained in writing the consent of the school board.

10. The principal has full and independent authority for the rights and duties contained in these statutes. The school board may set policies (in accordance with statute 4 above) which limit the discretion proper to administrative authority, but may not eliminate the principal's discretionary authority. The school board may also request explanations for administrative decisions, but may not reverse or amend such decisions. The principal is bound to follow diocesan laws and the directives of the Bishop and the Superintendent. With these provisions and limitations the principal has the following rights and duties: the implementation of laws, directives, goals, and policies issued by proper authority; cash management of the operating fund; accounting and reporting for all diocesan Interparochial school funds; general management of the operating plant; employment and termination of all staff members; determination of curriculum; acceptance and expulsion of students; and all responsibilities of ordinary administration, especially those described in Canons 1284-1289 inclusive, of the Code of Canon Law.

11. The principal may delegate his/her responsibilities to a vice-principal or to other officers with the following exceptions: the employment and termination of staff members, the supervision of administrative personnel, and the authorization of cash disbursements from operating funds. Permission of the Superintendent is required before anyone other than the principal can be authorized to sign checks.

12. The principal has the right and duty of managing all restricted funds, restricted trusts, and endowment funds unless other arrangements are made by written agreement with the Bishop. The finance committee of the school board may request the Bishop to authorize in writing a subcommittee to manage these funds. Disbursements from these funds can be made only by the principal; however, if written agreements with the Bishop authorize separate management of the funds, disbursements can be made by the principal only upon written authorization by the Chair of the managing group. Such written agreements with the Bishop shall not affect the rights and duties of the principal given in statute 10. The principal must submit to an audit at any time it is request by the Superintendent.

13. Implementation of these statutes will require the preparation of new by-laws by each Interparochial Catholic school. It is the sole right of the principal to convene a group of not less than five persons for the purpose of studying these statutes and formulating by-laws consistent with them. These by-laws must be approved by the Superintendent before they become effective.

14. In the event that the public juridic person should become extinct, its assets will be equitably allocated to the parishes represented on the Board.

DIOCESE OF LANSING
8/15/87

Appendix C2
Diocesan High Schools
(Separate Juridic Persons)

A LETTER CONCERNING THE CATHOLIC SCHOOL SYSTEM
(Diocese of Nashville)

Greetings in the name of our Lord Jesus Christ!

In accordance with my canonical responsibilities to govern the Catholic School System of this diocese, I hereby issue Directives for the Governance of Parish and Diocesan Schools. These are to be understood as laws of the diocese which become effective June 1, 1985. I call upon all those concerned with our Catholic School System to accept these directives and to implement them in a generous spirit of cooperation with our common task to promote the Mission of the Church.

Some of these directives specify the requirements of Canon Law. Some include the norms contained in our Statutes for Parishes. Some of these directives supplement provisions of our Statues for High Schools, especially with reference to the role of the Superintendent of Schools; high school principals should apply these directives in their relationship to the Catholic School System. Included with these directives is a more complete description of the Office of the Superintendent of Schools. The rights and duties of the Superintendent and of his assistant are clarified so that these important officers can function efficiently within our Catholic School System.

Given this first day of June in the Year of Our Lord One Thousand Nine Hundred and Eighty-five from the Chancery of the Diocese of Nashville.

James D. Niedergeses
Bishop of Nashville

ATTEST:

Chancellor

DIRECTIVES FOR THE GOVERNANCE OF PARISH AND DIOCESAN SCHOOLS

1. The Code of Canon Law imposes on bishops and pastors the duty to provide Catholic education for the faithful. Every reasonable effort should be made to maintain the Catholic School System as it presently exists in this diocese. Therefore, no parish is permitted to close a schools without permission of the Bishop, and such permission will be granted only if it is clear from all available evidence that the parish is incapable of subsidizing the school operations and other resources are not available. Likewise, no parish is permitted to open a school without the Bishop's permission, which should be granted only if the parish can show its ability to finance this program. In other words, any act of extraordinary administration requires permission of the Bishop.

2. Canon Law requires that all Catholic schools in a diocese be subject to the supervisory and regulatory authority of the diocesan bishop and his representatives. The subsidiary autonomy enjoyed by parishes and other juridic persons must not prejudice this centralized diocesan authority over the Catholic Schools System. These directives and the legitimate acts of the Bishop, the Episcopal Vicar for Education, and the Superintendent of Schools are binding on all parish and school officers.

3. Canon Law requires the episcopal conference to issue general directives for religious formation and education. The Catechetical Directory issued by the National Conference of Catholic Bishops is binding on all parish and diocesan schools.

4. The Bishop alone has the right to issue rules, regulations and policies for Catholic schools in accordance with Canon 806. Such documents have been approved and are currently binding on all

parish and diocesan schools. The Superintendent of Schools has primary responsibility for monitoring compliance with these norms, and he may also issue guidelines to interpret them and promote their implementation. The purpose of these documents is to promote the quality of education in accordance with the requirement of Canon 806, Section 2.

5. The Commission on the Teaching Office of the Church has the right to recommend rules, regulations, policies, and other value statements for the governance of Catholic schools. These are developed by the Schools' Committee of the Commission and are referred by the Commission to the Bishop for approval and implementation.

6. Canon Law reserves to the Bishop and his Vicars the right to name or approve teachers of religion and likewise to remove or to demand that they be removed if it is required for reasons of religion or morals. The values promoted by this canon are generally fulfilled through the diocesan program of certification for teachers of religion.

7. The governance of diocesan high schools must accord with Statutes for High Schools, laws of the Diocese of Nashville which are binding on all concerned.

8. Article 7 of our Statutes for Parishes lawfully requires that the policies and administration of parish schools must conform to diocesan laws and regulations. The pastor, principal, parish education commission (and school committee), and parish council enjoy only those rights and duties which are given in the Statutes and in these directives. The promotion of our common Catholic School System requires the cooperation of all in compliance with these respective rights and duties. The Superintendent of Schools has primary responsibility for monitoring compliance.

9. The pastor enjoys the certain rights and duties with respect to financial administration of the parish school as given in the Parish Statutes article 7.1. Other rights and duties enjoyed by the pastor may be exercised only in consultation with the Superintendent of Schools and the parish education commission, as follows:
   (a) To supervise religious education and formation programs.
   (b) To hire the principal or to contract with a religious institute for a principal.
   (c) To supervise and evaluate the principal.
   (d) To terminate the employment of the principal with the additional requirement of consultation with the Episcopal Vicar for Education.

10. In addition to certain rights and duties of financial administration, the principal enjoys the following rights and duties:
    (a) To employ all teachers and other employees exclusively involved in school operations in consultation with the pastor and in accordance with diocesan regulations issued by the Catholic Schools Office.
    (b) To supervise and evaluate all teachers and other school employees.
    (c) To terminate the employment of school employees with the consent of the pastor.
    (d) To formulate policies for consultation by the education commission.
    (e) To propose teachers' salaries and other budget items for consideration by the education commission.
    (f) To implement regulations and policies approved by diocesan authorities and the parish council.

11. The education commission or the school committee of the parish council may be given the following rights and duties in the operation of the school:
    (a) To approve policies for the school in conformity with diocesan laws, regulations, and policies, sending a copy of approved policies to the pastor, the parish council, and the Superintendent of Schools.
    (b) To propose an annual budget to be integrated in the total budget of the parish.
    (c) To suggest to the parish council provisions for the school committee's organization and procedures to be incorporated in the bylaws of the parish council.

12. The parish council has the following rights and duties in the operation of the school:
    (a) To determine the organization and procedures of the education commission (and school committee) to be incorporated into the bylaws of the parish council.
    (b) To participate in the decision concerning the subsidy to be made by the parish for school operations.

13. Non-compliance with these directives or other issues may occasion complaints at the local level. These complaints should be settled at the local level using available resources. Otherwise, complaints should be directed to the Superintendent of Schools who will study the issue and attempt to reconcile

the parties through his office. The Superintendent may issue a written judgment in the matter, a copy of which must be sent to the Episcopal Vicar for Education. If these attempts at conciliation fail, or if the parties refuse to accept the judgment of the Superintendent of Schools, the issue may be referred to the Episcopal Vicar for Education who may accept reference of the issue if it is contended that the judgment of the Superintendent involved a violation of law or personal rights.

14. The Superintendent of Schools exercises the following rights and duties in the governance of schools:
- (a) To represent the authority of the Bishop and the Episcopal Vicar for Education as given above in these directives.
- (b) To represent the diocesan Catholic School System to state and federal authorities, and certify that institutions within the System are in compliance with state and federal regulations.
- (c) To issue guidelines for the implementation of rules and regulations, and for the development of curriculum and for the general improvement of the diocesan school system.
- (d) To monitor compliance with diocesan norms and, when necessary, to issue in writing mandates requiring compliance with a copy sent to the Episcopal Vicar for Education.
- (e) To interpret programs and policies of the school system to personnel, to parents and to interested groups.
- (f) To develop and publish guidelines for school calendars, and to approve the calendar for each school.

OFFICE OF THE SUPERINTENDENT OF SCHOOLS

The relation of the Superintendent of Schools to all schools in the diocese is clarified in "Directives for the Governance of Parish and Diocesan Schools." In addition to the rights and duties of governance which are contained in Article 14 of that document, the Superintendent exercises the following responsibilities in service to the school system.

1. To supervise the development and implementation of the in-service training of school administrators, school staffs, and office personnel.
2. To conduct or attend such educational meetings and conferences that relate to the welfare and improvement of the school system.
3. To plan and supervise the testing program and facilitate the interpretation of the results.
4. To remain informed with current trends in education and to communicate this information to principals and school personnel.
5. To encourage innovative and experimental programs in all the schools, and to approve the formulation and implementation of such programs.
6. To publish an annual statistical and interpretative report of all schools.
7. To facilitate the recruitment and promotion of qualified, certified teachers.
8. To prepare the programs and budgets for the services under his supervision.
9. To collaborate in the selection of staff for services under his supervision.
10. To supervise the services of the Assistant Superintendent of Schools and other personnel in the Catholic Schools office.
11. To direct the development of curriculum with the cooperation of the Assistant Superintendent, and to monitor the implementation in each school.
12. To evaluate school facilities and resources and to recommend improvements.
13. To mobilize the support of the community for the development of Catholic educational institutions and programs.

The Assistant Superintendent of Schools shall assist and represent the Superintendent and shall give educational leadership and guidance consistent with the philosophy, goals and policies of the Catholic Schools. The Assistant Superintendent is directly responsible to the Superintendent. The Assistant Superintendent must have a graduate degree, be a practicing Catholic and have proper credentials for Tennessee certification.

Duties of the Assistant Superintendent include:
1. Organizing and supervising the work of curriculum committees.
2. Coordinating curriculum programs in the elementary and secondary schools.
3. Administering the implementation of text book adoption.
4. Reviewing proposals and evaluations of innovative and experimental programs used in the

schools.
5. Reviewing and revising, as needed, forms and publications of the Catholic Schools Office.
6. Attending various educational meetings and serving on committees as designated by the Superintendent.
7. Maintaining a current curriculum library.
8. Assisting the Superintendent in the following tasks:
   (a) Offering supportive professional assistance to principals and teachers.
   (b) Visiting schools for consultation with principals on overall school conditions and with individual teachers in areas where needed, for demonstration lessons for teachers new to the Catholic schools system.
   (c) Providing orientation for new principals and assisting, as required, with pre-school faculty needs.
   (d) Coordinating, interpreting and evaluating the administration of the diocesan testing program.
   (e) Planning and evaluating in-service programs for administrators and teachers.
   (f) Reviewing and evaluating various reports submitted by the schools.
   (g) Coordinating information received from the schools and preparing reports for the Catholic Schools Office.
   (h) Developing criteria and procedures for planning and projections for Catholic schools.
   (i) Managing acquisition and distribution of instructional materials for the Catholic Schools Office.
   (j) Organizing and distributing teaching materials provided to the educational program of support institutions.

STATUTES FOR DIOCESAN HIGH SCHOOLS

1. These statutes are laws of the Roman Catholic Diocese of Nashville, promulgated by the Bishop of Nashville in his legislative capacity, and become effective on July 1, 1982.
   1.1 All existing constitutions and bylaws now being used by diocesan high schools are hereby revoked. New bylaws consistent with these statutes must be developed and must have the approval of the Bishop's Delegate for Education (hereinafter "Delegate"); such bylaws are binding as laws only insofar as they reflect the provisions of these statutes.
   1.2 High school administrations may request the Delegate to grant a dispensation from a particular provision of these statutes. The request must be in writing and signed by the administrator, and must contain the reasons for the request. The Delegate must inform the Bishop of any dispensations granted.
   1.3 The implementation of these statutes shall be without prejudice to legal rights acquired by written agreement between the Bishop and the trustees of restricted funds owned by high schools.
   1.4 Questions concerning the interpretation of these statutes should be referred to the Vicar General (Moderator of the Curia).
2. Each diocesan high school is a separate juridic person, incorporated in accordance with the common law of the Roman Catholic Church, a subject of rights and duties distinct from all physical persons, and subsidiary to the Diocese of Nashville. The rights and duties of governance of a diocesan high school are shared by the administrator and school board in accordance with the provisions and limitations of these statutes.
   2.1 Each diocesan high school is juridically independent of parishes. However, it has long been customary for parishes to support the high school of their metropolitan area by subsidizing its operations and by otherwise promoting its welfare. The leadership of each high school is expected to maintain relationships of effective communication with parishes, and to make responsible accommodations to the judgments of pastors and parish councils.
   2.2 The principal is the administrator of the high school unless another provision is made by the Bishop. The Bishop has the exclusive right to appoint and remove a principal or administrator, but he will consult with the Delegate and the school board before doing so.
   2.3 High school administrators act on behalf of the juridic person except for specific rights and duties expressly given in these statutes to the school board or, by virtue of written agreements with the Bishop, to a committee or subcommittee of the school board.
   2.4 Robert's Rules of Order should be used for all meetings of the school board and its com-

mittees in order to insure the validity of official actions.
3. Administrators and school boards are bound not only by these statutes and other diocesan legislation, but also by executive directives of the Bishop and Delegate. Decisions of administrators and school boards may be appealed to the Delegate, and upon a showing of a violation of a law or directive, the Delegate may intervene and reverse or amend such decisions. Administrators may request from the Delegate a dispensation from a particular diocesan directive. Such requests must be in writing and signed by the administrator, and must give the reasons for the request. Dispensations may be granted only in writing. The Delegate must inform the Bishop of all dispensations granted.
4. Policies are acts issued by policy-making authorities within their limits of competence whereby guides are established for the discretionary authority of administrators.
- 4.1 High school boards may not establish policies that are inconsistent with policies issued by the Diocesan Board of Education. Exceptions to this rule may be granted only by the Delegate upon written request from the presiding officer of the school board, and the reasons for the request must be stated. The Delegate must inform the Bishop and the Board of Education of any exceptions granted.
- 4.2 Policies are legitimate expectations of administrators but are not laws, and a violation of policy would not justify an appeal unless it could otherwise be shown that a right has been violated by an administrative decision.
- 4.3 If an administrator decides to act contrary to a policy, he should notify the school board and the Delegate in writing of the reasons for his decision.
- 4.4 A violation of policy may occasion a complain to the Delegate and the Delegate may attempt to mediate such disputes, but he cannot reverse or amend the administrative decision which occasions the complaint. Consequent disputes between the administrator and the Delegate should be referred to the Bishop.
- 4.5 The norms given above in 4.1 through 4.4 apply also to the implementation of guidelines issued by administrative authorities to guide the implementation of diocesan policies.
5. The school board is to be constituted in accordance with the following provisions.
- 5.1 The school board consists of two committees: the policy committee and the finance committee.
- 5.2 The policy committee should be representative of the community, and its members should be elected or chosen in accordance with local bylaws. There should not be less than nine nor more than fifteen members of the policy committee.
- 5.3 The finance committee should consist of not less than three nor more than nine persons appointed in accordance with local bylaws. Those appointed should be experts in finance or management.
- 5.4 The finance committee elects its Chair from its own members. The Chair, in consultation with the other members, may appoint sub-committees for preparation of the budget, and for the promotion and management of endowment and development funds. The Chair may appoint persons other than the members of the finance committee to serve on the subcommittees, but at least one member of the finance committee must be appointed to each subcommittee. The implementation of this norm shall be without prejudice to the special provisions of the following norm.
- 5.5 The boards of trustees which presently exist in virtue of written agreements with the Bishop of Nashville will continue to operate in accordance with their approved bylaws. For the purpose of these statutes, however, they will be understood as subcommittees of the finance committee, even though their members are not appointed by the Chair of the finance committee. The trustees are encouraged to elect or appoint one member of the finance committee to their board.
- 5.6 The Chair of the policy committee, elected by the members of the policy committee, also serves as the Chair of the school board. The administrator serves as Executive Secretary of the school board. Agenda for meetings of the school board are determined jointly by the Chair of the policy committee, the Chair of the finance committee, and the administrator.
- 5.7 No committee or subcommittee is empowered to act independently of the entire school board unless otherwise provided in these statutes.
6. Each juridic person is capable of acquiring capital. Ownership of capital in church law belongs to the juridic person which acquired it. Internal questions of ownership are always adjudicated in the context of church law. Legal title to all church property in this diocese is held in the name of "N.N.,

Bishop of the Roman Catholic Diocese of Nashville and his successors in office." Ownership of real estate in the name of the Bishop and his successors in office is treated by the Bishop as a trust in state law, with the Bishop as legal owner and the juridic person as equitable owner. For purposes of protecting the diocese and its subsidiaries in questions of potential liability, the Bishop is presumed solely liable.

7. The following definitions and norms are to be used in deciding questions of ownership and administration of assets.

- 7.1 Operating funds constitute capital which is cash on hand for operating purposes (undesignated funds), or money temporarily set aside for future needs (designated funds). The school board has the right to designate funds for specific purposes.
- 7.2 Restricted funds constitute capital that is available to meet current expenses but only in compliance with restrictions specified by contributors or grantors. The income from a restricted fund may be designated by the school board or undesignated.
- 7.3 Restricted funds constitute capital donated or bequeathed for a restricted purpose for which the income also is to be restricted.
- 7.4. Endowment funds constitute capital donated by gift or bequest with the stipulation that the principal be invested and maintained intact and in perpetuity, with only the income available for expenditure. The income may be restricted (by the donor), designated by the school board or undesignated.
- 7.5 Term endowment funds constitute capital donated with the provision that the principal may be released from its inviolability and expended, all or in part, upon the happening of a particular event or the passage of a stated period of time. The income may be restricted or unrestricted. When these funds are released, they are transferred to operating funds unless other provision is made by the school board.
- 7.6 Stable capital is money which has been stabilized as the essential financial base of the high school in one of three ways: (a) by permanent investment in real property to be used for school purposes (not for temporary investment); (b) by addition to unexpended plant funds and thus made available for construction, replacement, renewal or acquisition of land, buildings, equipment to be used for school purposes or for the repayment of debt incurred for the same purposes; (c) by creation or addition to quasi-endowment funds so that only the income is available for expenditure. Capital remains stabilized if it is transferred from one form to another.
- 7.7 Restricted funds, restricted trusts, and endowment funds created by gift or bequest to a high school are owned in church law exclusively by the high school. By diocesan law, however, such funds and all surplus funds of the high school must be placed on deposit with the Governance and Service Offices in the Deposit and Loan Fund for which the Bishop and Diocesan Finance Board act as trustees.

8. A budget must be prepared annually by the Finance Committee for all items of ordinary administration. The school board must approve the budget before it becomes effective; the administrator must inform the Delegate if this approval has not been granted before the beginning of the fiscal year. Ordinary administration includes whatever is necessary for the preservation of church property, whatever actions are required to collect income, pay bills, make ordinary repairs, keep records, and transact customary business.

9. Administrators act invalidly when they exceed the limits of ordinary administration without the written approval of the Bishop. Extraordinary administration includes such acts as do not occur at regular intervals and are of their nature of greater importance. All acts of extraordinary administration can be divided into two categories: the destabilization of capital, and other major transactions.

- 9.1 Since stable capital constitutes the essential financial base for the high school, any act whereby it is destabilized requires the written approval of the Bishop. Such acts would include the sale of operating property without stabilizing the proceeds in unexpended plant funds, and the transfer of plant funds or quasi-endowment funds to operating funds.
- 9.2 Other major transactions, especially acts which would endanger stable capital, also require written permission of the Bishop. Such acts include the purchase of immovable property, the mortgaging or leasing of immovable property, the incurring of any indebtedness, the signing of any contract for the development of a capital project, the approval of any capital improvement or repair exceeding a cost of $5,000, initiation of any lawsuit, and announcement of public fund drives.
- 9.3 The Bishop will not accept a request from an administrator for any act mentioned in these

statutes unless the administrator has obtained in writing the consent of the school board.

10. The administrator has full and independent authority for the rights and duties contained in these statutes. The school board may set policies (in accordance with statute 4 above) which limit the discretion proper to administrative authority, but may not eliminate the principal's discretionary authority. The school board may also request explanations for administrative decisions, but may not reverse or amend such decisions. The administrator is bound to follow diocesan laws and the directives of the Bishop and the Delegate. With these provisions and limitations the administrator has the following rights and duties: the implementation of laws, directives, goals, and policies issued by proper authority; cash management of the operating fund; accounting and reporting for all high school funds; general management of the operating plant; employment and termination of all staff members; development of job descriptions and supervision of all staff members; determination of curriculum; acceptance and expulsion of students; and all responsibilities of ordinary administration.

11. The administrator may delegate his/her responsibilities to a vice-principal or to other officers with the following exceptions: the employment and termination of staff members, the supervision of administrative personnel, and the authorization of cash disbursements from operating funds. Permission of the Delegate is required before anyone other than the administrator can be authorized to sign checks.

12. The administrator has the right and duty of managing all restricted funds, restricted trusts, and endowment funds unless other arrangements are made by written agreement with the Bishop. The finance committee of the school board may request the Bishop to authorize in writing a subcommittee to manage these funds. Disbursements from these funds can be made only by the administrator; however, if written agreements with the Bishop authorize separate management of the funds, disbursements can be made by the administrator only upon written authorization by the Chair of the managing group. Such written agreements with the Bishop shall not affect the rights and duties of the administrator given in statute 10.

13. Implementation of these statutes will require the preparation of new by-laws by each high school. It is the sole right of the administrator to convene a group of not less than five persons for the purpose of studying these statutes and formulating bylaws consistent with them. These bylaws must be approved by the Delegate before they become effective.

Given this thirteenth day of May in the Year of Our Lord Nineteen Hundred and Eighty-two, in consultation with the Council of Priests, from the Governance and Service Offices of the Diocese of Nashville.

James D. Niedergeses
Bishop of Nashville

ATTEST:

James K. Mallet, Chancellor

Appendix D—The Catholic School Principal

Appendix D1
PRINCIPAL'S JOB DESCRIPTION

(Catholic Schools of Arkansas
Diocese of Little Rock)

PRINCIPAL'S JOB DESCRIPTION
Qualifications: Certified by the State Education Department and approved by the Diocesan School Superintendent.
Contract Time: 10 1/2 months
Functions: Executes Board policies and administrative regulations in the area of assignments and assumes administrative responsibility and instructional leadership in the school. Is responsible for the planning, operation, supervision, and evaluation of the educational program.

The school principal is responsible for the leadership and the administration of the Catholic school which seeks to offer high quality academic programs that are integrated with religious truths and values. The principal strives to provide opportunity for the students to be prepared for life in today's Church and society through a strong basic and contemporary curriculum and through instruction and formation in the beliefs, values, and traditions of Catholic Christianity.

In general, administrative tasks include: organization of the school so that appropriate learning can take place; development of a competent faculty and staff; development and implementation of a balanced curriculum; provision for the safety, welfare, and care of the students while they are attending school; management of the physical facilities of the school; management of the financial and business affairs of the school; and development of good school-community relationships.

The minimum expectations for achieving the above tasks are the following:

GENERAL RESPONSIBILITIES
- a) Administers the school according to Diocesan and local policies.
- b) Gives leadership for achieving the goals of Catholic education.
- c) Shows evidence of a knowledge of the Catholic philosophy of education.
- d) Works toward the creation of a Christian community within the school.
- e) Provides opportunities for liturgical expression and experience for staff and students.
- f) Maintains open channels for two-way communication with all segments of the school clientele.
- g) Shows respect for individuals and fairness in dealing with others.

RESPONSIBILITIES TO THE SUPERINTENDENT
- a) Coordinates efforts of the school with the philosophy of the diocesan school system as outlined by the superintendent.
- b) Maintains a record system and make reports as required to the superintendent's office.
- c) Appraises and evaluates the instructional program provided by the school and reports findings to the superintendent of schools.

RESPONSIBILITIES TO THE PASTOR
- a) Works cooperatively with the pastor in the formulation of regulations and procedures for the school.
- b) Furnishes data and makes recommendations to the pastor concerning the operation of the school.
- c) Keeps pastor informed of the status of the school, the faculty, and the students.
- d) Administers and is accountable for the receipts and disbursement of all internal funds such as books, fees, supplies, etc.
- e) Implements programs recommended by the pastor who is the chief teacher in the parish.
- f) Maintains collaborative relationship between the religious education program of the school and that of the parish.

RESPONSIBILITIES TO THE CONSULTATIVE SCHOOL BOARD
- a) Works cooperatively with the school board in the implementation of school policies.
- b) Furnishes data and makes recommendations in preparation for the annual budget.

c) Makes periodic reports to the board on the financial status of the school if principal is responsible for finances.
d) Works with the chairperson of the board to develop agenda for the meeting.
e) Keeps the school board members informed of the general operation of the school.
f) Updates the board on current educational trends, issues, new laws, and other inservice matters that will be useful to them.

RESPONSIBILITIES TO THE FACULTY
a) Hires and assigns teachers in accord with diocesan and state policies.
b) Is responsible for the supervision of the instructional program and works cooperatively with the faculty in the accomplishment of this function.
c) Provides in-service workshops before the opening of school each fall and whenever the opportunity or need arises during the course of the school year.
d) Holds regular faculty meetings each month that are geared towards staff development.
e) Visits classes periodically to coordinate the total curriculum.
f) Provides planning periods by having teacher-aides supervise the students to relive the teachers during lunch and play periods.
g) Provides textbooks, materials, and supplies for each classroom.
h) Encourages systematic and well-developed lesson plans.
i) Maintains accurate personnel files that include records of all sick leave, emergency leave, and substitutes needed.
j) Is available to the teachers for consultation when needed.
k) Works cooperatively with the parish religious education coordinator.

RESPONSIBILITIES TO THE STUDENTS
a) Establishes with the faculty a curriculum that meets the needs of individual students.
b) Administers school policy relating to the admission and assignment of present and/or incoming students.
c) Holds an official registration for students each year.
d) Oversees all student activities in the school including athletic activities, assembly programs, and social functions.
e) Draws up class rosters at the beginning of each school term.
f) Establishes guidelines and enforces the discipline policy of the school.
g) Plans, conducts, and reports fire and safety drills in accordance with adopted policies.
h) Enforces immunization and other health requirements set by the state department of health and sees that health records are maintained and kept up-to-date.
i) Establishes and makes known to all teachers the routines for handling student sickness and accidents.

RESPONSIBILITIES TO THE PARENTS
a) Is responsible for communications between the school and home.
b) Schedules and participates in, when advisable, parent conferences.
c) Schedules a conference with all parents to meet with the teachers of their children at the end of the first and third quarter.
d) Encourages and cooperates with organizations dedicated to the improvement of the school.
e) Designates someone to work with the news media in releasing news items on a regular basis concerning school activities.
f) Establishes and makes known the procedures for hearing complains and suggestions from school patrons.
g) Is available for conference at any time by appointment.
h) Develops and maintains public relations with and among appropriate publics.

Appendix D2
OUTLINE FOR A PORTRAIT OF THE
CATHOLIC SCHOOL PRINCIPAL

Qualities and Competencies—Self-Evaluation

Qualities
Qualities are basic characteristics. These fundamental attributes or traits describe what the principal should be.

Spiritual
The Principal
- Is committed to the Lord Jesus as a believing and practicing Catholic
- Is prayerful, faithfilled and committed to spiritual growth
- Is loyal to the Church and accepts its authentic teaching

Professional
The Principal
- Is committed to the philosophy of Catholic education which underlies Catholic schools
- Is broadly educated
- Is open to professional growth, familiar with professional literature, and committed to self-evaluation
- Is able to articulate educational values
- Is an active member of professional organizations
- Has successful teaching experience, preferably in Catholic schools
- Has the requisite, formal academic preparation
- Has leadership capabilities

Personal
The Principal
- Is mature and open to growth
- Is intelligent
- Is organized and flexible
- Is caring and supportive
- Is challenging
- Is a person of hope and trust
- Is a critical thinker
- Possesses a sense of humor
- Possesses an interest in youth and in their future
- Possesses verbal and written competence
- Possesses a positive self-concept

Competencies
Competencies are statements of fundamental goals. These describe what the principal should be able to do. One should view the strengthening or acquisition of these competencies as developmental; however, the applicant can assess the present level of competency by circling the appropriate number following each statement.

Pastoral	High to Low Scale			
The Principal:	(4)		(1)	
• Is familiar with and creates and environment where the process of faith and moral development as it relates to working with youth and adults can be applied.	4	3	2	1
• Is familiar with and creates an environment where the content and methods of religious education can be applied.	4	3	2	1
• Knows and applies Church documents and other religious resources that relate to schools	4	3	2	1

- Is capable of providing opportunities which foster the spiritual growth of faculty, students, and other members of the school community — 4　3　2　1
- Is capable of leading the school community in prayer — 4　3　2　1
- Is capable of integrating gospel values and Christian social principles into the curriculum and the life of the school — 4　3　2　1
- Is capable of articulating the Catholic educational vision and directing its accomplishments — 4　3　2　1
- Is capable of recognizing and providing for cultural and religious differences within the entire school community — 4　3　2　1

Professional Educational
The Principal: **High to Low Scale**
　　　　　　　　　(4)　　(1)
- Is capable of working collaboratively with a variety of parish and/or diocesan groups, especially governance groups — 4　3　2　1
- Is capable of promoting staff morale and a sense of Christian community among teachers — 4　3　2　1
- Is capable of providing leadership in curriculum development in general, including the integration of Christian values — 4　3　2　1
- Is capable of shaping, sharing, and implementing a school philosophy which reflects the unique Catholic character of the school — 4　3　2　1
- Is capable of initiating and conducting appropriate staff development activities — 4　3　2　1
- Recognizes, respects, and is capable of facilitating the primary role of parents as educators — 4　3　2　1
- Possesses a general variety of educational/pedagogical skills — 4　3　2　1
- Is capable of initiating and conducting evaluations of students, staff, and innovative programs — 4　3　2　1
- Is capable of providing effective instructional leadership and supervision of staff and programs which reflect the unique Catholic character of the school — 4　3　2　1

Professional Managerial
The Principal: **High to Low Scale**
　　　　　　　　　(4)　　(1)
- Is capable of planning and managing the school's financial resources — 4　3　2　1
- Is sensitive to the demands of justice in making financial decisions, especially as they relate to the Church's social teachings — 4　3　2　1
- Is capable of providing leadership for long range planning and development activities — 4　3　2　1
- Is capable of providing an orderly school environment that promotes student self-discipline consistent with Gospel values and Christian principles — 4　3　2　1
- Knows current school law as it applies to the Catholic school — 4　3　2　1
- Knows and can apply group dynamics, conflict management, problem solving, and other organizational development skills — 4　3　2　1
- Knows how to delegate responsibilities appropriately — 4　3　2　1
- Knows how to relate the service dimension of the school to the civic community — 4　3　2　1

(adapted from *Those Who Would Be Catholic School Pricipals*, NCEA 1985)

Appendix D3
THE PRINCIPAL'S LEADERSHIP OF AND SERVICE TO THE SCHOOL BOARD

1. **The principal gives direction to the school board.**
   a. Together, principal and board president build the board's agenda.
   b. Principal identifies school needs for the board's attention.
   c. Principal prepares an initial school budget draft for board consideration.
   d. Principal offers ideas for (and, when asked, makes arrangements for) the board's inservice study.
   e. Principal makes policy recommendations to the board for consideration.

2. **The principal provides the board with timely, thorough, and clear information about the school.**

   Principal prepares a written or oral report for each board meeting. This should include information useful for formulating policies, for evaluating previous board decisions, and for keeping informed about curriculum, staffing, activities, services, regulations, special events, facilities, and school-wide problems or concerns.

3. **Cooperation, mutual respect, and trust should characterize the relationship between principal and school board.**
   a. Principal owes to the board and its individual members public loyalty and respect.
   b. Principal should see that the board has adequate clerical assistance and help with arrangements for its activities.
   c. Principal should assist the board in recruiting new members.
   d. Principal should see that committees of the board have adequate assistance (data, personnel, materials) to carry out their tasks.

4. **The principal demonstrates accountability for the job that has been asked of him/her.**
   a. Principal has a responsibility to fulfill the job description in a satisfactory way.
   b. Principal is responsible for implementing the board's policies.
   c. Principal is responsible for completing the tasks assigned him/her as an outgrowth of the board's formal goal-setting session.
   d. Principal is responsible for compliance with diocesan directives.

Appendix D4

GUIDELINES FOR PRINCIPAL EVALUATION
(Archdiocese of Oklahoma City)

Archdiocesan evaluation forms are to be used. Additional items may be developed on the forms to meet specific needs at the local level—provided those areas were set by the Board and the Principal at the beginning of the term.

I. The Principal's evaluation consists of four parts:
   A. The Principal's self evaluation based on the Archdiocesan job description.
   B. The individual Board members' evaluation.
   C. The Pastor's evaluation.
   D. The individual faculty members' evaluation.
II. The Board members' evaluation of the Principal includes:
   A. The Principal's job description as it pertains to the Board.
   B. The goals and objectives for the year as determined at the beginning of the term by the Board and the Principal.
   C. The relationship of the Principal to the Board.
III. The Pastor's evaluation of the Principal includes:
   A. The Principal's performance in relation to the parish as a whole according to the Principal's job description.
   B. The collaboration/visibility of the Principal in parish life.
   C. The relationship of the Principal with the Pastor and the total religious education program in the parish.
IV. The faculty's evaluation of the Principal includes:
   A. The Principal's job description as it pertains to the faculty.
   B. The relationship of the Principal with the faculty.
   C. The faculty's perception of the Principal as the educational leader in the school.
V. Procedure to be followed:
   A. The Board president calls for the evaluation through a letter to all parties in the evaluation process.
   B. Evaluation forms are sent with the letter.
   C. Completed forms are returned and summarized by _____ (person designated).
   D. The Board discusses the SUMMARY in executive session and shares the results with the Principal.
   E. The Principal responds/clarifies if necessary.
   F. Strengths are celebrated; goals are set for the remainder of the year in areas where growth is needed.
   G. All summary sheets and the individual evaluation forms are destroyed.
   H. The Board minutes indicate that the evaluation of the Principal took place and should indicate the process used.

N.B. It is understood that the entire process is a means to help acquaint the Board more fully of the broad scope of the responsibilities on the Principal's job description, the many and varied expectations that are placed on the administrator, and the need the Principal has for clear direction, support and encouragement by the Board.

PRINCIPAL'S JOB DESCRIPTION
(Archdiocese of Oklahoma City)

The school principal is responsible for the leadership and the administration of the Catholic school which seeks to offer high quality academic programs that are integrated with religious truths and values. The principal strives to provide opportunity for the students to be prepared for life in today's Church and society through a strong basic and contemporary curriculum and through instruction and formation in the beliefs, values and traditions of Catholic Christianity.

In general, administrative tasks include: organization of the school so that appropriate learning can take place; development of a competent faculty and staff; development and implementation of a balanced curriculum; provision for the safety, welfare, and care of the students while they are attending school; management of the physical facilities of the school; management of the financial and business affairs of the school; and development of good school-community relationships.

The minimum expectations for achieving the above tasks are the following:

GENERAL RESPONSIBILITIES
1. To administer the school according to Archdiocesan and local policies.
2. To give leadership for achieving the goals of Catholic education.
3. To show evidence of a knowledge of the Catholic philosophy of education.
4. To work toward the creation of a Christian community within the school.
5. To maintain collaborative relationship between the religious education program of the school and that of the parish.
6. To provide opportunities for liturgical expression and experience for staff and students.
7. To maintain open channels for two-way communication with all segments of the school clientele.
8. To show respect for individuals and fairness in dealing with others.

RELATIONSHIP WITH BOARD OF EDUCATION
1. To be accountable to the Pastor and the Board for all matters that concern the operation of the school.
2. To report regularly to the Board regarding implementation of policies, curriculum development, evaluation, and school concerns.
3. To prepare the necessary background material for policy formation and for long-range planning.
4. To update the Board on current educational trends, issues, new laws, and other inservice matters that will be useful to them.
5. To assist the Board in the preparation of the annual budget and to administer the approved budget within the designated parameters.

LEADERSHIP OF FACULTY AND CURRICULUM DEVELOPMENT
1. To hire and assign teachers in accord with Archdiocesan and State policies.
2. To provide orientation and on-going inservice for the faculty according to their needs.
3. To direct and involve the faculty in an on-going program of philosophy evaluation, curriculum assessment, and planning for instructional improvement.
4. To assist the faculty in the integration of Christian social principles in the curriculum.
5. To promote the growth of the teachers through on-going supervision and evaluation.
6. To diversify the curriculum to serve the scope of abilities, talents, interests and needs of faculty and students.
7. To be familiar with all textbooks and instructional materials used throughout the school.
8. To assist teachers in the guidance, assessment, and analysis of student achievement.
9. To provide the faculty with materials and resources necessary for their assigned tasks.
10. To conduct regular faculty meetings and to provide opportunity for faculty involvement in the agenda preparation.
11. To oversee scheduling of classes and daily lesson planning by the teachers.

MANAGEMENT AND RECORD KEEPING
1. To develop and communicate routine procedures for the operation of the school.
2. To publish rules, regulations, schedules, and procedures, and to be consistent in expectations

regarding them.
3. To maintain discipline throughout the school so that a learning environment prevails.
4. To unify expectations for high academic standards throughout the school.
5. To implement fire, tornado, health and safety codes in the school and on the school grounds.
6. To provide adequate maintenance and cleanliness of the school for the safety and well-being of the students.
7. To meet deadlines with official school reports and statistics as required by Archdiocesan and State personnel.
8. To keep school files organized in a professional manner.
9. To maintain an up-to-date professional file on each teacher.
10. To be responsible for overseeing that accurate and up-to-date cumulative, attendance, and health records are kept on every student.

PARENTAL INVOLVEMENT AND PUBLIC RELATIONS
1. To provide opportunities for regular conferences and meetings of parents and teachers.
2. To provide channels for parent involvement and input in curriculum and school policies.
3. To alert parents to the special needs and/or problems of their children.
4. To keep parents informed through regular school bulletins.
5. To cooperate with, and help to promote, the various programs existing in and for the parish.
6. To represent the school to outside agencies.
7. To develop and maintain public relations with and among appropriate publics.

PRINCIPAL'S EVALUATION: PASTOR'S SURVEY

Instructions: Circle the number which most accurately reflects your opinion of the principal's performance. Your response will be treated confidentially.

	OUT-STANDING	SATIS-FACTORY	UNSATIS-FACTORY	UNABLE TO EVALUATE
1. Gives leadership for developing and maintaining strong religious education in the school.	1	2 3 4	5	0
2. Has a collaborative relationship with total religious education in the parish.	1	2 3 4	5	0
3. Provides opportunities for Eucharistic celebrations with staff and students.	1	2 3 4	5	0
4. Involves students and teachers in the preparation for liturgical celebrations.	1	2 3 4	5	0
5. Guides the spiritual development and prayer opportunities of students and staff.	1	2 3 4	5	0
6. Keeps clientele informed through regular bulletins.	1	2 3 4	5	0
7. Sees school in relation to total parish.	1	2 3 4	5	0
8. Promotes and cooperates with programs and projects existing in the parish.	1	2 3 4	5	0
9. Cooperates with other members of the parish staff.	1	2 3 4	5	0
10. Contributes positively during parish staff meetings.	1	2 3 4	5	0
11. Represents the school positively with outside agencies.	1	2 3 4	5	0
12. Meets necessary deadlines as they pertain to parochial matters.	1	2 3 4	5	0
13. Participates in parish activities and services.	1	2 3 4	5	0
14. Gives Christian witness in accord with position held.	1	2 3 4	5	0
15. Is open to suggestions and shows cooperative spirit.	1	2 3 4	5	0

COMMENTS/EXPLANATIONS:

_____
Signature

PRINCIPAL'S EVALUATION: FACULTY SURVEY

Instructions: Circle the number which most accurately reflects your opinion of the principal's performance. Your response will be treated confidentially.

	OUT-STANDING	SATIS-FACTORY	UNSATIS-FACTORY	UNABLE TO EVALUATE
1. Provides orientation and on-going inservice according to needs.	1	2 3 4	5	0
2. Involves faculty in study and formulation of school's philosophy.	1	2 3 4	5	0
3. Is open to faculty assessment and development of curriculum.	1	2 3 4	5	0
4. Assists teachers in improving instruction and methodologies.	1	2 3 4	5	0
5. Helps staff in integrating Christian principles throughout the curriculum.	1	2 3 4	5	0
6. Provides regular and on-going supervision of teaching and learning.	1	2 3 4	5	0
7. Conducts two formal evaluations yearly for faculty growth.	1	2 3 4	5	0
8. Shows concern for meeting needs of students with varying abilities.	1	2 3 4	5	0
9. Is sensitive to the abilities, needs and interest of the faculty.	1	2 3 4	5	0
10. Is knowledgeable about textbooks and instructional materials used in classrooms.	1	2 3 4	5	0
11. Provides for and guides student testing and interpretation of scores.	1	2 3 4	5	0
12. Provides materials and resources necessary for teaching assignments.	1	2 3 4	5	0
13. Conducts regular faculty meetings.	1	2 3 4	5	0
14. Involves faculty in preparation of the agenda for the meetings.	1	2 3 4	5	0
15. Is available for faculty consultation.	1	2 3 4	5	0
16. Shows interest and concern for daily lesson planning.	1	2 3 4	5	0
17. Works toward well-balanced academic schedules in the classrooms and in the school day.	1	2 3 4	5	0
18. Develops and communicates expected routine procedures and rules.	1	2 3 4	5	0

	OUT-STANDING	SATIS-FACTORY	UNSATIS-FACTORY	UNABLE TO EVALUATE
19. Is consistent in enforcing the published procedures and rules.	1	2 3 4	5	0
20. Takes measures necessary to maintain discipline in the school.	1	2 3 4	5	0
21. Works to achieve high standards and to unify teacher expectations.	1	2 3 4	5	0
22. Is conscientious in implementing safety codes and conducting fire and tornado drills.	1	2 3 4	5	0
23. Is concerned with adequate cleanliness and maintenance of the school.	1	2 3 4	5	0
24. Provides opportunity for parent-teacher conferences and meetings.	1	2 3 4	5	0
25. Maintains composure in stressful and/or unexpected situations.	1	2 3 4	5	0

COMMENTS/EXPLANATIONS:

_____
Signature

PRINCIPAL'S EVALUATION: BOARD MEMBER SURVEY

Instructions: Circle the number which most accurately reflects your opinion of the principal's performance. Your response will be treated confidentially.

	OUT-STANDING	SATIS-FACTORY	UNSATIS-FACTORY	UNABLE TO EVALUATE
1. Administers the school according to Archdiocesan and local policies.	1	2 3 4	5	0
2. Shows willingness to be accountable to Pastor and Board for duties assigned.	1	2 3 4	5	0
3. Attends Board meetings and assists in preparation of the agenda.	1	2 3 4	5	0
4. Reports regularly to the Board regarding implementation of policies.	1	2 3 4	5	0
5. Keeps the Board updated on curriculum development.	1	2 3 4	5	0
6. Informs the Board in a general way of teacher evaluations and student achievement.	1	2 3 4	5	0
7. Prepares necessary material for the Board and assists in long-range planning.	1	2 3 4	5	0
8. Updates the Board on current issues and trends in education.	1	2 3 4	5	0
9. Keeps the Board informed about new laws and issues affecting the school.	1	2 3 4	5	0
10. Assists in preparing the annual budget and operates within the approved parameters.	1	2 3 4	5	0
11. Hires and assigns teachers in accord with Archdiocesan and State requirements.	1	2 3 4	5	0
12. Provides channels for parent interest and involvement in school affairs.	1	2 3 4	5	0

COMMENTS/EXPLANATIONS:

_____
Signature

PRINCIPAL'S EVALUATION: GENERAL RESPONSE
(Pastor, Board Members, Faculty)

Instructions: Circle the number which most accurately reflects your opinion of the principal's performance. Your response will be treated confidentially.

	OUT-STANDING	SATIS-FACTORY	UNSATIS-FACTORY	UNABLE TO EVALUATE
1. Gives leadership for achieving the goals of Catholic education.	1	2 3 4	5	0
2. Evidences a knowledge of the Catholic philosophy of education.	1	2 3 4	5	0
3. Works toward a Christian community within the school.	1	2 3 4	5	0
4. Maintains two-way communication with school clientele.	1	2 3 4	5	0
5. Shows respect and equity of treatment to all individuals.	1	2 3 4	5	0
6. Is fair and objective in dealing with others.	1	2 3 4	5	0
7. Communicates ideas effectively and consistently.	1	2 3 4	5	0
8. Follows through on decisions.	1	2 3 4	5	0
9. Is generally cheerful and positive.	1	2 3 4	5	0
10. Demonstrates ability to organize and manage effectively.	1	2 3 4	5	0
11. Maintains professional decorum in carrying out responsibilities.	1	2 3 4	5	0
12. Respects confidentiality and safeguards the privacy of students.	1	2 3 4	5	0

COMMENTS/EXPLANATIONS:

_____
Signature

Appendix D5
PRINCIPAL CONTRACT
Archdiocese of Oklahoma City
Catholic School Department

This agreement is made this _____ day of _____, 19 ___, by and between _____, hereinafter called the "School" and _____, hereinafter called the "Principal."

The School hereby employs the Principal in this Catholic School for the school year 19___ - 19___, beginning _____ and ending _____, and for such times prior and subsequent to said period as are necessary to perform the duties hereinafter set forth to the School's satisfaction.

COMPENSATION

For services rendered in accordance with the following terms, the School agrees to pay the Principal the sum of $_____ for such year, to be paid in _____ installments for _____ months, in the sum of $_____, the final installment of which is to be paid upon satisfactory fulfillment of all obligations. The Principal shall also be offered the opportunity to participate in the insurance and retirement benefits as established by the Archdiocese of available to the faculty of the School to the extent of the Principal's qualifications thereto and to enjoy additional benefits as described in Supplement "A" attached hereto.

RESPONSIBILITIES

1. For the aforesaid compensation, and in consideration of the mutual covenants herein, the Principal hereby agrees to administer said School to the best of his/her ability with responsibility for giving leadership in the educational program and fulfilling the duties listed on the job description attached hereto as Supplement "B"*; to perform such other reasonable duties as may be required for the success of the School; and to comply with the established policies, rules, and regulations expressed in the Archdiocesan Handbook of Policies for the Catholic Schools and the local School handbook. (*cf. Principal's Job Description in Appendix D4, "Guidelines for Principal Evaluation.")

2. In carrying out the aforesaid duties, the Principal agrees to give leadership in building the Christian Faith Community in the School, to show respect for Catholic beliefs, to work for the achievement of the goals of Catholic education, and to aid in the Christian formation of the students by exemplifying in his/her own actions the characteristics of Christian living.

3. The Principal agrees to provide regular faculty inservice and opportunities for parent-teacher meetings as a part of the School program. He/she also agrees to provide ongoing Christian formation of the faculty and to hire only such teachers as can meet the expectations of a Catholic School.

4. The Principal shall be allowed one day of sick leave (cumulative to 60 days) without salary reduction for each month of service up to ten days a year. For absences taken beyond the stated number of days, proportionate salary deduction shall be made. Such sick leave is granted for the personal illness of the Principal and for serious illness or death in the Principal's family.

TERMINATION

1. This contract is for one year and does not imply an automatic renewal for another year. It shall be renewed only upon the written agreement of all parties. Notification of intention not to rehire the Principal will be given by certified or registered mail by April 30.

2. The School may terminate this agreement at and upon written notice to the Principal for failure to comply with the terms of this agreement, for ineffectiveness in the performance of duty, for lack of professional conduct, or for living a lifestyle incompatible with Catholic moral principles.

3. The Principal may appeal such termination to the local School Board within ten (10) days from the date of termination. In the event that the Principal receives an adverse decision at the local level, the Principal may have further recourse to the Board of Appeals of the Archdiocesan School Office. Such appeal must be made in writing and it is agreed specifically that the decision of the Board of Appeals shall be final and binding.

4. In case the Principal resigns, vacates, or is removed from his/her position prior to completion of the term of service, said Principal shall have no claim or right to any further salary payments or other

benefits under this contract except the proportionate part to the date of termination, less any offsets at the time of discharge.

5. Casualty to the school properties requiring a complete cessation of the school operations shall immediately and automatically terminate this contract.

ACCEPTANCE

The Principal shall file this contract with the School within fifteen (15) days after receipt of this contract. Failure to file the contract within such fifteen (15) days shall be taken as refusal of the Principal to accept this contract.

IN WITNESS HEREOF, the School has caused this instrument to be executed in its name, by its proper officials, and the Principal has executed the same, all on the dates indicated hereto.

PRINCIPAL　　　　　　　　　　　　　　　SCHOOL

_____　　　　　　_____
　　　　　　　　　　　　　　　　　　　　　　　　　　　Pastor

　　　　　　　　　　　　　　　　　　　　_____
　　　　　　　　　　　　　　　　　　　　　　　　Chairman of Board

Date:_____　　　　　Date:_____
White copy: School　　　　　　　　　　This document is not to be duplicated
Pink copy: Principal　　　　　　　　　or altered without the written permis-
Green copy: Catholic School Office　　sion of the Superintendent of Schools
Yellow copy: Pastor　　　　　　　　　　of the Archdiocese of Oklahoma City

.Appendix D6
SAMPLE INTERVIEW QUESTIONS

Reflecting on Spiritual Qualities and Pastoral Competencies

Questions which encourage expression:
- Briefly share with us some of the most important ways in which you are committed to the Lord Jesus as a believing and practicing Catholic.
- In what ways do you provide for your own spiritual growth?
- How would you describe your relationship with the Lord?
- In what ways are you involved in your parish community?
- How can you help a school community grow in its relationship to the Lord?

Questions which discourage expression:
- When was the last time you participated in a retreat?
- Do you go to Mass daily?
- How often do you pray?
- How many retreat experiences have you undertaken this year?

Considering Professional and Educational/Managerial Competencies

Questions which encourage expression:
- What do you think are the major features of the philosophy that underlies Catholic education?
- What are some elements you think essential to any philosophy of Catholic schools?
- In what ways are you committed to professional growth?
- What are those educational values which guide your decision-making?
- How do you describe your leadership style?
- What are your areas of professional strength?
- In what professional areas do you especially need to grow?
- Reflect on principals you've known and what it is you admire most in them.
- Give an example of how you organized and motivated a group to solve a problem.
- How have you demonstrated your interest in young people?
- What are some of the ways in which you would provide for the religious growth of the school community?

Questions which discourage expression:
- Do you read professional magazines and journals?
- To which professional organizations to you belong?
- Are you a leader?
- Are you committed to the philosophy of Catholic schools?

(from *Those Who Would Be Catholic School Principals*, NCEA 1985)

Appendix E—The Board and Evaluation

Appendix E1
PRINCIPAL'S EVALUATION

	Almost Always	Often	Seldom	Almost Never
The Principal gives diretion to the school board				
1. Together, principal and board chair build on the board's agenda.	1	2	3	4
2. Principal identifies school needs for the board's attention.	1	2	3	4
3. Principal offers ideas for the board's inservice opportunities.	1	2	3	4
4. Principal prepares an initial school budget draft.	1	2	3	4
5. Principal makes policy recommendations for board formulation.	1	2	3	4

COMMENTS: (optional except for ratings of 3 or 4)

	Almost Always	Often	Seldom	Almost Never
The principal provides the board with timely, thorough, and clear information about the school.				
1. Principal prepares a written or oral report for each board meeting.	1	2	3	4
2. Principal informs the board about evaluation of curriculum.	1	2	3	4
3. Principal keeps the board informed regarding results of national and/or diocesan testing programs.	1	2	3	4
4. Principal informs the board about school-wide problems and concerns.	1	2	3	4
5. Principal invites the board to special activities and events.	1	2	3	4

COMMENTS: (optional except for ratings of 3 or 4)

	Almost Always	Often	Seldom	Almost Never
Cooperation, mutual respect, and trust should characterize the relationship between principal and school board.				
1. Principal gives to the board and its individual members public loyalty and respect.	1	2	3	4
2. Principal sees that the board has adequate clerical assistance and help with arrangements for its activities.	1	2	3	4
3. Principal assists in recruiting new board members.	1	2	3	4
4. Principal sees that committees of the board have adequate assistance (data, personnel, materials) to carry out their tasks.	1	2	3	4

COMMENTS: (optional except for ratings of 3 or 4)

	Almost Always	Often	Seldom	Almost Never
The principal demonstrates accountability for the job that has been asked				
1. Principal is responsible for fulfilling the job description in a satisfactory manner.	1	2	3	4
2. Principal is responsible for implementing local and diocesan policies.	1	2	3	4
3. Principal is responsible for completing the tasks assigned as an outgrowth of the board's formal goal-setting session.	1	2	3	4
4. Principal is responsible for compliance with diocesan guidelines.	1	2	3	4

COMMENTS: (optional except for ratings of 3 or 4)

Appendix E2
THE INTERNAL FUNCTIONS OF THE BOARD

There are two major sections to be considered in the internal functions of a board: decision making and operations. Please rate each section by circling the appropriate letter according to the following scale:
A — Very satisfied
B — Satisfied
C — Somewhat satisfied
D — Not satisfied

Decision Making
1. How satisfied are you with the board's decision making?   A   B   C   D
2. How satisfied are you with the board's willingness to delay action for further discussion?   A   B   C   D
3. How satisfied are you with the time allowed to prepare for and discuss major decisions?   A   B   C   D

Please make suggestions which will improve board level decision making.

Operations
4. How satisfied are you with the board's leadership?   A   B   C   D
5. How satisfied are you with the composition of board?   A   B   C   D
6. How satisfied are you with the quality of board materials and information?   A   B   C   D
7. How satisfied are you that participation and comments of board members are encouraged and welcome?   A   B   C   D
8. How satisfied are you with the level of board member participation?   A   B   C   D
9. How satisfied are you with board members' preparation for meetings?   A   B   C   D
10. How satisfied are you with the structure of board committees?   A   B   C   D
11. How satisfied are you with the frequency and length of board meetings?   A   B   C   D
12. How satisfied are you with the board's participation in the evaluation of the principal?   A   B   C   D

Please suggest how board operations can be improved.

Appendix E3
THE EXTERNAL FUNCTIONS OF THE BOARD

The external functions of a board include areas of responsibility and relationships. Please rate each external function by placing a check in the appropriate column.

Areas of Responsibility

	Outstanding	Good	Fair	Poor

Strategic Planning
1. The board sets goals for the school and works toward the achievement of those goals.
2. The board involves other appropriate individuals and groups in its planning process.
3. The board accomplishes the activities for which it assumes responsibility in the goal setting.
4. The board has an active development committee.
5. The long-range plan for the school includes development efforts.
6. The mandate for the development committee includes its relationship to the finance committee.
7. The long-range plan for the school includes marketing efforts.
8. There are active public relations efforts on behalf of the school.

How can the board's role in strategic planning be improved?

Finances
9. The board has an active finance committee.
10. The board reviews, approves and monitors the school budget.
11. The finance committee's relationship with the parish finance council is clearly stated.
12. The board has developed policies for the financial management of the school.

How can the board's role in finances be improved?

Buildings and Grounds
13. The board has an active buildings and grounds committee.

158

14. The board has developed in its long-range plan priorities for capitol repairs and improvements.
15. The relationship between this committee and other parish groups is clearly stated.

How can the board's role in buildings and grounds be improved?

Policy Formulation
16. The board formulates policies in accord with diocesan policies and procedures.
17. The board uses opportunities for input into the policy formulating process of the diocesan board.
18. The board evaluates its policies regularly.
19. The board policies are systematically indexed, codified, and published in a board policy manual.
20. Board policies are communicated to those people who are affected by the decisions.
21. The board has a process for ensuring that the policies formulated are formally enacted prior to being implemented by the principal.

How can the board's role in policy formulation be improved?

Relationships
Please rate the board's relationship with the individual or groups by placing a check in the appropriate space:
I think that the board's relationship with the following people is...

	outstanding	good	needs improvement
1. principal			
2. pastor			
3. superintendent of schools			
4. parish pastoral council			
5. parish finance council			
6. parishioners			
7. parents			
8. civic community			
9. alumnae(i)			
10. faculty			
11. students			
12. others; please name			

How can the board's relationships with others be improved?

Appendix F—Board Membership

Appendix F1
BOARD MEMBER PROFILE GRID

Board Members (put X in appropriate column)

	John Jones	Sr. Mary Patricia	Mary Brown	Chris Sullivan	Sue Smith
KNOWLEDGE OF:					
Educational Process		X			
Human Resources			X		
Financial Resources	X				X
Community Resources				X	
EXPERTISE IN:					
Legal Affairs					
Personnel Management		X			
Financial Management	X		X		
Fund Raising					
Development Programs					
Public/Community Relations					
Field of Planning					X
Marketing					
Publications					
INFLUENCE WITH:					
The Business Community				X	
The Financial Community					
The Media					X
The Government					
Other Non-profit Organizations					
The Church Community		X			
MALE	X			X	
FEMALE		X	X		X
Under 21					
21-29					
30-39	X				
40-49		X	X		
50-59					X
60-69				X	

From National Association of Boards of Catholic Education/NCEA, July 1989

Appendix F2
CODE OF ETHICS FOR CATHOLIC SCHOOL BOARD MEMBERS*

As a member of a Catholic school board, I
- acknowledge that schools are a significant expression of the teaching mission of the Catholic Church and function within its structure;

- will become more knowledgeable about the mission of Catholic education, as expressed in this school, and sincerely promote it to the various publics with whom I have influence;

- recognize the need for continuing education about my responsibilities and know that I do not represent the board officially unless explicitly authorized to do so;

- will be fully and carefully prepared for each meeting by doing the required readings and completing necessary tasks for committee work and reports;

- support the principal in authorized functions and avoid intruding in administrative details unless requested to do so;

- will be loyal to board decisions even though personally opposed to the final recommendations and decisions;

- will be alert to alternate solutions to problems by keeping an open mind;

- will disqualify myself from discussion and vote on an issue where there is a conflict of interest with my family or business interests or if the outcome will grant me any pecuniary or material benefits; and

- pray often for other members of the board, this Catholic school, and the community it serves.

*Copies on stock are available from NCEA Publication Sales; cost $2.00; 10 or more $.70 each for members/$2.60 each for non-members.

Appendix F3
A BOARD MEMBER'S PRAYER*

I have been asked to serve, Lord, and I have agreed.

Help me to know my fellow board members: their gifts, their concerns, their lives. I am doing your work, Lord, and your love for me and for them is, above all, personal.

Help me to welcome conflict as a sign of the diversity in this board, as an opportunity to reach for creative solutions. Help me to recognize this diversity as a sign of your capacity to love us all and help me to cherish it as a great strength.

Help me to approach issues with an open, inquiring mind, free from prejudice, with my spirit depending on yours for the strength to make hard decisions.

Help me to listen; to know when and to whom I should listen.

Help me to learn to use my own gifts to promote thorough, thoughtful discussion of important concerns in our Catholic community.

Help me to develop my skills as a peacemaker, to know how and when to mediate, to conciliate, to negotiate.

Help me to enjoy doing your work and to remember your promise: whenever two of us are gathered in your name, you are with us. Sit with me now.

Amen.

*Copies on stock are available from NCEA Publication Sales; cost $2.00; 10 or more $.70 each for members/$2.60 each for non-members.

Appendix G—Meetings

Appendix G1
CHECKLIST FOR PLANNING A MEETING

Purpose of the Meeting
___ Decide reasons for having the meeting
___ Determine program content
___ Plan the agenda
___ Set yearly goals

Attendance
___ Decide who should attend
___ Determine the number of people expected

Resource People
___ Determine why you are inviting them
___ Invite them
___ Make arrangements for any special needs they have (equipment, transportation, lodging, etc.)

Time
___ Select the date; set timeline for year at the onset; emphasize and adhere to an annual Board calendar of activities
___ Select the starting and ending times

Place
___ Determine needs (seating capacity, arrangement of furniture, kitchen, audio-visual, accessibility, parking, restrooms, lighting, etc.)
___ Determine availability of particular facilities
___ Reserve space
___ Request any special set-up of furniture

Equipment
___ Order any equipment needed (projector, screen, microphone, record player, easel, blackboard, chalk and erasers, portable risers or stage, etc.)

Refreshments
___ Determine what you need (food, beverages, utensils, serving utensils, coffee pot, refrigerator, cups, etc.)
___ Make arrangements for what you need (purchase, borrow, reserve from the facility)
___ Make arrangements for the time and manner (preparation, serving, clean-up)

Publicity
___ Plan publicity (fliers, posters, ads, invitations, displays, gimmicks, etc.)
___ Carry out publicity plans

Evaluation
___ Review plans for the meeting; check that the program is really what you want; check that arrangements are completed)
___ Determine an evaluation tool which will help measure the success of the meeting.

Appendix G2
MEETING EVALUATION FORM

                                                          Poor   OK   Good   Great   N/A

THE MEETING WAS WELL-PLANNED
1. Members were notified in advance of meeting time and room

2. The notice included main items of business

3. There was a pre-arranged agenda

4. Officers and committees were ready to report

5. The meeting room was set up

THE MEETING WAS WELL-ORGANIZED
6. The meeting started on time

7. Guests were introduced and welcomed

8. The purposes for the meeting were made clear

9. There was a transition from the last meeting

10. The agenda was visible for all to see

11. One topic was discussed at a time

12. One person had the floor at a time

13. Members confined remarks to relevant matters

14. The chairperson summarized main parts of discussion

15. There was correct parliamentary action when needed

16. Good use of audio-visual aids was made

17. The meeting was moved along at a challenging pace

18. Committee assignments were complete and clear

19. Plans for the next meeting were announced

20. The meeting was adjourned with good timing

THE MEETING HAD GOOD PARTICIPATION
21. Members participated in discussion and voting

22. Members participated in planning the agenda

23. Members gave suggestions to committees on methods

	Poor	OK	Good	Great	N/A
24. Responsibilities were widely distributed					
25. The chairperson made good use of questions					
26. The "pro" and "con" of all issues were considered					

THE MEETING WAS VALUABLE
27. Progress was made toward goals

28. Something was learned

THE PROGRAM WAS WELL DONE
29. The members were interested and attentive

30. The timing was just right
(not too short/too long)

GOOD FEELINGS PREVAILED
31. Attendance was good

32. Everyone was present and on time

33. The members knew one another

34. There was some humor during the meeting

35. Members and officers helped one another when needed

36. There was an atmosphere of free expression

37. Volunteers for committee appointments came quickly

38. There was evidence of group unity on group goals

This is adapted from *Leadership Is Everybody's Business* by Lawson, Griffin and Donant, 1976.

Appendix G3
MINUTE-TAKING REMINDERS

Person assigned to take minutes should be willing to assume this all-important task and be clear as to reporting format at the outset.

It should be clear to all that the approved minutes are:
- official record of all motions adopted or disapproved;
- official record of member attendance;
- not the school's policy manual. Policies that affect the schools should be extracted and properly bound for appropriate referral.

Minutes should be:
- signed by pastor or appropriate person
- distributed with agenda for next meeting
- available for appropriate constituents

Minutes should:
- emphasize motion or action items, isolating them from the major text of the minutes for easy reference
- be clear and concise, not lengthy transcripts of discussions that took place

Example of poor minutes:
(Partial) *Finance Report:* Father John presented a list of repairs that may be needed in the school and what needs to be done on the roof, to meet fire regulations, etc. A restructure of the budget was briefly discussed to provide for capital improvements.

Example of good minutes:
(Partial) *Finance Report:* The chair of the Finance Committee made a motion that the $40,000.00 in the capital improvement fund be directed toward the following:
1. $29,000.00 — repair of roof on Learning Center (details discussed in 4/20/87 meeting)
2. $ 5,000.00 — renovation per fire marshall directive (see March and April meeting)
3. $ 6,000.00 — remain in capital improvement fund (proposal presented at last month's meeting.

Motion seconded. No discussion. Motion passed unanimously.

OR

The Board reached a consensus and approved the acceptance of the Finance Committee's recommendations.

Appendix H—Alternative Tuition Plans

Appendix H
ALTERNATIVE TUITION PLANS

Contact the following dioceses or schools for further information:

Parent Income Weighted Tuition
Rev. Walter Brunkan
Columbus High School
3231 W. 9th Street
Waterloo, Iowa 500702
(319) 233-3358

Negotiated Tuition/Fair Share Tuition
Mr. Michael Franken
Catholic Education Vicariate
200 Josephine Street
Denver, Colorado 80206
(303) 388-4411

Entirely Prepaid Non-Discounted with Commercial Borrowing
Rev. John A. Thomas, Ph.D.
Superintendent of Schools
436 West Delaware Avenue
Toledo, Ohio 43610
(419) 255-8282

Entirely Prepaid Non-Discounted with Low Interest Loans
Mr. Myles Seghers
Archdiocese of New Orleans
7887 Walmsley Avenue
New Orleans, Louisiana 70125
(504) 861-9521

Appendix I—Five-Year Development Plan

Appendix I
FIVE-YEAR DEVELOPMENT PLAN

Cite the task or objective to be accomplished each year in an effort to improve the overall development position of the school.

	School Year (date)	School Year (date)	School Year (date)	School Year (date)	School Year (date)
Quality Catholic Education					
Business Management					
Public Relations					
Parent-Student Fundraising					
Alumni Activities and Fundraising					
Annual Giving Programs (other than parents and alumni)					
Business and Community Cultivation & Investment					
Newsletters and Other Communications Vehicles					
Foundation Grants					
Endowment Program (Establishment of advisory committee and program)					

Note: Cite Specific Activities

Appendix J—Church Documents on Catholic Education

Appendix J
CHURCH DOCUMENTS ON CATHOLIC EDUCATION

Listed below are the significant Church Documents issued since Vatican Council II related to Catholic schools. In each case the general content of the document is described, and salient ideas are quoted.

Declaration on Christian Education is one of the documents of the Second Vatican Council. It was issued in 1965. The text reflects on the duties of parents, the civil society, and the church in education. It speaks to the Catholic school as being of "utmost importance" and urges "pastors and all the faithful to spare no sacrifice in helping Catholic schools fulfill their function in a continually more perfect way." Identified as the distinctive function of the Catholic school are these purposes: "to create for the school community an atmosphere enlivened by the gospel spirit of freedom and charity,...to help the student in such a way that the development of his own personality will be matched by the growth of that new creation he became by baptism...(and) to relate all human culture eventually to the news of salvation" (art. 8). Teachers are especially challenged in their vocation which "demands special qualities of mind and heart, very careful preparation, and continuing readiness to renew and adapt." The declaration also has encouragement and advice for Catholic colleges and theological schools.

General Catechetical Directory was issued in 1971 by the Sacred Congregation for the Clergy in Rome. "The intent of this Directory," the forward says, "is to provide the basic principles of pastoral theology...by which...the ministry of the word can be more fittingly directed and governed." The document was written for all those who have some responsibility for catechesis (i.e., "ecclesial action which leads both communities and individual members of the faithful to maturity of faith"). The **General Catechetical Directory** speaks about revelation (how God's word comes to us) and about the hierarchy of faith truths (the four basic mysteries being the triune God who creates, the incarnate Christ, the sanctifying Spirit, and the Church). It offers some insights regarding the catechetical approach appropriate for different age groups; it emphasizes the importance of formal preparation for catechists; and it addresses in a general way structures and tools for carrying out catechesis.

To Teach as Jesus Did is a pastoral message by the National Council of Catholic Bishops which was issued in 1972. It identified three main goals for all of Catholic education: to teach the gospel message, to help people grow in the fellowship of the Christian community, and to remind the Christian of the obligation to service. It offered specific counsel to various components of Catholic education: adult education, college campuses, Catholic schools, CCD, youth ministry, etc. On the Catholic school, it sounded a very up-beat note: "Of the educational programs available to the Catholic community, Catholic schools afford the fullest and best opportunity to realize the threefold purpose of Christian education among children and young people."

Teach Them is a statement specifically on Catholic schools which was released by the Bishops of the United States Catholic Conference in 1976. It reaffirms the support of the American hierarchy for Catholic schools. "The reasons are compelling. Generally these schools are notably successful educational institutions which offer not only high quality academic programs but also instructions and formation in the beliefs, values and traditions of Catholic Christianity...They have a highly positive impact on adult religious behavior." The document encourages efforts to sustain Catholic schools which serve poverty areas. It also complements and challenges parents, teachers, administrators, and pastors.

The Catholic School was produced by the Sacred Congregation for Catholic Education in Rome in 1977. The document is a ringing endorsement of the pastoral value of Catholic schools. They are seen as places where faith is part of the school's culture and where "all members of the school community share this Christian vision." The schools are called upon to integrate "all the different aspects of human knowledge through the subjects taught in the light of the Gospel" and to help young people "grow towards maturity in faith." Teachers are particularly challenged to "reveal the Christian message not only by word but also by every gesture of their behavior."

Sharing the Light of Faith is also called the National Catechetical Directory (NCD). It was written by the United States Catholic Conference for the American bishops and was approved by Rome in 1978. Our country's sequel to the General Catechetical Directory, this is now one of the most important documents relating to our Catholic education.

It speaks first to some general principals on catechetics. For example, it defines the source of catechetics as "God's word, fully revealed in Jesus Christ..." and identifies the "signs" or manifestations of God's word as falling into four categories: biblical, liturgical (Mass and sacraments), ecclesial (e.g. creeds) and natural (God's presence in the world).

Next the NCD outlines the content of the catechetical message. This is a beautiful concise summary of Catholic faith. After this, there follow special chapters on catechesis for worship, for social ministry, and for faith maturity (including sections on conscience formation and sexuality).

Finally the directory offers some insight and guidance in the very practical areas of personnel, organizations, and resources for catechists.

In its guidelines for Catholic schools, the NCD advises schools "to have a set religion curriculum with established goals and objectives," to build and foster community among staff and students, to provide for "creative paraliturgies and sacramental celebrations," to introduce students to the practice of Christian service, and to develop in students "a social conscience sensitive to the needs of all." Of the Catholic schools' uniqueness the NCD says, "Growth in faith is central to their purpose." The schools are called upon to integrate their educational efforts with those of the parish(es), and teachers are charged with being witnesses to the Gospel and demonstrating commitment to community, service, and the teaching authority of the Church.

Lay Catholics in Schools: Witnesses to Faith was issued by the Vatican Congregation for Catholic Education in 1982. This document provides a theological rationale for the role of the lay person as educator. "The lay Catholic educator is a person who exercises a specific mission within the church by living in faith in a secular vocation in the communitarian structure of the school." The statement calls the educator, by his/her example, instructional methods, and personal contacts with students, to show respect for the individual dignity of each student, to provide principles by which students can think and act both critically and creatively within their culture, to communicate information truthfully, and to encourage students toward social awareness and responsible decision-making. The document stresses the importance of ongoing professional and religious education for educators. It asks "all believers (to) actively collaborate in the work of helping educators to reach the social status and economic level that they must have if they are to accomplish their task." This includes "an adequate salary guaranteed by a well-defined contract." Finally, the document states that the lay educator "should participate authentically in the responsibility for the school."

The Religious Dimension of Education in a Catholic School was issued by the Vatican Congregation for Catholic Education in 1988. Offered as guidelines for reflection and renewal, this document is addressed primarily to local ordinaries and the superiors of Religious Congregations dedicated to the education of young people and invites them to examine whether or not the words of the Second Vatican Council have become a reality. The distinguishing characteristics of a Catholic school are described as follows:

The Catholic school pursues cultural goals and the natural development of youth to the same degree as any other school. What makes the Catholic school distinctive is its attempt to generate a community climate in the school that is permeated by the Gospel spirit of freedom and love. It tries to guide the adolescents in such a way that personality development goes hand in hand with the development of the "new creature" that each one has become through baptism. It tries to relate all of human culture to the good news of salvation so that the light of faith will illumine everything that the student will gradually come to learn about the world, about life, and about the human person. In this statement, the Congregation states that the Council declared that what makes the Catholic school distinctive is its religious dimension, and that this is to be found in a) the educational climate, b) the personal development of each student, c) the relationship established between culture and the Gospel, and d) the illumination of all knowledge with the light of faith.

Each chapter addresses one of these distinctive characteristics and presents challenges and specific recommendations for evaluation.

Of particular interest to board members is the concluding section stating "that a Catholic school needs to have a set of educational goals which are 'distinctive' in the sense that the school has a specific objective in mind, and all of the goals are related to this objective. Concretely, the educational goals provide a frame of reference which:

- defines the school's identity: in particular, the Gospel values which are its inspiration must be

explicitly mentioned;
- gives a precise description of the pedagogical, educational and cultural aims of the school;
- presents the course content, along with the values that are to be transmitted through these courses;
- describes the organization and management of the school;
- determines which policy decisions are to be reserved to professional staff (diocesan staff, principals and teachers), which policies are to be developed with the help of parents and students, and which activities are to be left to the free initiatives of teachers, parents, or students;
- indicates the ways in which student progress is to be tested and evaluated."

Archdiocese of Louisville
(adapted from *Parish School Board Manual*)

Appendix K—Catholic Regional School Systems:
Pros, Cons and Alternatives

Appendix K
CATHOLIC REGIONAL SCHOOL SYSTEMS:
PROS, CONS AND ALTERNATIVES

by Neil Meitler, CMC
John Augenstein, Ph.D.
(September, 1989)

Introduction
The following observations regarding **CATHOLIC REGIONAL SCHOOL SYSTEM: PROS, CONS AND ALTERNATIVES** are opinions of the authors of Neil Meitler Consultants, Inc. They are based on their extensive experiences in working in the area of Catholic school planning.

The individual parish school model will continue to work successfully for some schools. However, it is no longer the best alternative for other schools at this point in history, and possibly in the future. Consequently, there is a need to consider other options.

Making changes in the present, traditional model of operating Catholic schools is a very difficult process and should be undertaken slowly, with the full understanding of all the issues involved. Most importantly, people's understanding and attitudes must be considered and sometimes new understandings and attitudes must be developed before changes can be implemented.

The issue is bigger than the elementary school alone. Any proposed changes affect the parish and its ministry, the role and authority of pastors, and must observe Canon Law. Some of the problems, as well as the solutions, lie within the parish and not only within the school.

Parish planning is as essential as school planning. Many, and perhaps most, of the problems related to Catholic elementary schools can be dealt with by the development of effective parish plans. Some parishes are in the process of long range planning, but long range planning has been limited in most parishes.

These issues and others are identified so as to help the reader understand the various dimensions of proposed changes in the way in which Catholic elementary school education is provided. Because there is need to contemplate new approaches, these observations are not meant to discourage continued investigation, but to aid in understanding the various alternatives as realistically as possible.

Periodic reference is made to "consolidation" and "regionalization" throughout this article. The following are the definitions of these terms:
— **Consolidation:** The agreement of a small number of parishes, located geographically close to each other, to combine their school programs, sometimes resulting in the use of fewer facilities. One of the primary motivations is often to respond to declining enrollment.
— **Regionalization:** The creation of a new governance structure, with a policy board (usually a board with limited jurisdiction), under which all Catholic schools in a particular geographic region are operated. It is within the authority and responsibility of the regional board to regulate finances, set policies, provide new programs, consolidate schools, propose new schools, and in other ways develop educational programs which meet the needs of Catholic parents and parishes.

ISSUES WHICH MUST BE CONSIDERED IN IMPLEMENTING NEW ORGANIZATION STRUCTURES FOR CATHOLIC SCHOOLS

Experience has shown that changes of organization or governance structures for Catholic schools and parishes have often been achieved with difficulty. Closing or consolidating schools and parishes, and other changes which affect the parochial structure to which people are accustomed, are almost always associated with a complicated mixture of challenge, resistance, hope, resentment and other emotions. Based on these experiences, it seems wise to list the numerous issues which must be considered in a proposed change of the traditional model of parish elementary schools.

A. Who Is Affected?
Many individuals and groups must be involved in proposed changes, and the various groups' viewpoints and expectations must be considered.
- Pastors
- Parish Members
- Principals

- Teachers
- Students
- Religious Communities
- Parish Councils and Parish Boards of Education
- Public School Systems
- Department of Public Instruction
- (Arch)diocesan Schools Office

B. What Is Affected?
Proposed changes impact on many aspects of the parish and school organization.
- Sources of revenue
- Expenditure decisions
- Budget planning and approval
- Bookkeeping and accounting systems
- Curriculum and instructional programs
- Religious Education (sacramental preparation)
- Personnel policies and practices
- Legal considerations
- Parochial identity
- Enrollment and marketing
- Transportation systems
- Facilities' ownership, use and maintenance
- Facilities' use for non-school purposes

C. How It Is Affected
Proposed changes in the organization structure result in changes in the ways in which decisions are made and impact on the authority and responsibility of individuals and groups.
- Present board, council or committee structures
- New board structures
- Property ownership and maintenance
- Board authority for implementing decisions
- Pastoral role and authority
- Canon Law
- Civil Law

CRITERIA FOR EVALUATION OF REGIONAL SCHOOL OPTIONS
Models can be developed which, in theory and principle, appear to be efficient. However, such models must be evaluated to determine if they will meet the long range goals for Catholic school education. In an effort to ensure that proposed models are adequately evaluated, a list of criteria is provided below:

1. **A regional system should not be developed on the assumption that it will save money.** Experience indicates that this is unlikely. The primary motivations for regionalizing schools must be to:
   - Improve and expand the educational program opportunities for children.
   - Utilize more effectively the resources and facilities.
   - Provide higher teacher salaries.
   - Develop new sources of revenue and increase enrollment.

2. **A regional system must include all parishes in the geographic region, both those with and without schools.**

3. **It is essential that most of the parishes choose to cooperate voluntarily and that relatively few parishes feel pressured into the system by the (Arch)bishop.** His approval will eventually be necessary, but should not result in pressure on a majority of the parishes to participate unwillingly in the regional structure.

4. **A regional system must be designed to retain and even expand parish "ownership" and commitment to the schools.** Catholic schools are, and must continue to be, a part of the mission and ministry of a Catholic parish. The school can be part of parish ministry only when it can be integrated into the ministry plan for parish members.

5. **A well developed, comprehensive written agreement must be signed by every pastor and

parish which will participate in the regional system, and the (Arch)bishop, to ensure a long term commitment to the structure and a clear understanding of all expectations and responsibilities.

6. **The regional school structure must have freedom to operate and potential for long term success, regardless of which pastors are assigned to parishes within the region.** In general, the concept of regional Catholic elementary schools needs to be supported by clergy throughout the (Arch)diocese, and be a part of the profile of participating parishes for personnel selection and assignment.

7. **A regional structure should be separately incorporated and established as a juridic person, according to Canon Law,** so that the regional entity has the governance authority within it to make necessary decisions, subject to approval of the (Arch)bishop. Parishes must be willing to transfer control of their schools over to a regional board in which all parishes have a direct or indirect voice.

8. **A regional system must have sufficient authority to develop standardization of financial policies** affecting tuition, salaries and benefits, tuition assistance, subsidy, etc.

9. **A regional system must have high potential for being marketable to parents and to the general community.**

10. **Improved tuition assistance programs should be an integral part of the objectives and funding structure** of a regional system to ensure that low income and minority families have opportunities to participate.

11. **An archdiocesan or religious community-owned high school located in a proposed region should be part of all discussions and related planning for the potential region.** The high school may or may not be part of the eventual regional structure, but it should be involved in all planning for it.

In summary, moving from a parish-based model to a regional model is experimental, few dioceses have tried it, and all existing models are new and have not stood the test of time. Consequently, any plan to move toward a regional model should be done slowly and with thought.

ADVANTAGES AND DISADVANTAGES OF REGIONAL SCHOOL MODELS

The following is a list of advantages and disadvantages of a regional Catholic school system. Although the list of disadvantages is longer than the list of advantages, this should not be viewed as significant. Both lists contain items that are more important than others, and the length of the list itself is not the important issue.

A. Advantages
- Potential to have more programs which are competitive with public schools.
- Potential to improve curriculum planning and coordination.
- Unified tuition, salary and fringe benefits.
- Potential for comprehensive financial development programs.
- Potential for comprehensive marketing and recruitment programs.
- Potential for coordinated expansion into other areas of need and service such as day care, preschool, before and after school programs, etc.
- Shared loss of present organization to gain an equal share of involvement in a new regional educational organization.
- Shared ownership by all parishes of the regional educational system.
- More effective and efficient use of school facilities within the region.
- Forerunner of future types of collaboration in other areas of parish life.
- Potential for better organization of the instructional system, i.e. primary, middle and secondary schools.
- Potential for higher teacher salaries.

B. Disadvantages
- Major change in the familiar, present structure, incurring the natural resistance to change.
- Potential loss of "ownership" of the schools by pastors, parish members and parents.
- Potential loss of the direct relationship of the elementary school to the parish mission and ministry.
- Possible reluctance of some parishes to transfer control of the parish school to another group.
- Possible reluctance of parishes without schools to see benefits in a change.
- Potential loss of uniqueness of the present system, resulting a system more like the public school structure.

- Possible decline of enrollments because of parish and parent reluctance to accept the new system.
- Possible continuance of financial problems for parishes now experiencing financial problems.
- Possibility of a regional system becoming too large and losing what the Coleman Research says is Catholic schools' largest asset—parent involvement and ownership of their own school.
- Difficulty in enforcing shared parish subsidy agreements.
- Initial difficulty of moving to a common salary schedule and tuition.
- Potential for some parishes to see this as a "way out" of their responsibility for schools.
- Fear by present staff of loss of jobs.
- Creation of a form of bureaucracy to run the regional schools.

POTENTIAL REGIONAL MODEL

Most present (Arch)diocesan systems of Catholic schools are "totally decentralized" whereas most public school systems are "totally centralized." The proposed structure presents a "partially centralized" school system for Catholic schools.

The following "potential" regional model meets most of the criteria for evaluation of regional school options and seeks to maximize the advantages and minimize the disadvantages cited previously.

Catholic Identity
- The Constitution and By-laws for the Regional system would state clearly that schools would be "distinctively Catholic" in their program, curriculum and staffing. Written guidelines defining "distinctively Catholic" would be developed by the Regional School Board and the Ordinary.

Involvement
- All parishes with and without schools which are located in the geographic area of the region would be required to be part of the regional system.

Governance
- The region would be separately incorporated with a constitution and by-laws.
- A Regional Delegate Assembly would meet two times per year. It would be comprised of the pastor and two representatives from each parish within the region. The role of the Regional Delegate Assembly would be to:
    1. Elect a Regional School Board from a slate of qualified candidates presented by a nominating committee after determining a means by which all parishes participate in the selection of the Board.
    2. Approve the annual budget.
    3. Be regularly informed as representatives and ambassadors for the schools in the region.
- The Regional School Board would be responsible for all operations of the regional school system including policy, finances, personnel, etc.

Regional School Board
- The Regional School Board would have 15 to 18 members, comprised of a fixed percentage of pastors and lay people from the region, e.g., one-third pastors, two-thirds qualified lay individuals, who bring special skills to the board.
- The Board would be responsible for the following:
    1. Development and presentation of the annual budget
    2. Approval of program plans
    3. Approval of changes in the school programs and structure
    4. Development of policy recommendations
    5. Recommend tuition and fee schedules
    6. Supervision of fund raising and development programs
    7. Recommend common salary schedules
    8. Other appropriate and necessary actions.

Administrative Staff
- The region would be serviced by a full-time Director, accountable to the Superintendent, to whom the principals would be immediately responsible.
- Secretarial and bookkeeping staff would be employed for the region. A Development Director would be employed by the region.

- Other staff, as may be deemed necessary by the Director and approved by the Regional Board, would be employed to provide educational services to all schools within the regional school system, e.g., reading teachers, special ed teachers, etc.

Relationship to the (Arch)diocese
- The region must work within the policy structure for Catholic schools which would be provided by the (Arch)diocese).
- The Regional Director would work as staff person for the regional schools. The Director would be hired by the Superintendent, in cooperation with the regional school board.

Financing
- A predetermined percentage of the regional school budget would come from parish subsidy, tuition and fees, and fund raising and development, e.g. 30%/60%/10% or 40%/50%/10%.
- A subsidy formula would identify the share of subsidy to be provided to the regional system by each parish within the region.
- Financing and accounting would be centralized. Tuition would be collected centrally, bills paid centrally, etc.
- Payroll would be centralized in the regional office.
- Provide a region-wide tuition assistance program.

Program and Curriculum
- Curriculum would be planned on a regional basis within guidelines of the (Arch)diocese.
- Inservice for faculty and staff would be provided within the region, as well as by the (Arch)diocese.
- There would be shared staff between the schools within the region; e.g. music, art, P.E., etc.
- The region would provide efficient and effective preschool programs.
- Middle school(s) within the region would be jointly sponsored, if appropriate.

Tuition
- A common tuition schedule would be developed for all schools within the first three years after the System was initiated.

Salary Schedule and Benefits
- A standardized salary schedule would be developed for all educational personnel within the region within the first three years after the System was initiated.
- There would be standardization of the benefit programs for all educational personnel in the region within three years.

Marketing and Recruitment
- There would be coordinated, regional marketing and recruitment programs for all schools.
- There would be coordinated regional development of brochures and other materials.

Development and Fund Raising
- Local fund raising by parents and children at each school would be used to buy particular things needed in that school, within guidelines established by the Regional School Board.
- There would be region-wide fund raising and development programs to raise funds to underwrite the regional budget.

Use of Facilities
- Parishes with school buildings which are used by the region would be paid a percentage of the utilities and maintenance costs for those facilities.
- The regional school system would pay for capital costs which are incurred specifically to make structural changes required for the educational program in a particular school building.
- Parishes would continue to pay for capital costs for major repairs of their buildings. These would be the type of costs which would be incurred regardless of whether the school were in the building, e.g. roof replacement, tuckpointing, etc.
- The host parishes would continue to have use of their school buildings for religious education and other parish programs, much as they do now.

Implementation Schedule

Two years could be allowed for planning the change, with implementation in the third year. The two years would be used to provide ongoing inservice for faculty, administrators, parents, board members and others to prepare them for the transition.

CONCLUSION

Most Catholic elementary schools in the United States are supported by a single parish. For generations, the parish-based elementary school has successfully and effectively provided Catholic elementary education. Only in recent years, when enrollments began to decline, have other alternatives been investigated.

Most dioceses have had an opportunity to consolidate one or more parish schools. Most of these consolidations were the result of declining enrollment and the need to re-evaluate the use of parish resources. Usually they affected only two or three schools in a limited geographic area.

There are some consolidated schools which are operating quite effectively and some which have met with marginal success. This observation is based on Meitler Consultants' work with dioceses throughout the country, and contacts with many superintendents regarding regionalized and consolidated schools. Many consolidations have failed to achieve their original objectives and are periodically bothered with lack of funding or support from pastors and participating parishes. This is a generalization, but it is a common experience in many diocese. The mixed success of many school consolidations have a close parallel to regionalization and warrant careful scrutiny.

Appendix L—Sample Diocesan Policies

Appendix L
SAMPLE DIOCESAN POLICIES

The following examples of diocesan policies are selected from among the many on file at the National Catholic Educational Association. Diocesan policies are guides for discretionary action by the administrator, and local policies must be in accord with them. Diocesan policies are formulated by diocesan boards, enacted by the diocesan bishop, and implemented by the diocesan superintendent of schools and staff. They are to be followed by all educational programs in the diocese.

ADMISSIONS (2.01)
The schools in the Diocese of Little Rock will admit students of any race, color, national or ethnic origin to all rights, privileges, programs, and activities generally accorded or mace available to their students. Every Catholic child has a right to religious instruction and formation in the Catholic faith. Enrollment in a Catholic school is a privilege. (Diocese of Little Rock)

APPLICANTS FOR PRINCIPALSHIP (3122)
Requirements (3122.1)
In a Catholic school, leadership shall include both the Catholic as well as the educational dimension. For that reason, principals in the Jefferson City diocese
- shall be practicing, committed Catholics in good standing with the Church;
- shall hold a philosophy of education that is consistent with this Christian conviction;
- shall have at least three years of successful teaching experience, preferably in a Catholic school;
- shall hold a Master's degree and a principal's certificate in the state of Missouri; occasional exceptions to this requirement may be made, e.g., if an applicant is nearing completion of a Master's degree or has the equivalent of such requirements;
- shall hold or be working toward the appropriate level of Religious Education Certification according to diocesan norms. (Diocese of Jefferson City)

ARBITRATION COMMITTEE (3.05)
If an arbitration committee is needed, the school board will recommend to the pastor names of persons to serve on this ad hoc committee. The arbitration committee will be composed of three members. Board members may not serve on this committee. it is recommended that the committee be represented by legal counsel. (Diocese of Little Rock)

CHILD ABUSE REPORTING (2.16)
Every person having reason to believe that a child under the age of eighteen years has had physical injury or injuries inflicted upon him or her by other than accidental means, where the injury appears to have been caused as a result of physical abuse or neglect, shall report the matter promptly to the county SCAN (Suspect Child Abuse or Neglect) or Social Services Office in the county wherein the suspect injury occurred. It shall be a misdemeanor for any person to knowingly and willfully fail to report any such incident promptly as provided above. (Diocese of Little Rock)

CHRONIC INFECTIOUS CONDITIONS (4000.4)
Each individual situation involving a chronic infectious condition (such as AIDS and Hepatitis B) shall be carefully considered on a case-by-case basis. The membership of a team to meet with and advise the administration shall be designated in school board policy. The team shall consider the current recommended policies and procedures of the Missouri Department of Health that are applicable to the situation.

A suggested team to meet with and advise the administration regarding a staff members could consist of the staff member, the person's physician, and the pastor(s) involved. To guard the person's right to confidentiality, the number of people who are aware of the infected person's condition should be kept to a minimum needed to assure concern for the person and to detect any extraordinary situation that may present a potential for transmission.

Ordinary social contact between children and persons infected with the AIDS virus is not dangerous. Therefore, persons seeking new or continued employment in or related to the school shall not be excluded on the basis of AIDS, unless the nature and extent of the illness reasonably precludes the performance of such employment or impairs any of the operations of the school. (Diocese of Jefferson City)

CONTAGIOUS AND COMMUNICABLE DISEASES (4000.3)

Any person who is liable to transmit a contagious disease through day-to-day contact (such as measles, chicken pox, tuberculosis) shall not be permitted at school or school-sponsored activities as long as the possibility of contagion exists.

To determine the diseased condition or the liability of transmitting the disease, the principal may require a staff member to be examined by a physician and, if the diagnosis is positive, shall exclude the person from school as long as the danger of disease transmittal exists. (Diocese of Jefferson City)

FAITH COMMITMENT (4000.1)

All persons within the Catholic school setting share in the basic mission of Catholic education. For that reason, all shall demonstrate by their attitudes, words, actions, and the integrity of their lives that they support the beliefs and values that underlie this form of education. They shall be either Catholics in good standing who are committed to the Catholic faith and to Christian living, or others who have a positive attitude toward the Catholic faith and a commitment to Christian living. They shall work with others within and beyond the school setting in a spirit befitting a Christian faith community. (Diocese of Jefferson City)

MOST REVEREND BISHOP (1010)

The Bishop of the Diocese holds the first responsibility for all Catholic educational programs within the limits of his diocese. As the chief teacher of the Diocese, the Bishop is responsible for providing Catholic formation for all his people, young and old. Because it is impossible for him to discharge this duty personally, he uses the services of the faithful — priests, religious, and laity — but the responsibility for the formal religious instruction of the faithful remains always uniquely his. As to Diocesan Schools, the Bishop is the legal employer and as "Corporation Sole" owns all assets of the school and the Diocese. (Diocese of Manchester)

OPPORTUNITIES FOR SPIRITUAL GROWTH (2.05)

Opportunities will be provided to enable the student's faith to become living, conscious, and active through instruction. The faculty will work together to provide a religion program for the students that will become a powerful force for the development of personal sanctity and for the building of community. (Diocese of Little Rock)

PROFESSIONAL ORGANIZATIONS (3.05)

It is recommended that every school in the diocese hold institutional membership in the elementary and/or secondary school department of the National Catholic Educational Association. Schools are encouraged to hold membership in professional organizations and to subscribe to educational journals. (Diocese of Little Rock)

RESPONSIBILITIES OF PASTOR (3010)

The Pastor, appointed by the Bishop, holds the rights and responsibilities specified by Canon Law. As the administrator of the parish, the pastor holds an important role in relation to the parish school. Most of the educational responsibilities of this role the pastor delegates to the school principal and faculty who collaborate with the Diocesan School Office. He does, however, maintain certain responsibilities related to the school:

Religious areas (3010.1)

By virtue of his position of spiritual leader of the parish community, the pastor is responsible for those matters within the school which affect religious education, worship, and the spiritual welfare of the students. It is his duty to see that the teachings of the Church are clearly and accurately presented.

Contractual responsibilities (3010.2)

The contract for either a principal or teacher is an agreement entered into by and between the educator and the Catholic Diocese of Jefferson City. The pastor is the agent at the local level, the superintendent at the diocesan level. The contract is not accepted and binding on any party until it has been signed by the diocesan superintendent of schools.

Local policies (3010.3)

The pastor works closely with the parish school board and officially enacts policies of the parish school board. He is ultimately responsible to see that local policies are in accord with those of the diocese, the diocesan school office, and the religious education office.

Delegation to principal (3010.4)

The pastor delegates the immediate direction of the school and its instructional program to the principal, who leads the school in accordance with the policies of the diocesan school office and the parish school board.

Financial responsibility (3010.5)

The pastor in consultation with the parish finance committee is responsible for the financial support of the school. He delegates all or at least the instructional part of school budget development to the principal with the school board. As specified in Canon Law he relies upon recommendations of the Finance Committee or Parish Council regarding the total parish budget. Consideration of any major change regarding the school shall include consultation with the diocesan superintendent and may be effected only with the expressed approval of the bishop. (Diocese of Jefferson City)

SEARCHING STUDENT LOCKERS (5142.1)

Students "own" their lockers against other students, but they do not have exclusive ownership against the school and its officials. The school does not supply lockers to students for illicit use.

School principals may, and should, search a student's locker on the basis of prior rights of the principal if and when the principal has evidence to suspect that the locker contains illegal or harmful material. If such material is found, it may be turned over to the police.

General search of all lockers in reaction to a bomb threat or widespread drug abuse can be justified as proper exercise of school authority.

Search of a student's locker by the police may be made only with a valid warrant or in connection with a valid arrest. Where police are involved, parents/guardians shall be notified immediately. The principal or other school official shall be present as police make the search.

Ordinarily, the student shall be present as the locker is searched.

A third party shall be present as the school principal searches a student's locker.

The principal need not secure a student's permission prior to searching that student's locker. However, such permission will assist in maintaining good student-principal relationship. (Diocese of Manchester)

STANDARDS OF GROOMING AND DRESS (4160)

Teachers in schools within the Archdiocese of Kansas City in Kansas shall always maintain high standards of personal cleanliness with respect to their physical person and wearing apparel. Dress and grooming shall be such as to maintain high standards of professional dignity and command the respect of students, peers and patrons and to establish a standard worthy of emulation by students. Standards of dress and grooming shall be established and appropriately modified to conform to the demands of the specific assignment and activity by the principal of the school. (Archdiocese of Kansas City in Kansas)

TUITION AND FEE POLICIES (632.1)

Catholic schools normally are financed by subsidies from parishes and other sources as well as by tuition from parents of enrolled students. It is recommended that local boards of education annually perform a budget analysis and provide parents with information about the actual cost per student in relation to tuition. In this process local boards may encourage the option of negotiated tuition amounts based on whatever portion of the actual cost that parents are able to pay.

Catholic elementary and secondary schools in the diocese are to establish tuition amounts and announce these publicly prior to the registration of students for the following year.In order to assure that all interested Catholic children are able to attend a Catholic school, each board of education should adopt and regularly publicize a policy which clearly states that no child shall be refused admittance because of inability of parents to pay any or all of the education cost.

It is recommended that each Catholic school establish an organized schedule for collecting tuition and fees. This should be published in parent handbooks. (Diocese of St. Cloud)

TUITION-FREE SCHOOLS AND CHURCH CONTRIBUTIONS (632.2)

1. Schools which do not charge tuition normally are financed directly from parish funds (subsidy) and other sources (diocesan, fundraising, etc.) rather than by direct tuition from parents. All parishioners therefore contribute to support the parish and the various activities which it sponsors, including the school.

2. Contributions made directly to the parish are voluntary charitable donations and may be claimed

as charitable deductions for income tax purposes.

3. It is recommended that the parish board of education should annually announce what is the actual operating cost per student and what amount the parish actually pays toward this cost in the form of subsidy to the school. Thus all parishioners not only should have a better understanding of the total parish commitment to Catholic education but also should be motivated to respond by contributing more generously to the support of the total parish and its needs.

4. It is recommended that all parishioners frequently be reminded of their responsibility to support the parish and its activities. If the parish school has a policy of charging no tuition, this means that the school's operating cost will be derived from the church contributions of all the parishioners. Therefore, parents with children enrolled in the school should *not* be obligated to a special level of church contributions simply because their children attend the school; to do so is merely construed as tuition by the Internal Revenue Service and not as a voluntary charitable deduction. (Diocese of St. Cloud)

BIBLIOGRAPHY AND RESOURCES

Becoming a Better Board Member: A Guide to Effective School Board Service. Washington, DC: National School Boards Association, 1982. (Prepared for public schools, this has some practical information and clever cartoons suitable for all boards.)

Brent, Daniel and Jurkowitz, Carolyn. *School Board Study Programs: Board Member's Manual Series I and II.* Washington, DC: The National Catholic Educational Association, 1983 & 1984. (A flexible series of study lessons for board member orientation and training.)

CACE/NABE Governance Task Force. *A Primer on Educational Governance in the Catholic Church.* Washington, DC: The National Catholic Educational Association, 1987. (This book presents models of governance for Catholic elementary and secondary schools and parish religious education programs that are in conformity with the laws and traditions of the church and sound educational management.)

Catholic High Schools and Their Finances. Washington, DC: The National Catholic Educational Association, 1988. (These biennial reports offer precise information about tuitions, salaries, per-pupil costs and financial aid.)

Catholic Schools in America: Elementary/Secondary, NCEA/Ganley's 1989 Edition. Montrose, Colorado: Fisher Publishing Co., 1989. (Diocesan and state statistics on Catholic elementary and secondary schools, enrollment and teachers, as well as an individualized directory of all Catholic schools, principals and diocesan school offices.)

Clearing House Files. Washington, DC: The National Association of Boards of Education/NCEA. (Some diocesan policy files and *PolicyMakers.*)

Code of Ethics for Catholic School Board Members. Washington, DC: The National Catholic Educational Association, 1988. (On sturdy cardboard, appropriate for presentation at commissioning ceremonies or board retreats.)

Convey, John J. "Research on Catholic Schools." *The New Catholic Encyclopedia, Vol. 18.* Washington, DC: The Catholic University of America, 1989. (A summary of current research on Catholic schools in the United States.)

Development Series:
    Rogus, Joseph and Yeager, Robert J. *The Development Director, Making Each Moment Count.*
    Yeager, Robert J. *Volunteers.*
    Gibson, Amy. *Student Recruitment.*
    Appell, David L. *Marketing.*

Cushman, Charles P. *The Alumni Program.*
Yeager, Robert J. *Resources for Development.*
Gary, Barbara Stewart. *Seeking Foundation Grants.*
Burke, Richard J. *Understanding & Implementing Development.*
Campbell, SP, Cathy. *Public Relations.*
Stuhr, Robert L. and Jarc, Jerry A. *Annual Fund-Estate Planning.*
Yeager, Robert J. *The Case Statement.*

Washington, DC: The National Catholic Educational Association, 1984-1987. (These are prepared for administrators and boards.)

Dernovek, SNJM, Mary. *Letters to Catholic Parents of Preschool Children.* Washington, DC: The National Catholic Educational Association, 1989. (This booklet contains sample letters that principals can send to parents of children from the time of birth to age five. These letters, which can be personalized, inform parents of the developmental changes that are taking place in their children and serve as an aid in the recruitment of students.)

14 x 7 Building Better Boards. Washington, DC: The National Association of Board of Education/NCEA. (Unpublished workshop materials.)

Houle, Cyril O. *Governing Boards.* Washington, DC: National Center for Nonprofit Boards, 1989. (A project of the National Center for Nonprofit Boards, this book provides comprehensive, authoritative and up-to-date guidance for boards in nonprofit and public organizations.

Hughes, Jane Wolford and Barnds, Mary Lynch. *Partners in Catholic Education: Pastor, Professional, Parent.* Washington, DC: The National Catholic Educational Association, 1989. (A workbook for leaders in Catholic education which provides a step-by-step process designed to help pastors, professionals, volunteers and parents work as partners in building the Catholic educational community.)

Keynote Series:
McDermott, SJ, Edwin J. *Distinctive Qualities of the Catholic School.*
Buetow, Harold A. *A History of Catholic Schooling the United States.*
Jarc, Jerry A. *Development and Public Relations for the Catholic School.*
Drahmann, FSC, Theodore. *Governance and Administration in the Catholic School.*
McLaughlin, FSC, Terence. *Catholic School Finance and Church-State Relations.*
Travis, OP, Mary Peter. *Student Moral Development in the Catholic School.*
Raftery, SC, Francis. *The Teacher in the Catholic School.*
Kealey, FSC, Robert J. *Curriculum in the Catholic School.*
Hawker, James F. *Catechetics in the Catholic School.*
Welch, PBVM, Mary Leanne. *Methods of Teaching in the Catholic School.*
DiGiacomo, SJ, James J. *Teaching Religion in a Catholic Secondary School.*
Washington, DC: The National Catholic Educational Association, 1985-1989. (These booklets are written for the preservice and inservice of Catholic school teachers.)

Kurtz, Daniel L. *Board Liability: Guide for Nonprofit Directors.* Mt. Kisco, New York: Moyer Bell Ltd., 1988. (Published by the Committee on Non-Profit Organizations of the Association of the Bar of the City of

New York, this book covers all aspects of board liability.)

McKinney, OSB, Mary Benet. *Sharing Wisdom: A Process for Group Decision Making.* Valencia, California: Tabor Publishing, 1987. (A process for group decision making is presented by this well-known Catholic educator.)

O'Brien, J. Stephen. *An Urgent Task: What Bishops and Priests Say About Religious Education Programs.* Washington, DC: The National Catholic Educational Association, 1989. (This study describes the views of bishops and priests who have the ultimate responsibility for catechesis in parishes, and gives some clues to the future of this ministry in the church.)

O'Brien, J. Stephen. *Mixed Messages: What Bishops and Priests Say About Catholic Schools.* Washington, DC: The National Catholic Educational Association, 1987. (Some topics covered are what bishops and priests say about the value and effectiveness of Catholic schools, their funding practices and future structures.)

O'Brien, J. Stephen and McBrien, Margaret (ed.). *Personnel Issues and the Catholic School Administrator.* Washington, DC: The National Catholic Educational Association, 1986. (Current church personnel practices are discussed and suggestions given on how administrators can carry out their responsibilities toward personnel. Topics covered include hiring, firing, salary benefits, and a plan for comprehensive diocesan models.)

Reck, SSND, Carlene and Coreil, MSC, Judith. *School Evaluation for the Catholic Elementary School: An Overview.* Washington, DC: The National Catholic Educational Association, 1983. (This publication includes the reasons for school evaluation, the steps in evaluation, the criteria for a Catholic elementary school, and a bibliography for other evaluation instruments).

Reck, SSND, Carlene and Coreil, MSC, Judith. *Verifying the Vision: A Self-Evaluation Instrument for the Catholic Elementary School.* Washington, DC: The National Catholic Educational Association, 1984. (A self-study process to help Catholic elementary educators and their school communities ask vital questions concerning the vision of their school, to verify progress toward the vision, and to plan for improvement. Includes special guide for visiting team.)

Recognition Certificates for Service to Catholic Education. Washington, DC: The National Catholic Educational Association. (NCEA helps people recognize the service others give to Catholic education. These certificates printed in green, burgundy, and gold help celebrate the gift of people who have given years of their lives to the church. The gold and burgundy certificates are used to recognize years of service; gold is for those who have served more than 25 years and burgundy is for those who have served 25 years or less. The green certificate is used to recognize service in a particular ministry (administration, teaching, board membership, catechist, pastor.)

Self-Study Guide for Catholic High Schools. Washington, DC: The National Catholic Educational Association, 1981. (This guide can assist the faculty of a Catholic high school and the entire community in using the self-evaluation process as an opportunity for renewal and improvement.)

Shaughnessy, SCN, Mary Angela. *A Primer on School Law: A Guide for Board Members in Catholic Schools.* Washington, DC: The National Catholic Educational Association, 1988. (This publication discusses types of Catholic school boards, laws affecting Catholic education in the U.S., tort liability of schools, duties and rights of school employees, duties and responsibilities of board members, conclusions and recommendations.)

Shaughnessy, SCN, Mary Angela. *School Handbooks: Some Legal Considerations.* Washington, DC: The National Catholic Educational Association, 1989. (This book provides school administrators with an outline of materials that should be incorporated into handbooks and provides guidance regarding the legality of what is written.)

Sheehan, RSM, Lourdes. *A Study of the Functions of School Boards in the Educational System of the Roman Catholic Church in the United States.* Virginia Tech dissertation, 1981. (This study includes a discussion of the authority structure of the Roman Catholic Church within which boards function and identifies phases and challenges of the board movement. Recommendations regarding appropriate structures are offered.)

Swanson, Andrew. *The Collected Board Sense: Common Sense for Nonprofit Board Members.* Rumford, Rhode Island: Community Services Consultants, Ltd., 1988. (This is a series of newsletters addressing a variety of issues of interest to boards.)

The Board Member's Prayer. Washington, DC: The National Catholic Educational Association. (A sturdy, colorful desk card with a suitable prayer for opening or closing board meetings. An appropriate item to present when commissioning new board members.)

The Code of Canon Law. Grand Rapids, Michigan: William B. Eerdmans Publishing Company, 1983. (An official English translation of the revised code.)

Trost, Arty and Rauner, Judy. *Gaining Momentum for Board Action.* San Diego, California: Marlborough Publications, 1983. (This publication offers a guide to increasing board effectiveness.)

United States Catholic Elementary Schools and Their Finances. Washington, DC: The National Catholic Educational Association, 1988. (These annual reports include analysis of national operating expenses, operating revenues, per-pupil revenues and costs, tuition ranges, and other data.)

U.S. Catholic Elementary and Secondary Schools. Washington, DC: The National Catholic Educational Association, 1988-89. (These annual reports include statistics on schools, enrollment, staffing, minority and non-Catholic enrollment.)

Information regarding NCEA publications, services and prices is available from:
    National Catholic Educational Association
    1077 30th Street N.W., Suite 100
    Washington, DC 20007-3852
    (202) 337-6232

ABOUT THE AUTHOR

Lourdes Sheehan, RSM, a Sister of Mercy, Province of Baltimore, is a native of Savannah, Georgia. She has been a Catholic school teacher, principal, diocesan superintendent of schools and director of education, and provincial administrator. Prior to assuming the position of Secretary for Education at the United States Catholic Conference, Sr. Lourdes was Executive Director of the National Association of Boards of Education at the National Catholic Educational Association.

She received a B.A. in history from Mt. St. Agnes College, Baltimore, Maryland, an M.A. in Colonial history from the University of Pennsylvania, and an Ed.D. in educational administration from Virginia Tech.